WHERE *the* ANGELS LIVED

Books by Margaret McMullan

EVERY FATHER'S DAUGHTER

AFTERMATH LOUNGE

SOURCES OF LIGHT

CASHAY

WHEN I CROSSED NO-BOB

HOW I FOUND THE STRONG

IN MY MOTHER'S HOUSE

WHEN WARHOL WAS STILL ALIVE

Praise for *WHERE THE ANGELS LIVED*

"Margaret McMullan has written a beautiful and heartrending account of her pilgrimage to Pécs, Hungary in the hope of retrieving what she can of the story of a distant (Jewish) relative, lost in the Holocaust. Written with her usual vividly realized, emotionally engaging prose, in which Margaret emerges as a protagonist with whom the reader identifies, *Where the Angels Lived* is a powerful testament of familial mourning as well as a vision of 20th century European history that is both searing and uplifting."

–Joyce Carol Oates

"An absolutely riveting story by an utterly engaging narrator—a triumphant blend of honesty, insight, research and imagination. The lethal, irrational hostility of one people towards another is movingly conveyed in all its appalling vividness, at the same time as a vein of humor and delight in discovering and recovering the past animates the prose. McMullan's best book."

–Phillip Lopate

"An impressive textual monument of the impact of Nazi genocide and the Shoah on individual lives and family, even three generations after the actual events. [McMullan] does not hesitate to point out the social dissonances, sometimes even in the form of "hatred", that still persist on many different levels as a consequence of this massive crime against humanity. Facing these dissonances is a necessary step towards a sustainable form of remembrance."

–Dr. Christian Dürr, Curator, Mauthausen Memorial

"McMullan beautifully pieces together a family history and the history of a country and its ethnic groups to create a stirring and highly informative narrative, full of information, wonderful wisdom and anecdotes, both sorrowful and joyful."

–Josip Novakovich, *April Fool's Day*

"Into this terrifying moment of severe intolerance in America, arrives this meticulously researched, soul-driven account of the generational trauma caused by another country that turned on and gave up its own. Margaret McMullan did not ask for the assignment that sent her and her family to Hungary to mourn an unknown family member lost to the Holocaust, but her radical courage, determination and stamina in the face of that assignment is breathtaking, insisting we pay attention, to the crimes of the past and our actions in the present, because, of course, it can happen here."

–Pam Houston, *Deep Creek*

"McMullan brings us along on a fascinating journey to discover the history of her once influential and industrious family—the Engel de Jánosis....They are entrepreneurs, musicians, lovers, builders and fighters, who, without the author's painstaking research, would have been erased from history forever."

–Eleni Kounalakis, Lt. Governor of California & U.S. Ambassador to Hungary (2010 – 2013)

"In this factional book you follow the Tragical Mystery Tour of the author from the USA to Pécs, Hungary, where she tries to find the traces of her Jewish ancestors killed in the Holocaust. My Jewish ancestors lived in the very same place and were also killed the same way. The similarities make me cry, the differences make me smile. Common fate—small comfort."

–Miklós Vámos, *The Book of Fathers*

Where the Angels Lived is an engaging, humorous account of one American's discovery of family roots and her personal struggle to understand the hate-filled history of 20th century Europe. Like Edmund de Waal's *Hare with the Amber Eyes,* McMullan pieces together the lost story of her forgotten ancestor and reminds us all how easy it is for humans to willfully ignore the murderous past and contemporary evil.

–Evelyn Farkas, Senior Fellow, German Marshall Fund;
National Security Contributor, NBC/MSNBC

"*Where the Angels Lived* is a powerful story of loss and remembrance, a journey to the past that informs our present. It is impossible to read this richly textured story and not be deeply moved by the lost voices who rise from the dead to speak in these pages. They, and we, should be forever grateful for their resurrection painfully and lovingly wrought by Margaret McMullan."

–Stuart Stevens, *The Innocent Have Nothing to Fear*

WHERE *the* ANGELS LIVED

One Family's Story of Exile, Loss, and Return

A Memoir by

Margaret McMullan

CALYPSO EDITIONS

CALYPSO EDITIONS
www.CalypsoEditions.org

By unearthing literary gems from previous generations, translating foreign writers into English with integrity, and providing a space for talented new voices, Calypso Editions is committed to publishing books that will endure in both content and form.

ISBN 13: 978-1-944593-08-7

Author photograph copyright © Pat O'Connor

Book design: Anthony Bonds
www.goldenratiobookdesign.com
Interior production: Seven Van Nort

For Richárd Engel de Jánosi
and
For all the other angels, lost and found

The Engel de Jánosi Family
Abbreviated

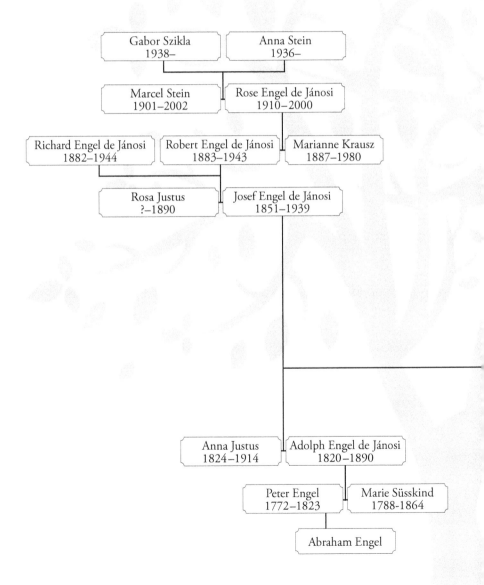

Gabor Szikla
1938–

Anna Stein
1936–

Marcel Stein
1901–2002

Rose Engel de Jánosi
1910–2000

Richard Engel de Jánosi
1882–1944

Robert Engel de Jánosi
1883–1943

Marianne Krausz
1887–1980

Rosa Justus
?–1890

Josef Engel de Jánosi
1851–1939

Anna Justus
1824–1914

Adolph Engel de Jánosi
1820–1890

Peter Engel
1772–1823

Marie Süsskind
1788-1864

Abraham Engel

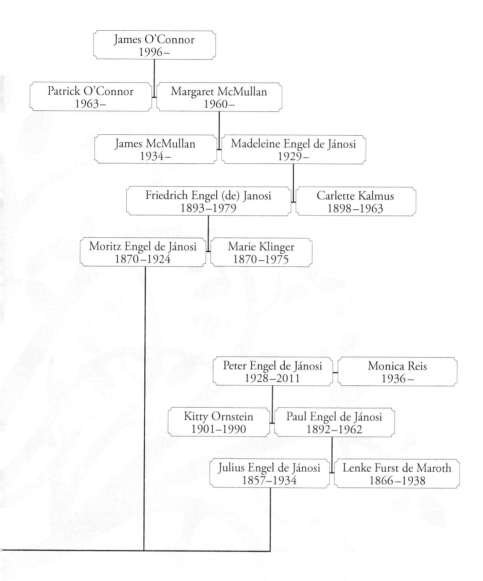

Contents

WHERE *the* ANGELS LIVED

Wall of Names, Yad Vashem

Part I

Israel 2008 and Indiana 2009

Israel 2008
Museum of Remembrance

I pass the pile of shoes, the empty suitcases, the propaganda posters, black and white photographs of ghettos and victims, the railroad tracks and the one old wagon. I try to ignore the hanging sign saying *Arbeit Macht Frei—Work Makes You Free.* I head straight back to the underground archives at Yad Vashem in Jerusalem. I don't have much time left.

I'm here as a visiting writer with The Writers Gathering. My hosts, Cindy and Gary, a Christian couple have brought me to Israel along with a movie director and a playwright to meet with representatives from Jewish, Christian, and Muslim faiths so that we all might get ideas to write inspirational stories. No pressure to produce, just creative diplomacy. Gary and I met while serving on the board of an organization interested in promoting good playwriting. I feel lucky to visit a country on someone else's dime.

This morning has been set aside for the Holocaust Museum. I realize now this is why I came to Israel, why I said yes to Gary right away when he called to invite me to explore what he calls "this place of stories." Fifteen years earlier, when I was researching my mother's family in order to write a novel, Yad Vashem was still under construction.

I descend. These archives were built underground to survive any blast, even nuclear. Yad Vashem's intentions are clear: no one will forget the Holocaust, and no one will forget its victims. This building is about remembering.

The playwright and I take our seats in front of the computers in the bunker-like library. Two men sit nearby. I read the instructions out loud in a whisper because this is the only way I can focus. I don't know why I'm shaking. The accent marks above the letters are impossible to type in, so I stop trying. I try *Engel de Janosi* first and get *"We are sorry, but we cannot find any results that fit your query."*

When I type *Engel Janosi*, over a thousand names appear, all of them Engels, from countries all over central and Eastern Europe. I try the less likely part of the name, *Janosi*. Six names appear on the screen. I recognize Pécs, Hungary, the town where my grandfather's family came from. The name on the screen is *Richard*.

"Who's Richard?" I say out loud. Nobody looks up. They are deep into their own searches.

When I was growing up, first in Mississippi, and then in the WASPy North Shore of Chicago, my mother was the most interesting person I knew. She brought out her childhood stories at our highly polished dining room table in the same way she laid out the good silver. It started when she was 12. She never talked about her formative years in Vienna.

She was an only child of a professor named Friedrich who researched and wrote about papal history and taught at the University of Vienna alongside Sigmund Freud. Her mother was from Paris and helped run a large parquet floor factory in Vienna, a business that had been passed down to Friedrich, who was more interested in teaching and writing history. My mother lived in an estate called the *Hofzeile* with maids and a cook and a groundskeeper, also passed down to her father. By her own account, my mother lived a fairy tale life. They were minor nobility, but nobility nonetheless.

Hitler marched into Vienna in 1938 and changed everything. My mother remembers a tense, chaotic time—mysterious phone calls, visits to passport offices and banks, whispered travel arrangements.

Friedrich left Vienna first, alone, leaving behind his mother, his wife, and his only child, my mother who was nine years old. Later, I pieced together the exact nature of my mother's exit.

When my mother first told me parts of her story, I wondered why a Catholic family would have to flee Nazis, but my mother reminded me that Hitler wanted to wipe out *all* religions, including Catholicism. "Look at *The Sound of Music*," she said. Jews weren't the only ones persecuted. This was true.

When I was sixteen, my great-grandmother, Marie, asked my mother and me to come be with her at the Lisner Home in

Washington, D.C. She knew she was dying. She was 105 years old. When we arrived, she stretched out on her bed, and spent the next two weeks falling in and out of sleep, reliving her life in order to die. That week, the week my great-grandmother was dying, she woke up, and each time she woke, she spoke a different language, believing that she was in a different country. She had gone into hiding during the war years, but I didn't know the specifics. It was spring then in D.C., and the cherry trees outside her bedroom window were beginning to bud.

On the last day, a man in a black suit wearing a skullcap came to pray over my great-grandmother. Later in college, when I took a Hebrew Scriptures class, I recognized the man's Hebrew prayers. The man in the black suit had been my great-grandmother's Rabbi, but back then, at the Lisner Home, I was clueless. My mother and I said our Catholic prayers right alongside my great-grandmother's Rabbi. It felt perfectly natural. What mattered was that we were praying for my great-grandmother, but I wondered, were we all praying to the same God? I started making the connections: Hitler and his henchmen had not been after my mother and her family because they were Catholics. If they were Jewish, but converted to Catholicism, what did that make me? I felt smart for figuring this out on my own, back then, but I also felt deceived. What other secrets was my mother keeping? What else did I need to figure out?

After the Rabbi left, my great-grandmother pulled off all her clothes. The nurses tied a sheet to the hospital bars on her bed to cover her body. Evidently, they didn't like her naked. My great-grandmother scratched at the sheet ends tied in knots. "*I shall not be caged in,*" she cried. My mother and I picked at the knots with our fingertips until they loosened, and, finally, my great-grandmother slept peacefully.

She was beautiful. Her thin body was more like a child's. There were no scars or liver spots. Her skin was loose, and she was a light beige all over. Whatever hair she had left was white down.

"Margaret," she said, waking up, recognizing me, speaking for the first time in English. "How good of you to come. But isn't the sun lovely?" Her eyes were as blue and clear as they had ever been. "Can you hear the birds?"

When I bent down over her to hug her frail body, I felt the weight of what I was embracing and I did not let go. Her chest warmed against mine, her heartbeat strong and startling. I could not understand how someone so alive could die. Her heart beat and beat and beat until hers made the same time as mine, and mine hers, and, as I held her, I thought surely one of us was giving life to the other, though I did not know which. As I held her, I felt as though I were holding on to everything my mother had left of her family.

Later, my grandfather Friedrich, who had moved back to Vienna, reminded my mother that after he died, she would be the last Engel de Jánosi. Everyone on the Engel de Jánosi side was gone. Growing up, my mother frequently reminded me of this: *she was the last.*

I spent five years researching and recording interviews with my mother, who was reluctant to reveal too much, if *reveal* is the right word. There's a great deal my mother simply did not know or perhaps did not *want* to know. When she had hip replacement surgery, I came to help out. Pain killers made her talkative. "Mind if I take some notes?" I said, shamelessly.

I applied for and received grants to trace my mother's exodus in 1939 by train from Vienna to Switzerland, to France, England, New York and finally to Washington, D.C. I interviewed my grandfather's former students at the University of Vienna, his second wife, and my godmother, Anna Corinth, an Austrian archivist who helped him with his research.

In My Mother's House is a fictionalized telling of my mother's emigration from Vienna and a daughter's quest to learn the secrets of her mother's past in order to gain an understanding of her own heritage.

As a novelist, I start with what I know, and use research and imagination to create a story that is emotionally true and honest. I devised personas for the mother and daughter, and I wrote what I knew: curiosity, playing the guitar, my own emigration from Mississippi, my mother, myself. I also wrote about what I did not know: Judaism, blindess, playing the viola d'amour, speaking

German, my mother, myself. In the novel, after seeing the Rabbi pray over her dying great-grandmother, the fictional daughter learns that her fictional grandfather converted to Catholicism in middle-age, quite possibly to avoid persecution as a Jew.

When our son was born, my husband and I gave him an extra middle name, Engel de Jánosi, to honor my mother and to keep her family name alive. Naming James felt right and even courageous. I was the Engel ancestor unafraid and unashamed of her heritage. Our son would be just as proud and defiant.

When the book came out in 2004, a man who said he was my mother's cousin, Peter de Jánosi, emailed me. "I read your novel," he wrote. "What's *not* true?" Even some of the facts I made up turned out to be true.

I asked my mother about Peter, and she assured me that he must be a very distant relative, no one who could have mattered. I asked Peter about his exact ties to the family and he sent me the Engel de Jánosi family tree, something I did not have access to when I wrote my novel. Peter's father was Friedrich's first cousin. Peter and my mother shared a great-grandfather. They were second cousins. I'm from Mississippi. Second cousins count as kin who matter. Peter told me he knew my grandfather, Friedrich, very well, and that he had met my mother once in D.C. Maybe my mother had forgotten Peter. *Willingly or accidentally.* On the subject of who might be the last Engel de Jánosi, it was clear that my grandfather, a man of facts, a well-known historian, lied. But why?

I stayed in touch with Peter because staying in touch with the remnants of my mother's people felt important, perhaps because it was not so important to my mother or her father. I also knew that finding out anything more about this side of my family would be up to me and only me. Eventually though, I stopped collecting stories about the Holocaust and Austria. Staying in touch with Peter felt oddly disloyal to my mother, so I shut the door. But I never turned the lock.

"Richard?" I say again in the Yad Vashem archives. I never heard of a Richard. When had I not been listening? Next to his name I read: *Source: List of murdered persons.* I press the "print" button and hurry to the information desk to pick up the printout.

The archivist pushes a box of tissues at me as she tells me to collect myself. She uses this word *collect* and she says it beautifully, extending the *l's*. She wears a headscarf and her English is careful and deliberate. Brown curls fall near her forehead framing her lovely dark eyes. She has seen my type before–Americans in Israel discovering their Jewishness and getting all weepy. *But no, that's not me*, I want to say. *I'm already collected. I know my story–Catholic with some mostly unacknowledged Jewish roots. That's all settled and I'm fine with all of it. My mother, not so much, but me?* I'm crying. I'm absolutely *leaking* tears. One word on a computer screen has reduced me to tears.

The archivist stares down at the sheet she printed out.

"Richard?" I repeat. I hadn't heard of anyone named Richard in my mother's family. The other names are exotic and European, names I often said out loud just to hear their sounds: *Moritz, Julius, Lenke, Sari, Ilona.*

"Richard," the archivist says, tripping over the *r*. "The Germans often renamed them. From Pécs. Pécs is one of the lost cities. You can find it in the Valley of the Communities." She points towards the *Exit* sign in the library, where apparently, the Valley of the Communities, a town of lost towns exists. Is she kicking me out? Does she want me to join the Valley?

I lean on her counter, trying to stop with the tears, but all I can think is, *he's gone.* Moments before I didn't know he existed, but now I know he's gone. Richard is gone and he's on this "list of murdered persons" and it's all so sad. It was a fact that has existed for years, before I knew, but now I know, and everything feels different.

The archivist reads aloud the single sheet of information:

Full Record of Details:
Original Record No.	*M-1/2*
Last Name	*Janosi*
Last Name	*Engel*

First Name	*Richard*
Sex	*Male*
Permanent residence	*Pécs, Baranya, Hungary*
Place during the war	*Mauthausen, Camp*
Place of Death	*Mauthausen, Camp*
Victims' status end WWII	*Perished*
Record Content Source	*Papp Kollezán Bertalan, Budapest, Pongrácz út 9.*
Language	*Hungarian*
Related item	*M.34—Card Catalog of Labor Battalions in Hungary*

Perished. The word is ridiculous; *perished*, as if he accidentally fell off a cliff.

The archivist checks her computer, then frowns, as if something is wrong.

"Look at me," she says. Her eyes are clear and brown. I take another tissue. "You are the first to ask about him. Do you understand? No one has ever asked about this man, your relative, Richard. No one has called him down. No one ever printed out his name. You are responsible now. *You must remember him in order to honor him.*"

"I don't understand," I say. "What do you mean?" *I must remember him.* How?

"Here." She gives me a form called Page of Testimony, which she says I *have* to fill out and send back to Yad Vashem, apparently so others can remember Richard too. Why is that so important? I glance over the form. *Victim's place of birth; first name of victim's father; first name of victim's mother; victim's profession; place of work; member of organization or movement; circumstances of victim's deportation.* I don't know the answers to any of these questions, and I have no idea how to get this information.

I have only heard about my mother's immediate family who got out, not much at all about the ones left behind. Why don't I know anything about the others?

Near the bottom of the form is a pledge: *I, the undersigned, hereby declare that this testimony is correct to the best of my knowledge.* I have *no* knowledge of Richard, and according to this archivist, this stranger, now I'm supposed to go find the answers?

The archivist slides the form across the counter towards me.

I want to say *Are you kidding me? I am not taking on this assignment. I don't want this assignment.*

I slip the form into the brown envelope she has given me and put it in my backpack.

"Thank you." It comes out a whisper.

With the playwright, I walk out of the archives, slowly this time, dazed.

"I didn't get a thing," the playwright says.

I'm envious.

"You?"

"She gave me homework." My backpack feels heavier. The envelope is next to a Ziploc bag of sharp, slate-colored rocks, souvenirs I labeled: *rocks from where King David encouraged his men to be mighty men.* Supposedly, David used one such rock to slay the giant, Goliath. I intend to give one of these rocks to my son, James when I get home. I will tell him, *Now you go and be a mighty man, too.* I will keep a rock for myself.

On the way out, we pass through the Wall of Names, a domed room covered floor to ceiling with names and pictures of Holocaust victims. There is detailed information about their lives and their deaths. People filled out their Pages of Testimonies. These victims have been remembered. This is where Richard should be, a place where I'm supposed to bring him.

". . . And I shall give them in My house and within My walls a memorial and a name . . . that shall not be cut off," reads the quote from Isaiah on the wall.

Remembering the dead, especially family members is important. I *know* this. Objectively, it is essential to commemorate the Jews murdered during the Shoah in order to refute Holocaust deniers and remind ourselves of our potential for evil. But in order to *remember*, you first have to *know*, right?

I grew up in Newton, Mississippi listening to elderly southern relatives on my father's side telling stories about relatives who had long since died. But my other, European grandfather, my mother's father, Friedrich, never felt this duty to remember, to honor the truth about his own family, and *he* was a historian. As I walk around the Wall of Names and read the facts, the stories, I imagine Richard among them. Remembered.

The playwright and I reunite with the group outside, and, on the way out, we pass the Valley of the Communities, a monument of stone markers commemorating the thousands of Jewish communities destroyed or damaged during World War II. *Pécs* is carved on one of the prominent tombstone markers, with *May 1944* in the second line, as though the date when all the Jews of Pécs were loaded onto trains and deported was the day the town died. Surely the town of Pécs doesn't exist anymore. How could it dare exist?

Our group gathers in front of a falafel stand up the street. I don't even like beer, but I drink beer. Then I drink another. I think, *if I have another beer and another, this assignment and all that I have to do will go away.* Gary asks how I'm doing, and I only nod. I should be telling them everything. Isn't this just the sort of "Israel story" they want? I don't want to talk and I certainly don't want to tell them about my assignment maybe because I don't know where to begin. Or maybe I'm just hoping it will go away. Here I am—on the sidewalk of the Muslim side of town, getting drunk on beer in order to forget what I've just learned about my Jewish relative from the museum of remembrance.

Back home in Indiana I return to the university teaching full time. We have a new department to run, programs to grow, grants to write. James has tennis, baseball, and drum lessons. I put aside thoughts about Richard. I am busy with the *living*. But then some nights, especially cold ones, I feel him shaking me awake. He tugs, sometimes from the inside, but I force myself back asleep, and that's when I walk behind him in black and white dreams in a village on broken cobblestone streets.

When I wake up, I know. I know what's going to happen next.

Indiana 2009
Parachute Jump

It feels rude to tell my mother about relatives in her family she doesn't know, but I call her to ask about Richard.

"Never heard of him," she says. I imagine her sitting at her desk, looking out the window at her rose garden.

"What about your father's relatives in Hungary? Did he ever talk about them?" I'm at the university in my office.

"You must have it wrong," she says. "I don't have time for this." She hangs up. My mother often hangs up on people. It's her way of staying in control. I don't take it personally. She has made me tough like that.

A few days later, she calls back and says she *does* remember her father complaining about family meetings in Hungary. The long lunches. The judgements. The interfering. "He went alone by train," she says. "He never took me or my mother."

Then my mother calls again, later that same day. She looked up Richard in her father's memoir, which he wrote in German.

"It says here Richard died in a concentration camp." My mother whispers this. I know she has her father's book open in her lap.

"At Mauthausen in 1944," I say. "Your father left Vienna in 1939, right? He said he was the last of his family. But Richard was still alive. And you were still alive. Why did he say he was the last? Did he think you were dead?"

"I can't answer for my father. I can't be expected to. He's dead. They all are. Leave it alone." My mother is 82 and she doesn't want to talk any more about the past. Not today. Maybe not ever. She hangs up. Again.

Before, I was driven by my own curiosity. Now I'm thinking of the lady archivist in Israel, waiting for my Page of Testimony. And I'm thinking of him: I'm thinking of Richard.

I will have to chip away for information, and I hate myself for thinking this way. I'm doing detective work, and somehow, I will have to trick my mother's memory into remembering, or at least tear down whatever walls she has up. My mother is a pro at keeping secrets. Before she married my father, she worked for the CIA.

My grandfather might have been wrong to forget about his Hungarian family and his family's past, but he instilled a forward thinking attitude in my mother that made her more advanced, determined, and hard-core ambitious than any other woman I know. She felt 100% loyalty to America for providing her and her family safe harbor, and like so many other thankful immigrants, she wanted to give back. After she finished her graduate degree at Johns Hopkins, she joined "The Agency," in order to "make the world safe for democracy." Her words.

Time is limited with my teaching schedule and so are my language skills. I don't know Hungarian, and, twenty years ago, I took one year of German, which doesn't help as I try to read my grandfather's memoir.

I'm in the middle of teaching world literature. At night, I go home and read the Nuremberg Military Tribunals. In class my voice cracks when we talk about the end of the empires. It's a survey class and we march quickly through history and literature: Pound, Joyce, Eliot, Lawrence, Yeats. Week five and we're in The Great War, as though any war could be called "great." It's all a set up. I want to go back in time, and stop the globe from spinning. My voice breaks again when we talk about the specifics of genocide, Zyklon B, the origin of pesticides, the race for some universities to hire the brilliant Jewish scientists, musicians, and scholars immigrating, and the Holocaust.

How did Richard "perish?"

According to Nuremberg trial testimonies, crimes committed at KZ Mauthausen Concentration Camp gained a reputation for brutality because of the use of slave labor. Men and women inmates were forced to work in the Wiener Graben quarry outside the walls of the camp, digging and cutting granite from the mines. The SS forced prisoners to carry heavy granite blocks up the stairs from the quarry to the camp, hence the nickname, "Stairs of Death." To amuse visiting dignitaries Heinrich Himmler and Adolf Eichmann, SS soldiers pushed inmates to their death, jokingly calling them "parachutists."

Hannah Arendt reminds me and my students about the "banality of evil." You get so caught up in the routine of the everyday, you don't notice little changes. You forget that both evil and good can just *happen*. There is the potential for both to exist side by side, for a long time. It's your choice. Not doing anything is also a choice. Ignorance is a choice, too.

I have been ignorant about the family I don't know for a long time.

Meanwhile, I have excruciating pains in my abdomen, and my doctor performs an ultrasound and finds a tumor. During spring break, to "celebrate" my birthday, I have it removed, in what the surgeon calls a "simple procedure." While under anesthesia, I dream of Richard, his face a pale blank. I lay facing him, sleeping outside in a ditch, while snow piles up all around. In the dream my blond hair grows longer so that it blankets the two of us. Even when I wake up, Richard is still with me.

In the weeks of recovery, I learn that Pécs, pronounced *Pay-ch*, is in southern Hungary in the county of Baranya. There is a University of Pécs. The Fulbright organization offers teaching opportunities, and I discover that there is an opening for a professor in the Department of American Literature. The information gives me goose bumps.

When I call the Fulbright offices in Washington, D.C., a woman named Muriel asks why I want to go to Pécs. It's spring but it's snowing, and I'm sitting hunched over the kitchen counter in a robe, flannel pajamas and fluffy slippers. I'm not feeling very intellectual or Fulbright-worthy.

I only feel pain and my own mortality, and, even though I am tumor and cancer free, the surgery felt like a wake-up call: I don't want to die without knowing about Richard and the story of my mother's family, or, as they say in the South, my "people." And I want our son, James, to know about all this too.

What if we lived and worked in Pécs on a Fulbright grant for a while? I could hunt for evidence, try to restore the pieces to this puzzle. I could *imagine* my way into Richard's life and death. How else do the living connect with their dead? Finding out about Richard and getting the assignment to remember him felt like a burdensome homework assignment, but now it feels like fate.

I've got the rock in the pocket of my robe, the rock from Israel, from where King David encouraged his men to be mighty men. I haul it around with me now wherever I go. James keeps his zipped in his tennis bag.

For some reason, I find myself whispering over the phone in a conspiratorial way. I tell Muriel I want to travel to Pécs, gather enough information to fill out the Page of Testimony for Yad Vashem, and maybe learn enough about Richard's life to write his story. I say all this out loud for the first time. *Write his story.* I secretly know that filling out the Page of Testimony is one thing, and figuring out who Richard was, is quite another. I might not get it right. Still, I can get close, can't I? Close enough to knowing this man, Richard? Surely, I can get to some sort of emotional truth about Richard. Isn't some version of Richard better than no version?

"You've got to do this," Muriel says.

I'm surprised that an official would say such a thing. *Why?* I want to ask. But I already know the answer. This isn't just about me discovering my roots. This has more to do with Richard, Hungary, history, and other lost, unremembered, unrecorded lives.

"I know," I whisper, the words hurting my throat. I'm holding the rock in the palm of my hand, squeezing hard.

Muriel tells me what forms I need, and who to contact at the University of Pécs. I can hear the energy in her voice. She says to be sure to apply for both the teaching and the research. She says to be sure to include my husband, Pat, and our son, James, in the application. "We want you *all* there," she says. Muriel and I are suddenly BFFs having coffee at the counter together, and I imagine she would even *like* my fluffy slippers if she saw them.

In the following weeks, I write the Fulbright application. My syllabi book lists read like wish lists of every book I've ever wanted to teach. I contact the head of the American Literature department in Pécs and she faxes a letter of invitation to teach there. Getting a

Fulbright is a long shot. The coincidence feels absurd—my need to research in Pécs and their need to bring in an American teacher to the University of Pécs? When does a match like this ever happen? Maybe more often than I know.

In the spring, news arrives in the mail. I stand in our driveway with the envelope, and when I read the letter of congratulations, I scream all the way back into the kitchen. I have been granted a Fulbright to research Richard in Pécs, teach Literature of the American South, the Contemporary American Novel and the first creative writing class at the University of Pécs, the second oldest university in Europe. The decision to accept the offer now depends on my husband and son.

When we met in graduate school, Pat and I took off by car to Mexico for spring break. After we married, we traveled to Bolivia, Italy, Ireland, France, and England all to teach, write, or make movies. When James was born, he came along. Once upon a time, Pat told me that being game and taking risks for the sake of art was what made the two of us tick. I adored him for not only living this way, but for seeing that we both could live this way.

He is game and willing to shutter his advertising and marketing business for five months. He buys books about Hungary and looks online for apartments in Pécs. James is entering the eighth grade and more than a little bored being in the same school he has attended since first grade. We work with his teachers to piece together a curriculum aside from the work he will do at a Hungarian school. His French teacher worries learning another language will be confusing. Everyone is concerned that James will fall behind in Math. We decide the experience of living in a different country outweighs all the other concerns.

That summer, when we visit my parents who live near Chicago, my father tells me he is having trouble reading, having trouble recognizing sentences. "The words slide off the page," he says. I drive him to see an eye doctor, who says he has dry eye, but the eye drops do nothing to improve the problem. He makes an appointment with his good friend, a cardiologist who holds up a headline from *The Wall Street Journal*. "It looks like Chinese," my father says. The cardiologist orders a CAT scan and my father is diagnosed with a brain tumor. Nobody calls it cancer. His Neurologist says radiation will shrink the tumor. He schedules the treatments to begin the week we leave for Hungary.

"You're never going to have this opportunity again," my father says. "Go. Tell us what you find out. We'll see you when you get back." He makes it sound like we're going out for groceries. Pat, James, and I spend two weeks at their house, cooking and freezing meals. We stack Ziploc bags of soups, stews, sauces, chicken pot pies, and meatloaf with spinach. I make loaves of my father's favorite gingerbread, banana bread, and six kinds of cookies. Comfort food. Pat gets my mother a new laptop computer and sets her up so she knows how to Skype. We tell her we're a computer button away.

My mother swears. She nags me about my clothes, my hair, even my passport picture. "You look jowly."

"Why is grandmother being so mean to you?" James asks.

"Being mean makes it easier for her to say goodbye."

Throughout my life, whenever I returned home, my mother would say in so many words, *Don't forget who you are or where you came from.* She didn't mean it in the way that my father meant it, to humble me, when he said as much: Remember, you're from Newton, Mississippi. My mother meant the opposite. You come from noblilty, so don't embarrass us. Now she's not sure what to tell me, or if she wants me to go disguised as someone else.

I buy them a crockpot and leave them with a split pea soup, which will be ready for their dinner that night. We try to make our goodbyes casual. No big deal. Just going to Hungary. Be right back.

Kossuth tér, 1908

Part II

Hungary 2010

August
Broken

We have been traveling now for sixteen hours. Past tired, we are catatonic. Outside the Budapest airport, Pat tries to speak to a cab driver in Hungarian, but his words are gibberish. We have less than an hour to get to the Keleti train station in order to catch the day's last train to Pécs.

There is no Rosetta Stone for Hungarian. Friends told us it's an impossible language to learn. One former Fulbrighter informed me in an email that I will never have a "meaningful" conversation with other Hungarians because I don't know Hungarian. *Even if they know English, your conversation will not have any full meaning.*

Still, over the summer, we cobbled together words listening to language CDs in the car. We learned that in order to pronounce "*Magyar*," the word for *Hungarian*, it helps to think of the word *endure.*

We know a few phrases. *Jó reggelt kívánok!* Good morning. *Köszönöm szépen.* Thank you very much. *Hol van a mosdó?* Where is the bathroom? *Hol van a férjem?* Where is my husband? *Hol van a fiam?* Where is my son? We have been practicing, but outside the airport, Pat is too exhausted to recall any Hungarian word. The cab driver stands listening, his arms crossed. He is in no hurry.

"We need to take a cab from the airport to the Keleti train station to get a train south to Pécs," Pat says.

The cab driver stares at Pat with his arms folded. "*Jó napot kívánok,*" the cab driver finally says.

"Excuse me?" Pat says.

"Good day. You tell to me first, good day, then make request."

"*Jó napot kívánok,*" Pat says. "Can you please take us to the Keleti train station? *Köszönöm szépen.*"

The three of us sit in the backseat holding hands. The driver turns on the radio, then turns it off. All I can think is *this guy hates us.* We can't believe he actually lets us out not just at a train station, but the one we asked for.

When we board the train, we collapse into our seats. I try *not* to fall asleep. The last time I fell asleep on a train in France, someone stole my backpack. I would most certainly never fall asleep again.

In the country, in between villages, our train stops abruptly. We all wake up.

"What's happening?" James asks, groggy.

From our window, we see there are no houses outside, just train tracks, onion and sunflower fields. The conductor makes a garbled, impossible-to-understand announcement in Hungarian.

"I fell asleep," I say, pinching my cheeks to wake up.

"Mom," James says. "Chill."

Everyone around us begins to collect their bags, and they get off the train. I worry that we may be on the wrong train, heading too far east, towards Russia. Maybe we're already *in* Russia. I curse myself for falling asleep. Is this one of those checkpoints my mother warned me about?

"Get your passports out and ready," I tell Pat and James.

James rolls his eyes, but still, he gets out his passport.

I unfold my Fulbright letter of acceptance. *Jó napot kívánok,* I practice. I consider ways to introduce myself: I am a teacher. *Tanár vagyok.* I am a writer. *Én vagyok író.* Which will keep us safe?

The political situation in Hungary is at a turning point. The new right-wing Prime Minister Viktor Orbán says he wants to abandon liberal democracy, preferring something akin to Turkey or Russia. Later, he will declare that his aim is "to keep Europe Christian." Political opposition has withered. An opinionated, decisive man like Orbán looks strong. He pals with Putin. The government has tightened its control over the press and state finances, weakening Hungary's system of democratic checks and balances. There is increasing discrimination against Jews, the Roma, and other minorities. The rising political party, the *Jobbik,* organize anti-semetic demonstrations in Budapest to deface synagogues with spray-painted swastikas.

And here I am with my husband and son, in Hungary to memorialize my Jewish cousin who was murdered in Mauthausen.

"Broken," a man says in English as he passes us on the train. We must look like the exhausted, clueless, Americans. "Broken," he says again, directing our gaze to the land, the train, and everything around him. We nod and heave our luggage off the "broken" train, dragging our bags over the train tracks and the gravel to board a bus.

"Pécs?" I ask the bus driver. He shrugs, turning the key. He could be taking us anywhere.

"You forgot to greet him first," James says.

The bus takes us to the next town, where we board another train headed south.

"Jó napot kívánok," I say to the ticket-taker. "Pécs?"

"Pécs," he says, unsmiling.

In Pécs, the head of my department stands on the platform of the train station, waiting for us. Her presence feels miraculous. Mária, pronounced MA-re-a, is an older woman with glasses, wearing sensible shoes and a blue dress. Her salt and pepper hair is pulled back. She has enlisted her colleague, László, to help. László looks to be in his thirties, with spikey hair, plaid shirt, jeans, and serious black boots. He speaks perfect English with a British accent. Pat and James look relieved to see him. We load up two cabs to drive the few blocks to the apartment that will be our home for the next five months.

Pécs is a medieval city surrounded by ancient, stone walls. The narrow streets open up into wide-open squares, flanked with old yellow and pink buildings, and everywhere, there are cafés and shops. Pécs was a sad, dark place in my dreams, but this lost city in Yad Vashem's Valley of Communities is sunlit, gorgeous, and alarmingly cheerful.

Our apartment is above an antique shop on the corner of Jókai utca, a street Mária says is named for Mór Jókai, considered the Hungarian Dickens. We haul the luggage up two flights of stairs, grateful for László's help. The place is clean and airy with plenty of sunlight. A slippery spiral staircase made out of what looks like old trombone parts leads to the two small bedrooms and bath. There is a little balcony and a dining room with a table, where we can all do our work. Mária looks around and says *Jó*, which means good. Later, we discover that Hungarians often say *Jó*, like saying *So*, to fill the space between sentences. My grandfather had this habit. *So*, he would say.

"*Jó*," Mária repeats. "Now we will have dinner."

László begs off and says he has to go. We are all tired and not in the least hungry, but we don't want to be rude to my new boss.

Down the street in an outdoor café, Mária complains about the newness of the town squares. Pécs has been spruced up because this year it is the European Capital of Culture. There will be festivals offering goulash, dancing, and songs and everything you can think of when you think of "Hungary." Only weeks before, city workers dug up what had been the square's paving stones, which were gravestones.

Fifty years ago the Soviets used gravestones in the main Széchenyi Square in Pécs because there was a shortage of concrete. Every day the people of Pécs walked over their ancestors' names. Mária says the color and age of the gravestones lent an old-world melancholy to the square, which she obviously prefers and misses. Now, they've torn up all the gravestones and laid out new stones, which are blindingly white in the late afternoon sun.

Mária points out the Zsolnay store nearby. The Zsolnay Factory in Pécs is famous for producing stoneware and other ceramics since 1853. Later I will read about the Zsolnay family and learn they were friends with the Engel de Jánosi family, working together on the same building projects.

All around there are Bauhaus-style public statues made of bright white stone—one of a chair, another of a thumb. I look at all the buildings. Where had Richard lived?

We have turned our clocks seven hours ahead. History has already taken place. What has happened has happened. Early in the morning the sun will rise orange and pink, mist coming up all around the ancient walls that surround this city. The family secrets I hope to uncover promise to be exotic, maybe even pleasantly global, for, as I learned in the South, dead relatives are much easier to handle than the living. And they can't hurt you. Every day I will walk the streets and the newly paved squares where Richard and the Engel de Jánosi family walked. I *will* find their homes and their graves.

We order goulash. James watches Mária dig into her plate of food—a wheel of fried Camembert cheese on a bed of white rice topped with a dollop of dark blue jam Mária calls "fruitgravy."

The following day, Mária walks me the ten blocks to the university so I'll know my way there. László said he has a better, quicker route, but Mária wants me to go her way. Outside the city center, she points out a building covered with cracks—a modern high rise she calls the "towering mistake," which I later discover is the tallest derelict building in Central Europe, a twenty-five floor concrete building, too dangerous to tear down because there are other buildings all around. Mária says the wiring in the cheap concrete is rotting, and it can collapse any minute. Evidently the Soviets had concrete issues. *NEED?* is spray-painted several times on the bottom half of the building. Some of the *NEED*s have exclamation points.

Mária shows me where I will teach—a newer building tucked between the older university buildings. She takes me inside and introduces me to the department secretary, Bea, a thin, dark-haired woman who has all the keys and chalk. As we shake hands, I can't help but notice Bea sizing me up.

I am a woman of a certain age wearing sensible shoes and a black cotton (read washable) dress. I carry a backpack. I would like to blend in. Most women my age here carry purses and teeter on high high-heels, even when they walk on the jagged cobblestone streets. Later, I am to understand that some of these women map out the easiest, often longer route in order to walk in their high heels.

I also have a job teaching while most men and women in Pécs and in Hungary are unemployed. Before WWII, when there were thousands of Jewish people living here, there was major unemployment. Then they kicked all the Jews out of Pécs, and, *boom,* instant job creation. I could be seen as an outsider now, a foreigner taking a job someone here wants. I could be easy for locals to hate.

Mária explains that I will need to come to Bea for chalk, paper, pens, and the correct key to unlock the classroom before every class. *Why?*

"Not everyone is to be trusted," Bea says, squinting.

As soon as we've unpacked and set up the apartment, we Skype with my parents. We can only see the tops of their white heads and their room's white ceiling. My mother is scared of adjusting the laptop because she thinks we will all get disconnected.

James tours them through the apartment, walking around with my laptop, and, at one point, he stands holding the laptop with the sheer curtains fluttering all around to give them that other-worldly Eastern European feel. He opens the refrigerator to show my father the harvest of cheeses, peppers, mushrooms, and fruits we bought at the market. My father asks that he close the refrigerator door. He's just back from a chemotherapy treatment. The sight of our new treasures makes him nauseous.

Over the summer we made contact with a small middle school near the university, and arrange to meet with the principal. She is a young woman dressed in a low-cut suit, revealing impressive cleavage.

Even though we have been emailing back and forth all summer, she now thinks James should go to the other school in town, a Hungarian school with more English speaking students, Apáczai Nevelési Központ, ANK for short.

"I don't understand," I say, "*Sajnálom, nem értem*. We have made all the appropriate arrangements. Why the sudden change?"

She is giving us a look, as if to say: *You are not wanted here*. I can't help but wonder: *Is it because we are American? Or does she know something about my past that she doesn't like?*

The principal calls to make an appointment for us at the "other" school. Even though we have been rejected, and even though we feel diminished and defeated, we thank her. As we leave, we re-read the graffiti on the school walls. *Need?*

"I feel like we've been fired," I say.

"She probably thinks we're just too much work," Pat says.

"I don't like this place any way," James says. "It's too small like my old school."

That's exactly why we liked it.

The following day, we take the bus to the ANK, a public K-12 school a few miles south of the city center. Surrounded by tall, affordable apartment buildings, the ANK is a three-story, split-level heptagon of linked structures. All the concrete gives it a prison, Soviet look. There are easily a dozen entrances and all of them are identical. We find one open door, and walk the hall maze and end in the hallway where we began. After wandering the halls for some time, we find an office.

The principal, a stern, older woman stands as we come in. A middle-aged woman with a stack of papers joins us and speaks English. Betti seems excited to meet us, happy to have an American student, a native English speaker who might help her other students. She brings in coffee and apple strudel. She offers to tutor James in Math, Hungarian, anything. The students and faculty are all Hungarian, but there is a strong emphasis on learning English at the ANK. A few of James' classes will be taught in English. As we stand to leave, Betti touches Pat's arm. "And you'll be teaching English for us, no?"

Their previous English teacher never returned. Betti doesn't say why. Later, we find out, that the previous teacher before also never returned, but that was because he died. Nobody mentions salary. Pat and I look at each other, and I can see that he's thinking, *there goes the sabbatical.* He reluctantly agrees, and the principal smiles for the first time.

As we leave, Pat and James discuss synchronizing their journey to and from the school. Classes begin at 7:15 a.m. They will have to get up at 5:00 every morning to catch a bus, but they will get out of school early, around 2:00. James is talking fast, which means he's excited. He says the school and the commute will be an "interesting challenge." It's everything he has never tried.

"I think we're making a mistake," I whisper to Pat.

"We don't have a choice," he whispers back.

They Will Grow Suspicious

"Relax," our language teacher tells us at orientation. We are back in Budapest for our first official Fulbright meeting. I sit with James and Pat in a big classroom in a nondescript building in the middle of the city with about fifteen other Fulbrighters. A few are here with their families too.

"Half knowledge is good knowledge when learning a language," our teacher says. "It's not so good if you're a surgeon, however." She talks about vowel harmony. She illustrates the darker sounds that come from the back of our throats, and the lighter sounds that come from up front. "It's not so very troublesome," she says when she sees that we are clearly having trouble.

We go around the table introducing ourselves, explaining the projects that brought us here. One young man is researching the Roma in Hungary. Another is translating a famous Hungarian poet. There are artists, academics, and a dancer. I am wary of talking about my research openly. A few state department officials sit at the table silently observing, and I worry that I might be "found out" by the current anti-Semitic government. Do they work for Viktor Orbán? My project might sound crazy, too. *She's looking for a dead relative she never heard of?* I worry that once they know about my research, which involves dredging up the sins of Hungary's past, they'll kick us out, or worse, make our stay miserable. I'm sure that any minute someone from Fulbright will call and say they've made a mistake, stuff us in a cab back to the airport, and put us on the next flight to the U.S.

I tell everyone my name and what I plan to teach. Period.

The dancer yawns.

We break for coffee and *pogácsa*, savory Hungarian scones.

"They're good," James says. "Are they supposed to taste old?"

As we eat, our language teacher discusses the "Hungarian attitude" with the class. She says Hungarians sometimes look and act as if nothing good will ever happen, not to them anyway. Every year on New Year's eve, most Hungarians stand up and sing the National anthem which ends *"Pity, O Lord, the Hungarians, who are tossed by waves of danger, extend over it your guarding arm, on the sea of its misery, long torn by ill fate, bring upon it a time of relief, they who have suffered for all sins of the past and of the future."*

The only translation for the English word *fun* means *nothing special* in Hungarian. "You are Americans, you want solutions," our language teacher says. "We are Hungarians. We are complainers. Complaining can be a form of happiness. Don't forget all our sufferings and the *t* in the endings. Our direct objects take the *t*."

Someone says that Hungary is supposedly not a very welcoming country. Hungarians like Hungarians. This makes complete sense. I was born in Mississippi, a state where even an Alabamian is considered an outsider. Here, we are the outsiders.

Another Hungarian Fulbrighter says that she has noticed that Hungarians don't smile much. Everyone in our class agrees.

"You don't want to overdo the smiling," another Fulbrighter says. He is from Hungary originally and has come back. "They will grow suspicious and you will be seen as hollow."

"It's like they just explained Grandmother," James whispers.

Several guest speakers come to talk about Hungary throughout the few days we are there. A contemporary Hungarian historian lectures about the tragic history of Hungary, saying that Hungary's "darkest" period was during the communist occupation. After class, I ask him about the Hungarian Holocaust. He says he doesn't know much about that period, but he knows enough to know that it was certainly not the "darkest."

"Why not?" I say. "Because they're all dead and they're not alive to remind you how bad it was?" Immediately, I regret my remark. I don't know if he even heard me because, already, I am out the door, heading to the lady's room to be alone. Who am I to say such a thing? Who am I to have this Hungarian chip on my American shoulder? Why am I shaking and why am I so . . . angry?

We learn the word for the poppy seed noodles my mother liked when she was a girl growing up in Vienna. *Mákostészta.* We learn what to say when we bump into someone, *Bocsánatot.* Then what to say for no problem: *Semmi baj.* We repeat the few phrases we already know when we don't understand: *Sajnálom. De nem értem. I'm so sorry, but I don't understand.* Our language instructor laughs with her eyes and asks us to repeat over and over. *Sajnálom,* we say again and again. *De nem értem. Sajnálom.*

After the language and history lessons, we fill out more forms for the Hungarian Fulbright office. They explain that even though we have all the appropriate papers, we will have to request a visa because of the extra three weeks in December we need to stay in Pécs in order to finish the semester. They tell us it's a minor inconvenience, that it will be no big deal, and that everyone goes through it. The Naturalization Office in Pécs will contact me.

When we get back to our apartment in Pécs, we Skype with my mother and father. They still don't want to adjust their computer's camera. My mother insists that connections are delicate. Sensitive. We talk to their ceiling and to the tops of their heads. We show them bottles of Tokay wine in the kitchen. James shows them forints and euros he's collected. He's taken to reading about the history of money.

"Don't tell people about your Jewish roots," my mother says to James and to me. "They'll come after you." She's not joking. The top of my father's pale head is shaking *no* as James does the same.

"Oh, Grandmother," James says.

Years ago back in Indiana, when I told him it wasn't safe to go door to door, campaigning for Obama in shady-looking, all-white neighborhoods with mostly McCain/Palin yard signs, James said, "Oh, Mom." He was ten years old. "The 1960's are over."

"Quit it, honey," my father says. "They know what they're doing."

I don't have the heart to correct him, to say *We don't have a clue.*

At the big farmer's market on Saturday, we get extraordinary cheeses, honey, apples, mushrooms, spicy smoked salamis and sausages, fish, flowers, and more peppers than we can possibly eat. My colleages at the university tell us to try and look less American when we shop, or else, the shopkeepers will charge more. Don't wear tennis shoes or backpacks.

Merchants see us coming, the Americans, and, they most likely hike up the prices. We don't know the language well enough to barter, but everything here is cheap anyway. We pay the extra forints willingly, forgoing the risky-looking "homemade milk," sold in recycled water and soda bottles. We find out later that "homemade milk" is unpasteurized. Pat takes pictures of the ladies chopping cabbage to make sauerkraut. They look ancient with their wrinkled faces, but they smile and blossom when Pat and James taste and buy their sauerkraut. From then on these women are known as The Cabbage Ladies and Pat and James visit with them every Saturday.

In the evenings we three work around the big dining room table. James does his homework for his Hungarian school and then his homework for his American school.

Pat has no curriculum to follow or textbooks from which to teach. He and Betti decide that the most valuable thing he can do with his students is to get them talking and writing in English with some vocabulary and grammar work thrown in. He designs strategies to teach English as a second language. One day, he uses Google Earth on his laptop to fly his students to our home in Indiana, zeroing in on our driveway and our home.

"Here is where our dog, Samantha, likes to sun herself," he says, pointing to the driveway.

He asks if there is any other place they want to see in the United States. "Hollywood," they say, and Pat tours them through Los Angeles, where he once lived.

I have re-connected with Peter de Jánosi in New York and he emails at least once a day. He says he can't believe we are in Pécs, the town where he grew up. He tells me he was the last Engel de Jánosi to be born in Pécs, and that he and his sister, Sissy, spent four years in hiding before they got to Mexico and then to the United States.

I think of Pécs in different times, when there were Germans in pike-gray uniforms. It's 1944, and some citizens wear canary yellow stars, each six-by-six centimeters, machine-hemmed onto coats and jackets, sewn tightly enough to keep a pencil from going under threads so you could not take it off when you felt like it. Hungary is a land of occupations, a kingdom without a king, but now there are no longer any occupying forces.

Peter writes that he is looking forward to sitting down with me to talk about Richard. I ask him if Richard had any girlfriends or boyfriends. Peter writes that Richard was a bachelor all his life. If Peter has any further details about Richard, he does not share them. He writes about one other living relative, Anna, who lives in Paris. *Another relative to tell my mother about?* Peter and Anna may be the last remaining relatives who knew Richard. Peter knows I am more than eager to sit down for this talk and I feel he is holding the golden ticket. I also feel he knows this. He and his wife, Monica, are making plans to come to Pécs for a ceremony to honor a family ancestor named Adolf, as soon as the mayor of Pécs schedules the date. It will be soon, Peter reassures.

Until then, Peter writes about which buildings once belonged to the Engels, as they were once known, and he provides his translation of Adolf's memoir, *Eletembol* or *My Life*. He also writes to me about Peter Engel, Adolf's father. Peter tells me to pay close attention to the fathers of the family. *Most everything in Hungary starts with the father,* he says.

With Peter's help and the memoir, I find out more about the Engel de Jánosi history and about Richard. I cannot know one without the other, Peter says. *Jó.* So.

At the big table, I read, grade, and prepare. Richard's Page of Testimony sits in the middle of the table, a reminder of what I came here to do. I look up from my work and stare at the word *victim* repeated so many times on the page.

September
It Starts with the Father

———————————————

My students keep trying to teach me how to pronounce their surnames. We go over the three different *o*'s, but I'm hopeless. I should do what Pat is doing with his students. He uses his iPhone to record video of his students introducing themselves so he can memorize their names and pronounciations.

In my creative writing class, we play the *What if?* game. *You got married last weekend? What if your groom hadn't shown up?* We all write different stories about the marriage that never was. One young woman says she does not like this "fiction" because it is lying. She drops the class. When I give an array of assignments, another student asks me to ask him a question to answer. That's the only kind of writing he knows how to do. "May I have a question?" he says. Some students come to my office to add my classes. Bea tells me not to be flattered. *They want to take your class because visiting professors are considered easier.* She reminds me to keep track of the chalk.

Then one day after my American Southern Literature class, a young woman stays to talk more about the similarities between the American South and Hungary.

"They both lost big wars," she says in English. "They both carry around a lot of guilt over the past."

Other students gather to get in on the conversation as I collect chalk for Bea. I wonder seriously what anybody would want with chalk if they stole it. Use it to write *Need?* on all of the walls?

"Why are you here? I mean, why would an American come *here?*" Dóra asks.

After our Fulbright orientation in Budapest, Pat gave me The Speech about not hiding anything. "Tell people why you're here," he said. "They can be helpful." He knows that my mother raised me to keep secrets. "People don't need to know anything about you," she said, which was helpful information growing up in Mississippi during the 1960's. As a result, I have tried to avoid the first person most of my writing life, unless it belonged to a fictional character.

"My mother's family is from Pécs," I say. "They were deported in 1944." Here, that's all you have to say. 1944. They don't talk about what happened, but they exchange looks. They know. I say I'm looking for information on one relative, Richard. I mention Adolf, Peter, and Bonyhád. I mention the Jewish cemetery there, saying I'd like to find Peter's grave.

Victim's Name. Engel. That's the first blank line to fill out on the Page of Testimony. To know Richard is to understand his father, and his father's father, and *his* father's father, and as far back as I can go.

That night, Dóra emails a map of how to get to the Jewish cemetery in Bonyhád, her hometown. She says she has never seen the Jewish cemetery herself, and that it's probably overgrown. It's late in the evening and the map she sends in her attachment blooms across my lit-up laptop screen.

That weekend, we rent a car and drive to Bonyhád to look for the cemetery and Peter Engel's grave. While Pat drives, I read from the stack of books I have in the front seat.

Richard's great-great-grandfather Abraham Engel lived in the 18th century village of Bonyhád, Hungary. Abraham had one son named Peter, who was born in 1772. Peter first sold rags approximately twenty-five miles south west of Bonyhád in Pécs. Pécs had laws that allowed Jews to come and sell their merchandise, but they were not allowed to live there without applying for permission. According to the earliest records, Jews lived in the county of Baranya, Hungary from the beginning of the 3rd century.

"It's just *Baranya*, not *Baaaranya*," James says from the back seat. "You don't have to exaggerate every sound or roll the *r* so much."

I continue, reading bits from a history book about the region.

The history of the Jews in Hungary stretches back to before the arrival of the original Hungarians, the Magyars, confirmed by a more than 2000 year-old Jewish gravestone discovered in Hungary dating from the time when the area was part of the Roman Empire.

In the late 17th century, after the Austrian Habsburgs captured Hungary back from the Ottomans, real hatred for the Jews grew right alongside hatred for the Turks. Maybe this hate came from the top down from the then King of Hungary and Habsburg Leopold I. Even though Leopold appeared to have no particular prejudice, his court preacher, Abraham, a Sancta Clara, was an anti-Semite, who hated both Jews and Muslims. Leopold's actions spoke volumes: he took money from the Jews to enlarge his palace and then sold their land to the burghers of Vienna, who immediately expelled them. But despite the anti-Jewish feelings, approximately 11,600 Jews lived in Hungary in the late 1600s.

"You know," James says. "Kids in my class drink alcohol. They all do, even the ones in 6th grade. Nobody can believe I'm going to a cemetery this weekend."

"You used to say Bud-leiser," Pat says.

The situation for Jews worsened during the reign of Maria Theresa back in the 1700's. Jews were forced to pay "toleration taxes" and were subject to persecution. The laws of the country permitted only a few Jewish families to live in towns. These few families were called "the tolerated ones."

Even though he paid tolerance taxes in Pécs, Peter Engel could not own property there. He was only allowed to travel *through* Pécs. Because Jews were often seen coming and going from town to town steering big carts, Hungarians furthered the stereotype of the wandering Jew, a homeless foreigner.

Peter must have been a great salesman, because he graduated from selling rags to trading grain. When recording the events of Peter Engel's life, a contemporary writer wrote that Peter's peers liked to "have jokes with him while working together." Maybe because he joked, Peter was allowed to buy crops from the best-run estates in the area.

"What kind of jokes?" Pat asks.

"It doesn't say." I'm staring down at the sheets of paper I printed out from documents my cousin Peter emailed me.

"Rag and grain jokes," James says.

"Do we know *any* Hungarian jokes?' Pat asks.

"The ones I know are like jokes we told about people from Alabama except they tell it about themselves. You know, How do you get a Hungarian out of the bath tub? Throw in a bar of soap."

"That's funny," James says, not laughing.

Peter met and married Maria Süsskind, an educated Jewish widow, who had inherited her first husband's house. At this time, in Pécs, when a husband died, the wife automatically was entitled to live in the house, but she could not own it. To legally own a house, the female purchaser had to apply for ownership with the city. Peter Engel was registered as a merchant in Pécs, but he was required to go before the town council to ask for permission to live there, and to register to live there in order to purchase his wife's property from the town.

It would have been easier to stay with his new wife every now and then, but Peter Engel wanted what he was not legally allowed to have as a Jew: he wanted property. To buy a home was a long, tedious, legal process. After years of haggling, delay, and lengthy litigation, Peter was finally permitted to live legally in Pécs, with his wife, and he also became the legal owner of Marie Süsskind's small house on a street that is now called Zrínyi Miklós utca 12.

Peter became the first Jew to own a house in Pécs, one room of which he transformed into a synagogue. He and other Jewish worshipers prayed there at least once a week, making it the town's first synagogue.

According to a speech delivered by the poet Henrik Lenkei in 1930, someone at the inauguration of the one-room synagogue said of Peter, "*Was dir einfäll, das baust du auf. Was du baust, das fällt dir ein.*" Or "What you build, collapses. What comes to mind, you build." Or perhaps more colloquially "Whatever you build, comes crashing down. Whatever pops into your head, you build."

"What does that even mean?" James asks.

"Have a vision, then go for it," I say, though I'm guessing.

There are no pictures of Peter. I imagine him with dark curly hair and a beard. In the years that followed, Peter became a wealthy man, despite the regulations against Jews in Pécs, and despite the infighting among the few "tolerated" Jews who lived and worked there.

"It was like that on Grandfather's side too. In Ireland," James says. "And practically at the same time." James wrote an oral history project for his history teacher the year before. My father told James about his ancestor John McMullan, who sewed sails for ships in Dublin with his brothers. James read about Ireland's British Penal Laws, which made it nearly impossible for Catholics to own land or have any political or social power. James told his grandfather that John was likely Catholic, which was why he left Ireland alone in 1760 when he was only eighteen. This was news to his grandfather, born and raised a southern Presbyterian.

Meanwhile in Hungary, Peter Engel's business floundered. In 1820, the year his first son, Adolf, was born, Peter bought a big shipment of wheat from a man named Czindery. Peter made a deposit of 1,000 forints, a large sum of money for Peter. Proceeds from the wheat sale would support his family for the rest of the year. Peter's fortune depended on this deal.

The day to deliver the wheat fell on Yom Kippur, the Day of Atonement, the holiest day in the Jewish calendar, a day of meditation, repentance and redemption. Many Jews spend this day at the synagogue or in a house of study, meditating, reading the Torah and chanting psalms together or quietly to themselves. It is a sacred day when a Jew does not work but prays. Who knows if Peter made a mistake when he scheduled the wheat sale. Regardless, on that day, Peter was not picking up the wheat he had purchased from Czindery. He was praying in his one-room synagogue.

The following day, Peter arrived to pick up the wheat and pay the remaining amount, but Czindery refused to honor the deal or return the deposit. *You're a day late,* he told Peter. As a result, Peter lost his year's income and the rest of his fortune. He went bankrupt.

"He should have picked up the wheat." James kicks the back of my seat, genuinely miffed.

"The Czindery guy could have waited," Pat says. "I mean. One day."

"There must have been some history between the two," I say.

Eventually, Peter had to sell his house back to the town in an auction, a public and private humiliation. After he lost his home,

Peter was a broken man. Marie gave birth to their second son, Simon, in 1822, but Peter's health failed quickly. A year later, he died. He was seventy-five years old.

Jews were not allowed to be buried in Pécs, so, Marie took Peter back to his hometown, Bonyhád, to be buried. Years later, his eldest son Adolf wrote in his memoir, *My Life,* that it was his father's wish to be buried in Bonyhád, even though his father never had a choice. Then again, why be buried in Pécs, a town that didn't even want him in the first place?

Maybe three-year old Adolf sensed that his father's death wasn't the end of something but the beginning, though he could not put into words what that something was. Is it possible that a family can pass along *a feeling* from one generation to another of being unwanted, rejected, *untolerated*? Did Richard feel this too?

When Peter Engel died, he left his family penniless. Maria and her two young sons, Adolf and Simon, were vulnerable without income. One year after Peter died, Maria Engel, married her third husband, an entrepreneur named Jakab Stern.

"The German word, *stern* means *star,"* I say.

"And *Engel* is *angel*," James says. "An angel with a star. Ha."

A few years later Jakab established a *Chevra*, a holy union among the different Jewish factions in Pécs to prevent bickering and to build strength in numbers. Jakab Stern also convinced the local magistrate to assign an acre of land next to the Catholic Cemetery in Pécs for a Jewish cemetery, which came to be on October 22, 1827.

Adolf inherited his father Peter's prayer book, which he kept all his life. Perhaps this one piece of inheritance served as Adolf's inspiration, and perhaps, it fueled what became his relentless ambition.

"Where's the prayer book now?" James asks.

"Who knows," I say.

Bonyhád is a hilly two-street town, and after we park, we trudge up and down the hills, through muddy cemeteries. We follow Dóra's map, searching in the brambles. At the end of the day, we come across what remains of the Jewish cemetery. The land has taken back the stones and we can't read any of the names or dates. Later, we discover that since World War II, Hungarian Catholics here bury their dead over the Jews already here, decomposing in the land.

The sun is setting and already it's cold. Our shoes are heavy with mud. We leave without finding Peter's grave. As we drive away from Bonyhád late that afternoon, there are three police cars with their lights on, while several policemen roam about the street. Some of them sip from their thermoses, the steam rising to their faces.

Pat slows and rolls down his windows, as though he is going through a check point. The police look at us and into our car. I think briefly that they might be after us for trespassing. Pat nods to them, rolls up his window, then makes the turn to get back on the highway.

"Should we stop somewhere for dinner?" I ask.

"Let's just get back home," James says.

Pat and I look at each other. We *think* James means our apartment in Pécs.

The marble halls are dark when we get back that night, but with each step, a light goes on. We smell the cabbage a neighbor is cooking. We have the wet, earthy smell of dirt about us. James sees an envelope slipped under our apartment door. He bends to pick it up.

Dear Neighbor,

I respectfully would like to welcome you as our house's new residents. I hope you're going to feel yourselves well in Pécs and we could be good neighbors with each other. In addition to the greeting, I am turning to you in favor of our peaceful and sound coexistence. My wife speaks English, but not too well, so we asked a friend of ours to translate this letter, to avoid using an even unintentionally offending style.

I would like to ask you a favor, as embarrassing for us as it is. Our family has lived in the mid-apartment of this house for two years. In the apartment, into which you recently moved, hasn't lived anyone. Perhaps that is why I realized just now that your second floor bathroom wall and our bedroom wall is the very same. In this wall run the water pipes. When you use the bathroom at 5:50 in the morning, it means to us that we shall get up as well because everything is heard in our bedroom so we cannot sleep.

As a musician and the director of the city's symphonic orchestra, I work a lot in the evenings; so I have to admit I am a late-in-the-bed-goer. It is really uncomfortable for me that I have to get up this early although I can't go to bed earlier, cause of my profession. I would respectfully ask if it's possible, that please use the ground floor bathroom in order to living next to each other undisturbed.

I am a believer in honesty and a very considerate person so I am confident that you understand and accept my request.

Let me also invite you to one of our next concerts with film music hits in symphonic orchestration, so your teenage child is likely to be able to enjoy it.

In our kitchen, we reheat leftovers and laugh about the letter, guessing at all the things The Maestro has overheard.

"Teenage child," Pat jokes. "Please pass the bread."

We catch up with the evening news on Al Jazeera. We find out about a Hungarian boy in Bonyhád who killed his father that day, cut up his body, to fit him into a home freezer, "marinating" the body parts in paprika. The reporter actually uses this word, *marinate*. The reporter is standing in front of police cars we all recognize.

"Where *are* we?" James wonders out loud after hearing the news story. He takes off his glasses and rubs his eyes. He needs a haircut. We all do. Even though the three of us know that such bizarre news events occur everywhere, any time, we all grow quiet as we prepare for bed. Am I the only one thinking about the boy's father in the freezer, wrapped in paprika?

Early the following morning, Pat and James use the less convenient, less modern, downstairs bathroom, and we all tiptoe around the apartment, careful not to disturb this Hungarian universe. We don't want to be The Loud Americans. We don't want to be butchered or marinated. We don't want to be unwanted. We aspire to be merely tolerated.

Punch Line

The Immigration and Naturalization Office in Pécs calls my office at the university. The Naturalization woman on the phone tells me in English that they are reviewing our "cases," and they request that I come to their office to fill out more forms. I am to report immediately to the *Bevándorlási és Állampolgársági Hivatal, Dél-dunántúli Regionális Igazgatóság* or the Immigration and Naturalization Office, South Transdanubian Regional Directors.

I find the way, looking for a low-to-the-ground, soviet-style, concrete building because that's what my imagination tells me it will look like. My imagination is correct. Their offices are a few blocks from the university, down the hill, past the cracked tennis courts. Inside, I stand in line for twenty minutes, considering the word *naturalization.*

To be naturalized is to be admitted to the citizenship of a country, but it also means to be altered so that one conforms. My father and I planted daffodil bulbs so that they could naturalize and spread. The idea is to establish the living thing in a region so that it can survive and prosper. *No big deal,* I say to myself over and over. But still, the fact is undeniable. Our right to be here in Pécs, to naturalize and spread, is in question.

When it is my turn, I stand before a woman standing behind a waist-high desk. There is no stool for her. I tell her my name. She gives me forms. As this woman holds the forms out, I see she is wearing very high red heels.

I think of this lovely dark-haired woman standing all day in red high-heels in The Naturalization Offices and I consider those shoes called Naturalizers. I want to make a witty remark, but I also know the joke will get lost in translation, and I really don't have a punch line, so I take the forms, thank the woman, and walk back to our apartment, careful not to walk too near the derelict building because one of my students said that chunks of concrete are falling from this building and one hit a passer-by, killing her. I don't even know if the story is true, but I don't want to die in Hungary from Communist concrete felled from "the towering mistake." There are better ways to go.

Our apartment in Pécs on Jókai utca is two blocks down from Zrínyi utca 12, Peter Engel's former home from 1820. When I pass the red, stuccoed house, I stop and stare. This was Peter's house and the first synagogue. There is no sign on it to distinguish it from any other building. Children bounce balls next door at the Catholic school playground.

There are two words for red in Hungarian—*piros* and *vörös*. *Vörös* is more blood-red. Peter's house is *vörös*. Some of the children look on suspiciously as I take pictures, then crouch near the base of the house to peel off a few chips of rust red paint from Peter's walls, secreting them in a plastic Ziploc bag. Most likely, the neighbors don't know anything about this house, but I do. Somewhere, there should be a signpost, a plaque or a gold stone at the threshold saying: first synagogue in Pécs; first house in Pécs owned by a Jew.

I get up, angry all over again. From now on, I promise myself, I'll take Zrínyi utca to and from school, just to pass Peter Engel's *vörös* house.

"We were held hostage today at school," James says, breathless, running down the trombone staircase.

"What?" I'm taking off my coat, putting my bag down. The Maestro's son practices his scales endlessly on the piano next door. We know better than to complain.

"It wasn't quite like that," Pat says. He's at the table, already working on more lesson plans. "We couldn't get into the school this morning. All the doors were locked."

"Then, when we finally found one open, the hall monitor wouldn't let us in," James says, unwrapping a piece of *Tejkaramella* candy. "She's this short, fat old woman, and she was *really* angry." He slows down, chewing the caramel. "She just kept shaking her head, *nem*. And then she spoke Hungarian really fast."

"We couldn't understand anything she said," Pat says. "I kept saying *Tanár vagyok* I am a teacher. She just said *Nem.*"

She led them into a tiny, windowless classroom and closed the door, leaving them to sit there alone in the dark. "At least she didn't lock it," James said.

After about twenty minutes, when it was clear she was not coming back, they peeked outside the door, and, seeing the coast was clear, they snuck out, and got to their classes late.

"Should I call someone? Betti?"

"We'll handle it, Mom," James says. He eats more candy.

"This is crazy," I say. Pat is pouring me a glass of *bor.* We're drinking more here.

"We weren't scared," James says. "It was more *annoying* than anything."

"Well," I say, heading towards the kitchen, moving away from the sound of the boy practicing the piano. "It wouldn't hurt to be more scared."

James rolls his eyes. "Real healthy, Mom."

At the university, before class, I go to Bea for chalk, the classroom key, and the boom box, and I start the Southern American Literature class with music my father taught me to love: Billie Holiday, Louis Armstrong, Ella Fitzgerald, Ketty Lester, Jelly Roll Marten's "Red Hot Peppers." The students laugh when I dance a little. Colleagues pause outside in the hall to listen. What do I care? We might get kicked out of Hungary any day. Might as well dance to Jelly Roll.

I learn later how much Hungarians love jazz and American blues music, music the Soviets allowed, which, ironically, became one more death knell for communism. Jazz, gospel, and the blues all have lyrics that inevitably urges you out of bondage and captivity towards freedom.

One student tells me proudly that he has already read William Faulkner's "As I Lay Dead." There is no present progressive verb in Hungarian, so I don't laugh. The closest Hungarian translation for *As I Lay Dying* is *As I'm Being Laid Out* or *As I Died.*

During our discussion, Zita says of Faulkner's Addie Bundren, "The mother is decomposing. The whole family is decomposing because their world has fallen apart."

I take a breath. "Yes," I say. We all think about what she has said, how things can suddenly all fall apart.

In the last class of the day, the class reads sections of Tennessee Williams' *Streetcar Named Desire* out loud. They read the part about what once belonged to Blanche, how she couldn't keep the house or the money, how she was left destitute and desperate, how she *had* to become a school teacher. For weeks, these students have talked to me about their own situations. Most of them live with a number of family members and grandparents in small houses or apartments.

"The melancholia of the American South, and so many women alone or orphaned or broken," Jùlia says. "I know this world." When Jùlia's mother died during the communist era, Jùlia was sent away because no one could afford to raise her. "Do you think Tennessee Williams meant to have Blanche represent so much that was lost?"

"Does it matter what the author meant?" Viktor, a body builder who's also in a rock band and has written beautifully in another class about growing up on his grandparent's fruit orchard, makes a convincing Stanley.

"Shtella!" he shouts.

The women argue about Blanche. The majority of them think Blanche deserves to get raped by her brother-in-law. "She was flirting," Barbara says. Barbara has just handed in a lovely piece about making apricot marmalade. "She was asking for it."

I want to say *you can't possibly think this way.* I wonder if I will ever understand them. We talk about Blanche and the power of memory to compensate for loss. We continue discussing loss until the bell rings.

Our apartment is above an antique shop, and I am thrilled when I finally step into the shop after the "Streetcar" discussion and after all my classes are over for the day. I run my hands along old, polished wood furniture that somehow looks familiar. I've withdrawn a hefty amount of forints and I'm ready to buy. I can figure out shipping logistics later. The handsome, dark-eyed owner rises from behind his desk as I greet him ever so carefully and politely in Hungarian. *Jó napot kívánok.* Then make a request.

I worry about my crinkled clothes, but I shouldn't because we are, in fact, looking more and more like everyone else in Pécs who have the same tiny washing machines that spin clothes until they're twisted and wrinkled. The first time we used the washing machine, it spun all day and all night, probably thumping near the sleeping head of The Maestro. When we take the clothes out of the machine, we untwist and hang them over the trombone parts of our spiral staircase in the apartment. There are no dryers. As a result, our clothes are wrinkled and misshapen, and, as James says, "crumbly."

The antique store-owner's dark hair is pulled back into a fetching ponytail. He too is wearing a dark wrinkled shirt. He takes me by the arm, as though he has just asked me to dance. Perhaps there is some very special armoire he would like me to see? He is walking me towards the front of his shop. Towards the silver in the window, maybe, or that antique Zsolnay vase I admired from the street. But no. He escorts me right out the front door and out of his shop. Then he turns to close and lock the door. I watch him return to his seat behind his desk. He sits down and begins reading his newspaper. I have no idea what I did wrong, or really, what just happened, or why. All I feel is shame.

He kicked me out of his shop.

I have never been kicked out of anything.

In the weeks to come, the antique store door remains closed, though the handsome owner is always behind his desk, reading the newspaper, ponytail snapped in place. Every now and then I see him talking to someone he has allowed inside. We learn that many Hungarian shopkeepers have not embraced western-style capitalism. They do not jump up to try and sell you their wares. They wait and *maybe* they will let you in or get up to help or to take your forints. Maybe not. But kicking out customers? It's impossible to make any sense of this. What am I not understanding?

Whenever I pass the antique store carrying boxes or bags containing purchases, I hold these high up in the air so that the handsome shopkeeper sees. In this way I am Julia Roberts in "Pretty Woman." *See? See what you're missing out on?* But he remains unimpressed and goes back to reading his newspaper. He probably has a story about me and my visit, which he tells at dinner parties. I have a feeling that I am the punch line to some Hungarian joke I will never understand.

My cousin Peter in New York emails that his friend, an "amateur historian" interested in the Engel de Jánosi family history, Christof from Düsseldorf, Germany is driving down to Pécs to meet me. Also, the mayor's office has scheduled the plaque ceremony to honor Adolf Engel de Jánosi for late September. Peter wishes the ceremony were earlier. Perhaps I know of a way to get to the mayor? *Me? Get an audience with the mayor? I can't even get into the antique shop downstairs.*

Rat Fortress

At the Zsolnay fountain, an older man holds up my grandfather Friedrich's memoir, *…aber ein stolzer Bettler,* as if he's in some Cold War spy movie. Peter explained in an email that this man, Christof, is retired and spends a great deal of his time researching the Engel de Jánosi's. He visits cemeteries all over Germany, Austria, and Hungary, and he uses the dates on gravestones, which sometime differ from dates written in articles and family trees. Gravestone dates are almost always more accurate.

We give each other two airy Hungarian kisses. He has with him his friend Renáta, a beautiful woman about my age with short, red-tinted hair and smiling eyes. Christof speaks Hungarian and German. Renáta, who lives in Pécs, speaks Russian, Hungarian and English. Renáta has agreed to translate our conversations.

We lunch at a Hungarian restaurant with an Australian cowboy theme. Peanut shells litter the wood floor and they serve rattlesnake and ostrich meat in addition to Hungarian goose with red cabbage and potatoes. The menu is as thick as a Hungarian history book. It comes with English translations. I order the chicken with "oily seeds on a sofa."

Christof considers me a relative, though at this point I'm not sure how. I attempt to relax with his affectionate familiarity as I enjoy my plate of chicken and spinach, which has neither oil nor seeds nor sofa. I have no idea how this day will unfold, realizing soon enough just how much has gotten lost in Google translations—Christof and Renáta have set aside not just lunch, but the entire day that runs into the evening and dinner.

Christof and Renáta walk me through Pécs, and introduce me to all the Engel de Jánosi buildings and homes I have passed every day, unaware of their relationship to me.

Adolf put his youngest son, Moritz, in charge of this building on the corner of Széchenyi Square. Moritz is the tallest son, with thick dark hair and no beard. Maybe it was a test. Moritz was twenty-four and this was his first major project. His father, Adolf, had already built several impressive buildings in Pécs, and Moritz could not let his father down with this structure, which was in the heart of the town, in the square named after Adolf's idol, Széchenyi.

Richard's uncle Moritz was my great-grandfather, married to my great-grandmother Marie.

I stand and catch my breath. Before me is something solid which connects me to them. Ornate and impressive, this massive building looks like The Flat Iron building in New York. Later, I discover that after Henrik Ibsen became friends with Moritz, and visited him, he thought of this building and the town when he wrote his play, *Wild Ducks*.

Moritz and Adolf hired the architect Ludwig Förster, who studied in Munich and Vienna and contributed to the Ringstraβe in Vienna, and the Dohány Street Synagogue in Budapest. When Moritz had his men level what they called the "Rat Fortress" to begin digging the foundation for the new building, they discovered a great deal of sand. Wood pilings had to be constructed. The project went over-budget and over-time. Nevertheless, people talked about Adolf and Moritz's first triumphant building project together for years–it was the first residential building in Pécs with an elevator. Adolf gave the building to his daughter, Bertha, when she married Leopold Loránt, a physician in town. The Rat Fortress became known as "Loránt Palota" or the Loránt Palace.

By 1885, Adolf was in the habit of buying estates and giving them to his sons and daughters. He bought Ócsárd-Pázdány from Count Draskovich for his son, Julius, later run by Julius' son Paul, who was my cousin Peter's father. Julius married Lenke Fűrst de Maroth and moved to Budapest, where he worked as a director at the Danube Steamship Company. Of course, this marital connection with the steamship company would help ensure deliveries for Adolf's lumber company in Vienna.

Maybe as a bonus for doing such a good job, Adolf invited Moritz to join him in establishing a new factory in Vienna.

The German Shepard at the Jewish Cemetery in Pécs growls and barks. The caretaker unlocks the gate, stands, and waits for Christof to dig into his pocket to give him a few forints. The caretaker says something and laughs. Christof waits for him and the dog to go back inside, then he takes a skullcap from his pocket, unfolds it and puts it on as we walk.

Christof explains while Renáta translates that the caretaker is not Jewish, and it is always a good idea to pay him a little something extra and to thank him so that perhaps he will keep the dogs off us, keep the graves tidy, and the vandals away. Am I growing too accustomed to this kowtowing, a version of tolerance taxes? Maybe James and Pat should give the hall moniter a few forints to get into school.

The Jewish cemetery in Pécs is old, shaded, and overgrown. I imagine it photographed in sepia tones. Some of the gravestones are nearly impossible to read, but Christof knows exactly where to find the Engel de Jánosi plot.

Not all of the bodies are here, but the names are and it means more than I could have known. I touch the obelisk stone with the Hebrew inscriptions, tracing names with my fingers. I will have them now to fill out Richárd's Page of Testimony. *First name of victim's mother:* Rózsika. *Maiden name of victim's mother:* Justus.

The stories and articles I have read have made my family real, but touching their names makes them even more real. This is why we have memorials. I find Richárd's name. The accent over the *a* is new to me. This is the first time I've seen his name in print outside of Yad Vashem. I say it out loud, the Hungarian way *Richárd* is supposed to be said, the *ch* a hard *c*. It feels like a prayer. I know his bones are not here, but his name is. Richárd. And his date of birth: July 31, 1882.

On Yad Vashem's typed sheet, Richárd's birthdate is July 31, 1892. *Approximate age of victim's death:* Richárd was, in fact, sixty-two years old, not fifty-two years old when he entered the gates of Mauthausen. Because there is so little information about Richárd, this new detail means the world to me. I will check to be sure, but if the date is right, I am both sad and relieved. He had ten more years of living than I thought.

We lay stones near the polished black marble oblisk, to remember the dead. We stand and breathe in the earthy smell of mud. *Yizkor*, in Hebrew, means "Remember" and it is the first word of a special prayer for the dead. The prayer implores God to remember our dead, and when the *Yizkor* is said, the connection, the bond, between us and the dead is strengthened. I whisper what I can recall of the prayer. *May God remember the soul of my father.* Right then and there, I feel them all gathering around us one by one in their long black coats. All the Engel de Jánosis. The men wear hats. Richárd is among them. So is his uncle, my tall great-grandfather, Moritz with his thick dark hair. I am in the right place at the right moment. I feel this with all my being. Ignoring the ants biting my ankles, I stare at my reflection over my ancestors' names in the smooth black marble of the obelisk.

We take a cab into the steep hills to Renáta's house, which overlooks Pécs. She has prepared a beautiful dinner of goulash, bread, and wine. Her husband Zoli, a bear of a man, greets me like a sister with a strong, warm hug. A historian at the University of Pécs, Zoli speaks German and Hungarian, but not much English. He knows the words, "My beautiful wife" and "OhMyGod" and he says these often. His specialty is the Danube Steamship Company and the history of coal in this region.

At the candlelit table, as Renáta translates, Christof explains that he discovered his connection to the Engel de Jánosi family about five years ago. His family's summer cottage was named Engel-Baiersdorf after Erna C. von Engel-Baiersdorf. Erna married Róbert Engel de Jánosi. Róbert was Richárd's brother.

Christof asks what brought me to Pécs. Is he suspicious or is that my imagination working overtime? Maybe it was the afternoon at the cemetery or the wine, but I tear up as I tell the whole story again about Yad Vashem and my search for Richárd, and as Renáta translates, she and I get into a talking rhythm that feels familiar and natural. In the candlelight, we drink the red wine, *bor*, and talk, and I grow awestruck with how we all came together at this table— strangers—all because of Richárd. Sometimes the dead bring the living together.

Christof brings out an antiquated laptop and even though it's slow to boot up, he begins to copy articles on a disk, there at the table. I tell him that whatever I find, I will send to him too. Later I will see just how much he gives—articles about Richárd's grandfather Adolf, and his great-grandfather, Peter, articles from all over Europe I never would have found on my own. Renáta offers to translate. Christof provides copies of photographs, time lines, documents from the city hall in Pécs, and blue prints of family homes. He even has a grainy black and white picture taken in the early part of the 1900's of the *Hofzeile*, my mother's childhood home in Vienna. During one of our Skype sessions, I email it to her and she weeps. She has never seen a picture of her home. The Germans bombed the *Hofzeile* after my mother left.

We talk until midnight, and after the *pálinka*, the thank-you's, and the farewells, Christof and I get into a cab, heading back down the steep hill towards the city center. The cab driver doesn't so much drive as he steers the car as though it were a sleigh. The night has grown cooler. Fall is in the air. Christof reaches across the back seat and takes my hand.

We are *sort of* related. And we are, after all, both on a mission to discover what remains of our families. My only promise was to share research, though now I worry if this too got lost in translation. I tell myself the hand-holding is more dear than creepy, more we're-in-this-together-so-let's-join-forces than "romantic," more European than American. This is my read of the situation, even as the cabdriver sneaks glances in his rearview mirror. When the cab stops in front of my apartment building, in front of the closed antique store, which is still off-limits to me, I turn the hand-holding into an American handshake, and I thank Christof over and over again. My ankles itch from the ant bites at the cemetery. I am more than eager to get inside, copy and save everything from Christof's disk, and start reading.

Pat and James open the door before I can put in my key.

"Where were you?" Pat says.

They tried to text and phone me, but my phone was not working. I apologize over and over.

"I should have called but I got so caught up."

"We were worried," James says, taking my phone. He sits down and gets to work to adjust the settings. "You're a grown woman, Mom. You should know how to work your phone."

In the following weeks I visit museums and libraries, collect the historical backstories, and spend evenings reading the articles about the town of Pécs, the early Jews of Pécs, and the Engels. On these evenings I feel the presence of Richárd in the room. I stay up late night after night in this city, the cradle of my ancestors, hoping to bring him back, both of us glancing at the Page of Testimony in the middle of the table, partially filled out. I want to ask him to be patient. *Wait a sec. I can almost see your face.*

Every few weeks, Pat, James, and I travel to Budapest and other Hungarian cities, where we pick up envelopes fat with forints from the Fulbright staff.

"Let me *see*," James says, shuffling through the colored bills. He reads through each one, a history lesson of people who gave their lives for Hungary. Everywhere I go, whenever I make a purchase, James calculates the forints for me.

"So you can work on your math skills," I say.

"So you don't have to think about numbers," he says back.

Getting these wads of foreign cash feels illicit. James counts out the appropriate sums. I deliver the cash to the department secretary Bea at the university so that she can pay our landlord for what we now know to be an overpriced apartment. We tell ourselves not to worry, not to feel as though we have been taken advantage of because we are Americans. I tell myself it's not because they know I'm an Engel, and, therefore, Jewish. I scratch at my ankles still dotted and swollen from the red ants in the cemetery. I tell myself we are paying rent, not *tolerance taxes*. I tell myself these things every day as I pass the antique shop, its doors closed shut to the likes of me.

Roots Run Deep

When he was eleven years old, Richárd's grandfather, Adolf, quit school to earn money. In his memoir, *My Life,* Adolf wrote, "For a few kreutzer, I bought some asbestos and sulfuric acid, which I filled into bottles, dipping wood sticks into them to make matches." He sold these matches, then pencils as well. It was 1831. Adolf's mother, his stepfather, Jakab Stern, and his little brother Simon were still living in Peter's house on Zrínyi utca in Pécs, a house they no longer owned. They had no heat and they were desperately poor. At eleven, Adolf was thinking what he had to do to own this house again, the home that broke his father's heart. Maybe Adolf believed if he sold enough matches and pencils, he could buy back the house.

Pécs is a small town, but it was even smaller back then. Everyone knew his neighbor's business. Peter Engel had lost everything and died shamed and penniless. His son, Adolf, carried the fear of poverty, homelessness, and perhaps, shame with him. When you lose all your money once, you don't want it to happen again. I see this fear of losing and financial ruin in myself and in my mother. Every day she worries over the smallest bills, even when my father, a successful businessman who worked hard all his life to give her everything, tells her she doesn't have to worry. But she lives to worry. She hunts for people and things to worry about, the way babies need pacifiers.

During Adolf Engel's lifetime, Hungary rode an economic roller coaster. In the first decades of the 19th century, when Austria ruled Hungary and the French Emperor Napoleon was attempting to conquer most of Europe, there was desperate poverty in Hungary. Trade, production, transportation and social and political life were at a low point. But in the 1830s, the Hungarian statesman, Istvan Széchenyi, inspired the nation with his writings, speeches, and leadership. Slowly the entire country began to show an interest in fostering employment and production. Adolf was eleven years old when he learned about Széchenyi's life and work. Everyone in

Hungary was talking about this great Hungarian leader and a can-do atmosphere of a rising middle class. Everything felt possible, even in Pécs.

Adolf added to his wares of matches and pencils. He began to buy and sell used clothing, and every day after his work during the cold, winter months, instead of going to his un-heated home, he went to the heated rooms of the bishop's library on Szepessy Ignác utca, the first public library in Pécs, founded in 1774 by Bishop György Klimo.

Klimo's library was open to the public in 1832, one year after Adolf quit school. Adolf took full advantage of this new library studying on his own, reading and learning geography, history, and languages. Adolf knew the sooner he sold his merchandise, the sooner he could warm up at the library. He sold his merchandise every day by noon. In four years he was fluent in German, French, Hebrew, and, of course, Hungarian.

Adolf was sixteen when he grew his business and began to trade tobacco. He traveled to tobacco farms in Godisa, Hungary, where he slept on straw in barns, eating bread and dried cherries he kept in his coat pockets.

At that time, there was little industry in Hungary, so it was not easy for people in Pécs to get furniture. At one point, Adolf sold his own bed, and slept on straw until he could afford to buy another bed. In 1838, when Adolf turned eighteen, he requested and received permission from the town of Pécs to open a store to sell old furniture.

People continued to buy clothes, furniture and tobacco from Adolf and his business thrived. When Adolf turned twenty, he hired two local men to teach him more about business practices. In 1844, when he was twenty-four years old, Adolf married Anna Justus. They were first cousins. There were many such marriages among family members in small towns during this time. It was considered preferable to marry within the family because you *knew* them and you knew what to expect. No surprises. In addition, family money remained within the family. The Engel's ancient Hungarian family history parallels with my father's ancient southern American family history of cousins marrying cousins. My father told me once about two brothers in his family who married two sisters. The two families lived across the street from each other for a decade, and then the brothers swapped wives and had more children.

In his memoir, Adolf wrote that Anna had a "good domestic education" and possessed all the fine qualities praised by King Solomon. She also had a tidy dowry of 500 forints, which, in 1844, was the equivalent of about $8 in America. Money was never far from Adolf's thoughts, most likely because he was still relatively poor. Still, even though he and Anna continued to live modestly, every evening Adolf invited poor local University of Pécs students to dinner for the company and good conversation, learning and challenging himself with new ideas.

Within four years, Adolf began to make a great deal of money selling and trading. At this time in 1848, when Adolf was twenty-eight, eighteen-year-old Franz Joseph came to the Habsburg throne in Vienna. Images of the young Habsburg trickled down to Pécs as early as 1835. In this old Empire, youth was no longer an impediment to success; it was a strength.

At the same time, the Austrian General Haynau imposed a mandatory payment on the Jews of Hungary, with the words that "they prove themselves as true patriots" to the Austrian-Hungarian Empire. Adolf contributed the equivalent of one million dollars in today's currency to the Empire. He had become wealthy in a short amount of time.

Perhaps as a result of political upheavals throughout Europe known as the Spring Revolutions in 1848, representatives of Hungary wanted their feudal Hungarian kingdom to be a modern constitutional monarchy. Influential Hungarian patriots forced the Imperial governor to accept their twelve points against the Habsburgs, an action which ultimately resulted in armed conflict between Hungarian and Austrian forces. Between 1848-1849, Hungary fought in a brutal war for independence in order to break from the Austrian Empire ruled by the Habsburg family.

Meanwhile, the Jewish community in Pécs grew as people moved there from all corners of the Monarchy, increasing diversity in religious viewpoints, and factions. There was a feeling among Reform Jews that if they let up on their strict religious laws, they might be viewed differently, perhaps less foreign, less "Jewish," and they might even get equal rights in their town and maybe even in their country. At this time, Jews were looked upon as non-Hungarian, foreign, and even to some, as somewhat otherworldly. Even creepy. Christians back then claimed they did not know exactly what went on during the Jewish worship services. There were rumors that Jews sacrificed Christian babies.

Hungarian laws forbade Jews to study law, but they could study medicine. Most Jews in Hungary were interested in progress and modernization, but the price for equality appeared to mean relaxing strict religious rules in order to "modernize" Jewish community life, which meant not keeping kosher and Shabbat so strictly. But the Conservative Jews of Pécs wanted to continue their laws of worship. Inevitably, the Jewish community of Pécs split into two camps: Reform and Conservative.

Adolf was one of the leaders of the Reform movement. He was devoted to Judaism, ate a strict Kosher diet, but he also believed in modern industry and hard work, both which helped his fortunes grow. He wanted to make Hungary as industrious, modern, and successful as Austria was becoming. After all, his father, Peter, had gone bankrupt because he devoted himself to prayer when he was supposed to pick up the wheat.

When the 1848 revolution broke out, many Hungarian Jews saw an opportunity to prove themselves to their fellow Christian citizens as Hungarians first, Jewish second. Even though he had already given one million guilders to the empire, Adolf turned radically toward the Hungarian side of independence, and joined up with the Hungarian National Guard from 1848-1849. At twenty-eight, Adolph was a self-made man. Against all odds, he had achieved so much. Maybe he felt invincible.

"A bunch of Philistines want to throw out the Jewish population," he wrote in his memoir in March of 1848. He insisted that his wife, Anna, who was nine months pregnant, flee Pécs with their four-year old son, Lajos.

Many Jews in Hungary participated in the 1848 revolution. But after Franz Joseph asked for help from Czar Nicholas I, and

Russian troops joined forces with Austria, Hungarian soldiers were outnumbered. As with all the wars Hungary has ever fought, their revolution failed, and the aftermath was brutal. Most of Hungary's leaders were tortured before they were put to death. Thirteen Hungarian generals were shot or hanged and about 500 death sentences were passed, of which 114 were carried out. Nearly 2000 Hungarians were put in prison. The seventy-five who fled the country were hanged in effigy. For months, Austrian troops conducted night searches, raping and stealing from Hungarians. In 1849, Austria imposed a dictatorship on Hungary, and judicial and economic restrictions were subsequently placed on the Jews. They were doubly punished—as Hungarians and as Jews.

After Austria crushed the smattering of Hungarian uprisings, Adolf and Anna Engel returned to Pécs. Anna gave birth to Helen. Soon after, they fled again. Serbian troops invaded in an attempt to make a grab for Pécs.

"The government lies." The boy with the long leather jacket and black lipstick has come to class for a change, and he's decided to speak. He sits in the corner next to a pretty girl who leans away from him. This boy unnerves his classmates. Today's discussion has veered from Shirley Ann Grau's novel to the American Civil Rights movement of the 1960's to governments in general. "All governments lie. Your own politicians in America caused the attacks on 9/11," he says.

"Why would they do that?" I ask.

"That's just a conspiracy theory," the pretty girl says. "He loves conspiracy theories."

"So they could blame it on the Muslims. So they could start a war. So they could get oil for themselves. Greed."

The girl next to him clicks her tongue and rolls her eyes. Others turn to me, waiting.

I ask him if he has any evidence. He shakes his head. My request is obviously pathetic. I am one more, brain-washed American.

"And then? They—your government? All governments." Black lipstick smudges his front teeth when he smiles. "They are so arrogant they don't notice us working against them."

After I return the classroom keys, chalk, and boom box to Bea, she tells me that the Immigration and Naturalization Office requests my presence as soon as possible. This is regarding my case.

In the rain, I walk to the Immigration and Naturalization Offices.

"*Jó,*" the woman official says when it is my turn. "So so wet." I have taken off my coat, but my clothes and hair are soaked. There are two stools at the desk, and the woman official sits with me this time. She slides the filled-out forms across the desk. Today the woman official is wearing black patent leather high heels. She asks that I please change the purpose of the visit of my son. "Please to write a letter requesting that the purpose of your son's visit is not "other" but 'family member.'" She smiles and crosses her legs.

In my mind, I see my student's blackened lips saying, "All governments lie."

I thank the woman, thinking all the while *no one really wants me or my family here. Ever again.* After all, I am not the original exile—I am merely a remnant. Surely I am here because I want something.

I get up to leave. Maybe The Immigration and Naturalization Offices are onto something. Maybe being a family member *is* purposeful. Being in Richárd's family, being an Engel de Jánosi is, after all, why I am here and why I brought my family here. Maybe I should do what Adolf's wife, Anna did—flee and stay away for a while and then come back when it's safe.

I walk back in the rain, dodging the derelict building. *Can't get me,* I secretly whisper to all the Communist concrete lurking around the towering mistake. I don't stop until I get to the Kafka Kafé. The Kafka Kafé used to be called Dante's Hell, but the Catholic diocese owns the building and would not allow the word *Hell* on its walls. So, the owner changed the name to the Inferno. But the Inferno went out of business. Then somebody else bought the Inferno, and apparently preferred Kafka and Jazz to Dante. Every Wednesday night, a Hungarian band plays American jazz, the music of freedom.

I decide then and there that the Kafka Kafé is just the right place to fill out the Naturalization forms and write the letter for the high-heeled woman official at the Immigration and Naturalization Office.

On Sundays we Skype with my parents, then, after talking to the tops of their heads and seeing that wide open ceiling again, I plead with my mother to move her laptop top forward so that we can better see them.

She leans in and her face comes into view. She looks pale and her hair is all white now. She stopped going to the beauty parlor, but she has put on lipstick, and she's wearing a nice brown silk blouse. My father stands behind her, holding his coffee cup, looking frail and less like himself. The radiation treatments are causing him to get thinner and he is losing his hair.

He has spent the better part of his life giving back to my mother all that she has lost--a beautiful home, antique European furniture, so many lovely things, a family, a country. And there she sits, my mother who has given him 100% of herself, and the kind of passionate love not readily reciprocated in his southern Presbyterian family.

I feel a pressing need to get Richárd's Page of Testimony filled out, put Hungary behind us just to get back to the states to help my parents. When I look at them, I see time ticking by. There are ancestors and then there is family. I want and need to be with my father more than I want or need to be with Richárd.

"We are *living* on your food," my mother says.

"The freezer is getting emptier," my father jokes.

I ask my mother if she would like to write a few words for the upcoming plaque ceremony, even though it has been postponed again and I seriously doubt it will ever materialize into an event of any kind. The mayor of Pécs has reassured Peter that the ceremony for Adolf will take place when the plaque is ready. The mayor's office realizes that already it's mid-September but the plaque simply is not ready.

My mother says she wants to do this because it will get her mind off "things." I know what she means when she says this. I know she means my father's cancer, even though no one is using the c-word yet.

"It's important," I tell her. "There's nothing here that says we were here." I am surprised to hear myself say *we*, knowing that I mean, *us, the Engels.*

Pat, James and I take the bus to James' ANK school for a charity event, where he has to perform a song with his classmates. On the bus, we meet up with one of James' friends.

Stigi is fourteen years old and he wants to be a chef. He likes to practice his English with Pat and James. He knows where all the good restaurants are and he has a recipe for *Kürtökalács*, which he pulls from his jeans pocket and gives to James. James calls *Kürtökalács* twirly bread because when you make it, you wrap it around a stick shaped like a baseball bat. Then you bake it over an open fire, sprinkle it with sugar and cinnamon. As you eat, it unravels. Once, at an outdoor festival, we saw a *Kürtőskalács* woman chef "quick-baking" her *Kürtőskalács* with a hair dryer.

We ask what today's school charity event is for.

Stigi moves his dark hair away from his forehead. "This charity is for the people without legs."

Women bring buckets of grapes from their gardens, apples and pears. The room is already filled with families. When we see the people in wheelchairs, we realize Stigi meant *handicapped.* There are pastries, almonds, cheese, homemade *pálinka* and *bor* for this Sunday's school event, way better than a bake sale at James' American school back in Indiana.

One of Pat's colleague's offers glasses of her red *bor.* Pat introduces me, explaining that I am Adolf Engel de Jánosi's great-great-granddaughter. Her eyes water as she smiles. She puts down her glass, straightens her hair and kisses me three times on the cheek. "Adolf," she says, backing away to get a good look at me. "He did give to my grandfather silver coins when my grandfather did do well on his school exams. I have these coins still. And now, you. *Jó.* Your roots run deep here."

James is already at the front of the auditorium with Stigi and his friends. There are about 100 other students lined up like birds on a telephone wire. They each have drums hanging round their necks. James and Stigi look humiliated. For them, this is childish. When their teacher signals, they begin singing in Hungarian, and every now and then, the students bang on their drums in time to the song. Maybe it's the *bor* or being "recognized" as Adolf's relative, but the song brings tears to my eyes. Everyone in the room sways to the music as they balance their glasses and plates of food. The "people without legs" dance in their wheelchairs.

We return to our apartment and to our laptops on the dining room table and I plunge into the articles Christof sent, some of which Renáta has translated. I piece together Adolf's life, telling myself that it's just as important to know and "remember" Richárd's grandfather so that I can know and honor Richárd.

At the university, Bea has a note for me from the woman from The Immigration and Naturalization Office requesting that I come to their offices as soon as possible. This is in regards to my case, which has been assigned a number, which I should write down.

How can I *not* feel unwanted here? The friendly, familiar streets of Pécs are less friendly, less familiar. Each time, I walk now to The Immigration and Naturalization Offices, it's raining, and the flat, grey concrete building a few long blocks away and down the hill from the university, has a third world feel, with its glass windows and back rooms into which "officials" disappear.

When I get there, after classes, I'm soaking wet. I am wearing the same black dress I always wear because I wanted to "pack light" for Hungary. This is a dress I can even wear inside out because inside, it's dark blue. I have worn it so many times, I can no longer tell the difference between the blue and the black. That morning I thought to wear this black dress inside out and back to front to save it from another washing and wringing in the torture device that is our washing machine.

The Immigration and Naturalization Office woman steps out from the back rooms bringing out my file folder, which has thickened. Today the woman official is wearing a different dark suit than the one she previously wore. This one has a shorter, tighter skirt and she is wearing high-heeled black boots. She looks like a Nazi porn star. I am convinced that she dressed this morning, knowing I was coming to her office. She wants to intimidate me. It's working.

The lady porn star official requests that I correct the forms I filled out, *here and here,* and sign them, *here and here.* She leans over the desk pointing to the blanks on my sheet and I see her impressive, pushed-together cleavage swelling with every move. She tells me to copy over what I have already filled out. I used pencil, *silly girl,* and they require pen. She smiles, her lips stop-light red. I realize just how misshappen my black travel dress has become, especially worn inside out and flipped, back to front. I feel like a flat-chested third grader, foolish and angry, and I want to stomp on this woman's high-heeled boots. There's another, more important form in the middle of our dining room table, at our apartment, a form from Yad Vashem I need to be filling out instead. The lady porn star gives me a pen, then stands over me, watching me trace over my stupid pencil letters in black ink.

He Who Rests, Rusts

After my visit with the lady porn star official at The Immigration and Naturalization Office, I am convinced that our time in Pécs is limited. I joke with Pat, knowing that I'm not really kidding. Not 100%. If we are lucky, we will get out alive and perhaps even relatively healthy, and I won't have to be exhumed from beneath the concrete rubble of the "towering mistake." Then we can all go home and tell stories about how the Engels got deported from Hungary. Again.

As I walk to and from the university, I look for Richárd in the faces wandering past. I'm looking for those who might have known Richárd in 1944, and for those who might have been the ones who tipped off the SS, who arrested him, or who saw him being taken away.

In a book about Hungarian Jews, I find a reference about an internment camp in Pécs. When did Pécs get rid of the internment camp where they may have held Richárd and 4,000 others? When I inquire at the city's museum about the internment camp, one assistant says it never existed. Facts about the camp's existence are nowhere in the museum or in any history book about the area. I email the archivist at Yad Vashem for more information about the camp.

I schedule lunch with a university historian. His specialty is Austrian history and the Jews of Pécs, but when I go to the restaurant to meet, he never shows. I eat "liver balls soup" alone. After more emails and phone calls go unanswered, I give up on him.

No one in Pécs seems to want to discuss what happened in 1944. The Municipal History Museum makes no mention of this period in the city's history. The archivist at Yad Vashem said to remember Richárd "properly," but history is so often written and manipulated by winners. History can't be written by the dead. Here in Pécs, I'm discovering that Hungarians, like everyone else in the world, have selective memories.

I stare at the blanks still left to fill out on The Page of Testimony. I have some of the answers, but hardly all. *Victim's place of birth:* Pécs. *First name of victim's father:* József. *Victim's profession; place of work.* I *did* come all this way for a reason, and the lady porn star official at The Immigration and Naturalization Office cannot stop me from doing what I came here to do.

I charge into further research about the family's lumber business, and, with Zoli's help, any articles I can get my hands on at the city museum.

Despite the restrictions and the violent, anti-Semitic atmosphere throughout Hungary in 1853, Adolf was always on the lookout for more land and more real estate. At a time when it was still against the law for Hungarian Jews to own a house, Adolf bought a house, just as his father Peter managed to do, legally. When he acquired and renovated his house in the Lyzeiumgasse in 1853, he also established a "wood business" he named Adolf Engel & Sons.

According to Adolf's memoir, a small circle of dealers ran the wood business at that time. They mostly sold boards and slats, which they procured in the Danube-Szabolcs-Dráva area. Wood for construction had to be brought in from Mohács by horse and wagon. Mohács is about twenty-eight miles from Pécs. The transportation costs were higher than the cost of the wood. Adolf noticed that despite the expanding wine-growing trade in Hungary, there was never enough wood for the wine barrels. In fact, even though there was a building boom going on throughout Europe, it was hard for Hungarians to get wood, even though it was growing all around them, miles away.

He spoke at length with carpenters and craftsmen to find out exactly what kind of wood they wanted and needed: they wanted more oak. Adolf bought acres of oak forests, and when he harvested, he had his workers replant so that he would have another harvest. He built a sawmill in the south part of Pécs, and there his workers cut Slavonian Oak, which soon become fashionable in all the bigger homes. Adolf also invested in the railways, building new tracks and stations in Mohács, Hamburg, and Styria where he knew he would be harvesting and transporting wood. Soon, Adolf owned every aspect of the wood business from start to finish.

Businesses all over Hungary and Austria continued to need more and more wood, mostly oak. They needed wood for railroad tracks, coalmines, streetcars, and all the new buildings going up in Budapest, Vienna, and Paris. Then there were the wood floors. Some of those new buildings needed elaborate, expensive parquet floors inlaid with mahogany designs. Other buildings for factory workers demanded "common parquet" floors. Adolf built a parquet factory near his sawmill in Pécs. He built warehouses to store his wood harvests, where carpenters cut the timber, then sent these long pieces of lumber by train. He used the dry steam from the parquet factory to heat a bathhouse next door. It was the Engel Bath, on a new street to be named—Fürdő utca or Bath Street. He built the bath house because he felt the people of Pécs "smelled poorly" and did not bathe frequently enough.

No one in Pécs denied Adolf the right to own a house, tracts of land, or businesses, maybe because by this time, Adolf Engel had made his mark as a supremely successful businessman and he was doing a great deal to make Pécs prosper. Maybe he was granted immunity as a Jew because he took such good care of his mostly Catholic workers. He built them homes, schools, bathhouses, and churches. He paid for their teachers and priests. He provided them with health care. When he went to Vienna on business, he brought back straw hats to protect them from the sun.

He continued to pay "tolerance taxes," huge gifts to a mostly Catholic town.

By 1855, Adolf's business had expanded to coal storage and he was housing his workers on a street in Pécs that bore his name. Adolf wrote in his memoir that the people of Pécs needed more exercise in order to live healthier and more productive lives. He wanted them to be more like him. And so, in 1857, he drained the Balokány swamp on the outskirts of Pécs, brought in wood by a steam railroad he had built, and had a large public swimming pool built for the people of Pécs.

How could this one man be this wealthy? There were rumors about Adolf in Pécs. While building one of his factories, he must have found hidden treasure left there by the Turks. Perhaps such magic was easier to believe than Adolf's ambition and energy. Perhaps Adolf made other, lesser men envious, jealous or ashamed. When Adolf was an older man, he wrote in his memoir, *Wer rastet, rostet.* Who rests, rusts.

Hungarians feared big industry. They still do. Big cities, innovation, new ideas reek of foreignness, otherness, and change. All that "otherness" felt suspect and Jewish to some, like those "wandering" Jews pulling wagons, coming in and out of their towns. During Adolf's time, something like 80% of Hungary's population was illiterate. Jews were simply not allowed to be illiterate. The law required Jewish men to read, write, and have a grade school education in order to run a business. This was not so with Christians. Illiteracy wasn't in the Jewish culture. Besides, logic and wits were the only way to survive in this system. It was no accident then, that some of the smarter, more educated Hungarians were Jewish and they became the more successful and wealthy Hungarians.

In 1857, four years *after* Adolf already owned several estates and most of the houses on what is now called Rákóczi út, the Viennese Court passed an ordinance rescinding an 1854 law, which forbade Jews to acquire "immobile property." Adolf was elected to the Hungarian Deputation so that he could express thanks to the Viennese Court for all Hungarian Jews. He refused. "When people have taken from me a natural right and have given it back again, I don't thank them for that," he wrote. No kowtowing for this guy.

Adolf continued to invest and acquire—houses, estates, farms, forests and land, including a lovely plot of land with gardens right next door to Adolf Engel & Sons. This is where he built his in-town house, a house he painted Wedgewood blue. At thirty-three years old, Adolf and Anna and their growing family lived in this house near Czindery Gardens so that he could keep a close eye on business and his 20,000 wood workers.

Czindery was the name of the landlord who had once sold wheat to Adolf's father, Peter, and then refused to honor the deal because Peter would not work on the sacred Day of Atonement. *Czindery*, who had driven Peter, Adolf's father into financial ruin, taking away the ownership of his home and driving him to bankruptcy. *Czindery*. When Adolf bought the *Czindery* property he did not change its name. Adolf loved to walk those gardens. Now *Czindery* is a shopping mall where we buy our groceries. Sometimes I think I can see Adolf in the garden, not *Czindery's* garden, but *his* garden. He is walking with his cane. He is kicking the dirt.

In 1859, Adolf worked with several other wealthy Jewish leaders in Pécs to build what he called "the best school building" for the Jewish students of Pécs, though he grew frustrated working with the town's magistrates. One Jewish friend became so enraged with the politics of building a Jewish school house, he was willing to mortgage his house to raise the necessary cash. "As long as there are men with such self-sacrificing devotion, the Jewish race is not lost," Adolf wrote.

Adolf remained deeply devoted to his religion all his life. He urged his children and his grandchildren to do the same. Perhaps he inherited his devotion from his father, Peter, who had opened the first Jewish synagogue in his own house. Whatever Adolf's *feelings* about his religion, at some point early in the 1860s, he was the first member of his congregation to pledge a large amount of money toward the construction of a synagogue that was needed for the rapidly growing Jewish population in Pécs. In 1865, Adolf became the founder and main financier for the synagogue known today as the Synagogue on Kossuth tér.

Both Clocks Ticking

The yellow synagogue on Kossuth tér was Richárd's synagogue. *Victim's place of worship.* Before 1944, there were four thousand members. Only four hundred and sixty-four of these members survived the Holocaust. Now, there are approximately three hundred members, but that's an overstatement. One person at the local museum says there are maybe forty members. Half of the synagogue is a used clothing store, which we pass on our way to the front of the building. In the store's front window, sun-bleached winter coats hang and lean into each other.

Because there aren't enough Jewish worshippers left in Pécs to justify turning on the heat, the synagogue remains unheated and is open now only on high holy days. In the winter, worshippers keep their coats on. It wasn't always this way.

In the 1860's restrictions against the Jews were lifted and they were allowed to settle anywhere and open businesses. The Jewish population in Hungary increased from 340,000 in 1850 to 542,000 in 1869. The synagogue in Pécs is still the biggest synagogue in this part of southern Hungary. A watchmaker from Pécs made the outside clock, which is set to Hungarian time. The clock inside is set to the time in Jerusalem, one hour ahead.

When we enter the synagogue, an elderly gentleman wearing a black skullcap gives Pat and James skullcaps made of black construction paper, stapled together. He gives me information sheets about the synagogue in Hungarian and in English, saying "Have a great lovely night," even though it's morning.

That the Jews of Pécs had this massive, richly-decorated synagogue built in the middle of the town in the middle of the 19th century reflects the relative stability and wealth of its Jewish community at that time. This building also reflects the acceptance or at least tolerance of Jews by the non-Jewish population of Pécs.

As electric lights lit up the best streets in Budapest during the late 19th century, millions of Hungarian Jews began to assimilate for various reasons. Many young Jewish adults married Christians. Some changed their names. Many who spoke Yiddish began to speak Hungarian.

The organ on the second floor was a show-offy piece, which Adolf bought for the synagogue to signal to the Christian community that the Jewish ceremony was not so mysterious or foreign. *See? We worship just like you Christians. With organ music! Never mind that there is no organ music in the Jewish ceremony.* Adolf's organ infuriated some Jewish members of the community back then, and even today, several orthodox Jews in Pécs *still* refuse to enter this synagogue because of the organ.

Church leaders from the Catholic cathedral and other religious groups from Pécs often gathered here in the synagogue for big occasions, and because Pécs was known to have very good, intellectual Rabbis such as Alexander Kohut and Albert Schweitzer, many Christians periodically attended Sabbath service.

At some point in the early 1980's, the gas lamp chandeliers in the synagogue were electrified. All around us now, the orange-red paint chips and peels on the walls, but the *Aron Kodesh* or Holy Ark containing the Torah scrolls is polished and gleaming. The red here is not the *vörös* red as it is on Peter's house. The red here is more orange: *piros*.

The Engel de Jánosi's spent a great deal of time in this synagogue. Adolf was head of the Jewish Community Council and Anna was head of the Women's Association. Because Adolf made the biggest donations and paid the most taxes, his vote counted more. Anna and her four daughters sat in the upstairs galleries among the other four hundred women, while Adolf and his four sons stood in the front row and davened before the canter with the other six hundred men. The synagogue held a thousand people, but it wasn't big enough. There were often so many people for Sabbath, worshippers stood crowded in the back. This is where Richárd learned to celebrate and worship with his family. This is where he learned to keep the Sabbath. This is where he also probably learned about religious fasting.

When Richárd was growing up, he spent most of his time at his father's home, which was next door to his grandfather Adolf's home. Every Friday Richárd went to the synagogue with the rest of his family. When he came of age, he attended the *Talmud Torah*, the Jewish School, which his grandfather built. Every day, Richárd was surrounded by Engels.

Adolf believed in educating his children and grandchildren, primarily his male children and grandchildren. Perhaps he saw it this way: Yahweh made a deal with the children of Israel: *his* devotion and loyalty in exchange for *their* keeping his law. Perhaps he made much the same deal with his own family. He saw to it that his sons and daughters were strictly disciplined in order to civilize them, and, in exchange, they were to keep *his* law. Adolf was no believer in the French, Rousseau-like upbringing popular at that time, where children run "wild" and learn at their own pace. Adolf believed in discipline and hard work. He taught his children and his grandchildren, including Richárd, to respect authority, especially the highest authority, in *his* order of importance, which was God, Rabbi, grandfather, father. *It starts with the father.*

At Richárd's place of worship, I stand with James in front, at the pulpit, before a glass-topped wooden display case attached to the Torah lectern. I can barely make out the staples in James skull cap, as I watch him bend to read.

Inside the display case is *The Book of Tears*. We are the only ones in the synagogue. Can he also hear the Hungarian and the Israel clocks outside and inside ticking? I reach into the display case, open the book, and begin reading the names listed in alphabetical order.

"Mom," James whispers. "Are you even allowed to do that?"

I shrug. "We are Engels."

He joins me in reading the information written in English about 3022 martyrs who perished in concentration camps—mostly in Auschwitz. 2711 were from Pécs. There is an inscription in *The Book of Tears*, taken from a memorial at the Jewish cemetery of Pécs:

"Blessed young mothers with their infants, budding humanity held to their heart, school-aged boys and girls, young men and women, the most beautiful in the Lord's garden; fathers and mothers, strong and weak, the sick and the innocent—amid terrible suffering and humiliation were all annihilated."

After the war, when the concentration camps were liberated, newspapers in Paris printed lists of survivors. The more lists there were, the fewer names the lists had. There were no such lists of names printed in Pécs because who among the Jews were left to read them?

The information sheet from the elderly gentleman and this list of names in *The Book of Tears* near the Torah is the first printed information we've seen about this particular time in Pécs' history.

We allow ourselves time at the pulpit to read through the list of Jews taken from Pécs in 1944. We turn the pages slowly, carefully, working our way through the alphabet. When we come to the *E's*, we slow down. James traces the names with his index finger.

There are more Engels on this page than I care to see, more names than had first appeared on the computer screen at Yad Vashem, but, once again, I have a strange sense of relief—*look, I've found them*, marked with sudden grief—*look I've found them*. Engel Mórné, Engel Alfrédné, Engel Erzsébet, Engel Richárd, Engel Ferencné, Engel Izidor, Engel Izidorné, Engel Tibor, Engel László, Engel Károly, Engel József, Engel Józsefné, Engel Sománé, Engel Alfréd, Engel Alfrédné, Engel Zoltán, another Engel Tibor, Engel Géza, Engel Sándor, Engel Mórné.

I recall that poem, "Easter 1916," when William Butler Yeats lists the names of all who died after he writes "our part to murmur name upon name." When I teach this poem to students, I always read it out loud, just to hear those Irish names, slowing down for each of them, to call them up, to remember, and to make the students remember, too. James and I put our hands on Richárd's name, as though it were an engraving. We both do this instinctively. Here, he is remembered.

What was it that Yeats wrote? *Was it needless death after all?*

There are at least fifty of our other relatives under the names of Stein, Stern, Justus, and Krausz that appear in *The Book of Tears*. But even this book of lists is not 100% accurate. And those who survived the camps are not listed.

James joins Pat to walk the tiled floors around the synagogue. I take a seat in a wooden pew where once only men were allowed to sit and pray. Here, I feel Richárd close by. He is becoming clearer and clearer, less black and white. More red. We are putting the puzzle together of a life, piece by piece, family member by family member. Isn't that what re-membering is?

Sitting there in the pew carved of Moravian oak, I start to shake. Inwardly, I curse every last Hungarian who deported or murdered my family. *See? Look at me. My mother got out and she had me and I had a son. You didn't end us.*

I pull down the wooden desk fixed on to the back of the pew in front of me. On it, someone recently scratched into the wood with a black ball point pen: *Aus Juden Seife Siede*. Roughly translated: *Boil soap out of Jews.*

Years later, I read Sándor Krassó's account of what he saw happen to the 48 Jews and Christians after they were rounded up in Pécs in March 1944. They were transferred to Tímár utca 5, the Jewish old age home, which the SS turned into Gestapo headquarters when they occupied Pécs. It was next to Richárd's synagogue.

They were called hostages. They were not questioned. They were beaten. Then they were transferred to the prison, guarded by the local Hungarian police. On April 4, 23 of the 46 were loaded up into cattle cars and transported by train to Mauthausen.

Outside, the uneven sidewalks and the concrete stairs leading from the back of the synagogue to the home for the elderly are cracked and beat up. We three try the door and a man, the director lets us in. I attempt to explain in Hungarian who we are.

"We're related to Adolf Engel de Jánosi," James says.

The director smiles. "Come." He speaks English. He would love to show us what is now a home for the elderly. Again.

After World War II and after the deportations, there were no Jewish children in Pécs to teach, so the building became a Croatian School, then, under the Soviet Occupation, a community house. Now the building is a "retirement home," or, better put, a home for the elderly, most of them women who returned to Pécs after World War II.

The director says the people on the second and third floors can't get down the stairs. Often, they are stuck in their rooms. They take their walks with walkers in the halls. There is no elevator or chair lift in the building, and they are hoping to raise enough money to put one in. I sense the strong hint, and the need here for more money. I can't help but think of everything else here that needs fixing.

Inside, the place is clean. The furniture and fixtures look to be from the 1950's. Old women stand motionless with their walkers or sit in wheel chairs in the dim halls. One white-haired woman stands in the middle of the second floor corridor, her eyes wide, as though she is surprised, her arms raised above her head.

James whispers to me that he thinks he might get sick, and would it be OK if he could please wait outside? I nod and watch him leave. I should go see about him, but I want to stay here, with this tour, with this building. "He'll be OK," Pat whispers.

The director tells us quietly that this woman married a Jewish man who was deported from Pécs to Auschwitz, and even though she is Christian and could have been exempt, she chose to be deported with him. She survived but her husband did not.

I greet the woman. "*Jó napot kívánok.*" I have no request to make. We stay with her. She presses her fingertips together as though she were imitating people talking. She stares out, past us, her eyes bright and blue like my great-grandmother Marie's. When she lets me, I hold her hand, and it feels as though we are praying.

Crossed Out

A colleague at the university tells me it's not a good idea to go to Komló. "There's nothing of value there," he says. "It's just a depressing mining town where everybody is out of work. The gypsies keep moving in and stealing things. You can't be there after dark." We are to call "Gypsies" *Roma* now, but I don't bother mentioning this to my colleague.

Renáta has offered to be our guide. Renáta and Zoli have become our close friends in Pécs. They love Pat and James; and Pat and James love them, their generosity, hospitality, and good sense of humor. Zoli invites us to every town event and regularly gets me into the city archives while Renáta offers to translate.

The three of us meet Renáta at the bus station on the edge of town and wait for the bus. We stand next to a big woman with red thong underwear peeking from the back of her jeans. Her boyfriend allows his hand to fall over her breast. They begin to make out.

"OK, then," James says, shaking his head. He whispers to Pat, "I mean. Who does that?"

There is no word in Hungarian for *privacy*. Only *magánélet*, which means private life. My students once explained to me that most families live all together in one house and there is no place to go and be alone with "a friend." We see a lot of couples in Hungary outside making out because they've had to take the private public.

Our bus arrives and James gets us seats far away from the couple making out. He puts in his earbuds, his hands tapping out whatever beat he hears. We travel through heavily forested rolling hills that remind us of Kentucky or Virginia. Of course there is coal here. Adolf knew. But, in the 1880's, Hungarian Jews were not allowed to own coalmines. They were, however, allowed to buy explosives. Adolf's business associates in Pécs asked him to go in on a coalmine with them, but he turned them down. If he was going to "do" coal, he would do it on his own terms, *köszönöm szépen*, thank you very much.

Adolf bought *Jánosipuszta*, his fifth estate, which came with the small village of Jánosi, not far from Komló. *Jánosipuszta* translates as land of Jánosi. He renovated the house, the town, and the Catholic Church. In 1892, while walking his land with his gardener, Adolf discovered traces of coal. He set out to build a coal plant and a coalmine in Komló, naming the mine *Anna akna*, Anna Mine, after his wife. He built houses for his workers, a school, and a 20 kilometer long railway. Legally or illegally, Adolf owned and ran his own coalmine in Komló, which became one of the largest coal mines in Hungary.

From our bus, we read the road signs telling us where we are and also where we are not. As we leave towns, there is a sign with the town's name crossed out. Renáta offers me dried appricots from her purse.

In addition to translating scores of English and American books into Hungarian, Renáta teaches in the secondary school in Pécs and two of her students are on the bus, teenage boys who take out their earbuds to talk with Renáta, whom they obviously respect. When Renáta smiles, her eyes disappear. We all introduce ourselves. Renáta explains my relation to Adolf Engel de Jánosi. The boys say *ah*. James leans in, taking out his earbuds.

The boys on the bus talk about a local alternative rock band in Komló called *Rózsaszín Pitbull* or Pink Pitbull who have a song about Adolf Engel-Jánosi. They promise to send lyrics. James is impressed that a punk band wrote a song about his great-great-great-grandfather.

Twenty kilometers north of Pécs, Komló was built on seven little hills to mirror Rome. There's not much more information about Komló. Our bus stops at Green Park across the street from Komló's town museum, which is also the town's library, bank, and art gallery. The building used to be the headquarters for the communist party of Komló. We smell cooking cabbage in the air.

Before they leave, Renáta's teenage students remind us to leave Komló before dark.

Renáta walks us over to the bust of Adolf in front of the museum. The bronze Adolf bears a resemblance to the young Emperor Franz

Joseph of Austria without the muttonchops. During the reign of the Hungarian Nazi Party, the coal miners hid the bust, and then, during the Rákósi period in the 1950's, when bronze sculptures were being melted down, they buried the bust in one of Adolf's mines. The bust was brought out and cleaned in 1985 for the 100th anniversary of the coal mine.

We stand in front of the bust now, and I can't help but wonder how often Richárd passed through this very patch of land in Komló. Later, when I post these pictures of us in front of Adolf's bust, Facebook recognizes and identifies James' face and Adolf's bronze face as my face.

Inside the Komló museum, we walk through rooms displaying rocks, ancient tools, coins, linens, lace, and costumes. Both Komló and the estate of Jánosi were inhabited during the Árpád Age (c.840-c.907). Down a long hall, we come to a room Renáta has brought us to see. She fetches the museum director, an older woman, who unhooks the red velvet ropes at the room's entrance.

The room is set up as Adolf's office when he owned the coal mines. The director claims that the furniture is Adolf's original office furniture - a heavy, dark, ornate desk, a comfortable sofa covered in green velvet with a matching set of baroque chairs and a high tea table in the center. Behind the desk and the sofa, stands a dark, heavily polished armoire, made by Adolf Engel & Sons, with wood from his parquet wood factory in Vienna.

"They made furniture too?" James asks.

The director invites us to sit, walk around, take our time. She provides us with a private viewing, even though we are the only ones there. I touch the smooth keys on the black manual Royal typewriter on his desk, the kind my mother once had, but this one has the Hungarian alphabet. These typewriters were made after Adolf died so this could not have belonged to Adolf, but still, I imagine Adolf at this desk. A coffee cup sits in its saucer near a pen and inkwell set. I open the desk's drawers and discover books and papers written by Engel de Jánosi's.

In the drawer of the highly polished baroque desk, I find a key that unlocks a side door, and there, I find more books, articles, and letters written by my ancestors, most of them in German beginning with *Liebchen* or dearest.

Flanked by the armoire's glossy, naked wooden cherubs, James sits on the green velvet sofa with claw feet, which look as if at any moment they might run away.

Pat takes a picture of a painting of a bearded, heavy-set man hanging above the desk, which the museum director says is Adolf. Renáta says how much I look like my great-great-grandfather, how our eyes are exactly alike. Pat and James agree. Even I can see the resemblance in our faces. Months later, Renáta asks the museum director for more information about the painting, and she emails to say there was a mistake: the portrait is not Adolf after all. On the back of the painting, written in pencil, the artist wrote in Hungarian, "The painting in question was painted by me. I would never deny it as it is the part of my life's work. Moreover, I think it's an important piece. I painted it in 1961 for the Foundation of Applied Arts, and it depicts the great social scientist, the well known Marxist ideologist, Friedrich Engels." For years, Friedrich Engels, the co-author of the *Communist Manifesto* passed as Adolf Engel, the capitalist. Shortly after the discovery, the painting of Friedrich, formerly known as Adolf is removed. Renáta and I laugh for days.

Certificates of nobility hang near the painting. In 1885, while Adolf was still busying himself with the reconstruction of *Jánosipuszta*, Franz-Joseph I, the Emperor of the Austro-Hungarian Empire began the process of granting Adolf and his heirs Hungarian nobility in "recognition of economic virtues." On Richárd's Page of Testimony there is a blank next to *Victim's family status*. I suppose I could write *nobility*.

On another wall, we see framed black and white photographs of all of Adolf's children for the first time—Adolf, Anna and their sons and daughters. His daughters are handsome with their dark, thick hair coiled into chignons. One could fall in love with that abundant, luxurious hair, their translucent skin, those almond eyes and their substantial, hourglass figures. My cousin Peter says, "the men were tall and the women were big."

I don't look at all like the daughters, but more like Adolf's sons, especially Moritz. Glass cases hold more recent Engel de Jánosi photographs. I recognize Moritz's son, my grandfather, Friedrich with his bushy eyebrows and his smiling eyes, and his second wife Christiane. Even though she was Austrian, Christiane stayed on the Russian side of Vienna during World War II, and, whenever my mother asked her more about that time, she implored to leave the past alone. Her mantra: "Think of hoppy things." Her "hoppy" for *happy* became a sort of joke between my mother and me. *Hoppy,* as in, hop right on over the truth and anything unpleasant.

I do not see any pictures of my mother's mother, Carlette. Christiane once told me that when she married Friedrich, she forced him to burn all but one of the pictures he had of Carlette. Christiane claimed Friedrich talked about Carlette altogether too much, and she was just trying to help him get over his wife's death. "He kept showing people her photograph," she once told me. "He kept her always with him in his coat pocket. It was morbid."

"There aren't any pictures of my mother," I say. "Or us."

"Maybe because we just found out about all this?" James has the camera now. He has the same dark brows and amused, crinkly eyes as the men in the photographs he's photographing.

"No need to get snarky, Mister," Pat says.

Who decides history? Those who write history, and those who stay in touch with museum directors, apparently. The only people I know who have been in touch with the museum director are Peter de Jánosi, Christof Baiersdorf, and the artist in Paris, Anna Stein. There are many pictures in the display cases of Peter's family and of Anna's family.

There is a family tree framed and hanging on the wall. Pat and James stand staring at their own names, surprised to see themselves, O'Connors, in a black web of Hungarian names, on a wall in a museum in a forgotten little coalmining village in Hungary.

We stand back and see the family crest partly designed by Adolf. An open-armed angel floats, her fingertips touching curled blue and gold leaves sprouting from a tree. One of the tree's branches is broken, representing the death of Adolf's first-born son, Lajos, the first Engel to be buried in the Jewish cemetery in Pécs. *Assiduo Labore* is printed in gold on blue at the bottom of the crest. *With Dedicated Work.* Because this all appears under the crown of Hungary with its crooked cross, the understanding is that this dedicated work is done for Hungary.

With nobility comes a title, the addition of *de* to the surname—of—but Engel *of* what? Even though Adolf had plenty of estates and cities from which to choose, he decided to be of Jánosi, or "de Jánosi." Of all his homes, Adolf imagined *Jánosipuszta*, the castle in Jánosi, where family would gather.

The nobility papers and the new seal of aristocracy were designed and signed, and the final granting of nobility came to Adolf and his descendants in 1886. There was and still is a joke made when people ask if someone was ennobled in Hungary before or after 1896, the year of the Millennium. Those who got the title before deserved it because their "excellence and work" were rewarded. With the Millennium came money, and many bought their titles. Nobility no longer involved traditional privileges, but it was a title that carried psychological and social weight. From 1860 to 1918 there were three hundred thirty-eight Jewish noble families. Many of them lived in Budapest.

Some family members chose the German *von Engel de Jánosi, von Engel,* or, during the Soviet occupation, when the *de* was no longer legal to use, *Engel-Jánosi.* Eventually having a *de* in their last name became illegal. Family members crossed the *de* out on their calling cards. My cousin Peter sent me Moritz's calling card, the *de* sliced with one black line, crossing it out, but still visable.

Adolf's name changed in this once dirty mining town. This is where he and everyone else in the family became "noble." For most of his adult life, Richárd was not just an Engel, but an Engel *of* Jánosi.

When Richárd was introduced, it was *Engel de Jánosi, Richárd* or perhaps even *de Jánosi, Engel, Richárd.* Richárd was only *part* of a bigger picture. His first identity belonged to his family first, which was a part of a place, Jánosi, and, of course, the very meaning of his family name is significant. *Engel* means *angel.* Angels are immortal. His story, like all family stories, goes on forever.

It starts with the father. Most Hungarian family stories do. Your surname comes from the father, and in Hungary, whenever you introduce yourself, your surname comes first. In Hungary, the most important part of your name is your last name, your family name. It's not who *you* are, it's who *you all* are. Even the personal pronoun "I" gets tacked on to the end of a verb. I can't help but notice that we say "I" less and less here.

It starts with the father. Maybe it ends there too. Or does it end at all? Friedrich ended the story with himself, for he was a father with an only daughter. He claimed to be the last Engel de Jánosi, and perhaps he felt he really was the last, because he was the male. Still, what about all the other male relatives he left behind? Even as a historian, he intentionally rewrote the family story.

In one of the glass cases, I find a photograph of Richárd.

It is a simple black and white headshot, perhaps used for a passport taken in 1939 when he was fifty-seven years old. His hair is cut short, a buzz cut the color of duct tape. Wearing a starched white shirt, a mouse-grey suit and dark tie, he looks like any businessman you might see today. I am disappointed with his thick Hitler mustache, fashionable during those days. He has sloping shoulders, the high Engel forehead, sad, scholarly eyes and two deep furrows between his brows, worry lines.

He looks to be the kind of relative I would have loved—tall, distant, cool. The quiet type, pensive and precise. I would have tried to make him laugh. I would have hugged him too long, too hard, served him extra helpings, fetched him water, brandies, smokes, thought of him in high-end stores for walking sticks, cufflinks and silk ties.

And there's another picture of Richárd standing in front of a garden. He looks American, maybe even a little Irish here, wearing an Irish style cap shading his eyes and just the sort of sporty tweed suit my father likes. Confident, more relaxed, he stands with his arms crossed. He could be on a holiday or he could be standing in the family garden. It looks like spring and everything around him is lush and green. He looks so sure of himself, even a little defiant, stubborn.

Maybe too proud. Maybe he believed too much in his own decency, maybe that's what got him killed.

Later, I find out that the picture was taken while Richárd was in Dubrovnik, Croatia on holiday. The date on the picture reads 1938, the same year the Hungarian parliament passed the first "Jewish Law," a year before my mother left Vienna. My father was four years old then, feeding chickens in Lake, Mississippi. And Hitler was going on and on about his vegetarianism and his German Shephard, Blondi.

I am leaning over the display cases, writing as much as possible as fast as possible to prove . . . what exactly? That Richárd had a life, was a life? That he in fact lived here? That they were all here once upon a time? They. The Engels, my family. Us.

In my writing classes, I often hand out old photographs of real people. Students answer their own questions about the person in the photograph before them. *Start with character,* I say. *Nothing you ask is irrelevant.* Hunting for secrets to Richárd's life, I can't help but play this game myself.

Did he play cards? Did he ever have longer hair that he wore slicked down with walnut oil? Did he wear spectacles? Did he sign his letters with *your most humble and most obedient servant*? Did he dance or flirt with women, offering his arm in the Biedermeier manner?

Did he walk with a cane? What was his favorite food? What was his favorite song? Did he have a smoking jacket he especially liked? Did he smoke at all? What were his favorite books? Where did he like most to have his coffee or tea in the afternoons? Did he wash his hands before morning prayer? What did his voice sound like?

Murderers always leave behind clues, don't victims?

Richárd's mother died in 1890. She was thirty years old. Richárd was eight. Richárd's sister, Natalie, died when she was five years old. Richárd was eleven then, and his brother, Róbert, was ten. A person has so few words when he is young, but when loved ones die, there are still fewer. Perhaps these two early deaths turned Richárd into a quiet boy. Richárd and his brother Róbert were without a mother for most of their lives.

Just as his father Adolf had taught him, József stressed modesty and restraint to his sons, Richárd and Róbert. It would not do to show too much emotion or flaunt one's wealth. Indeed, later, József refused to allow his sons to own cars, because owning a car was too flashy.

It's doubtful that the Engels were physically affectionate in public. They kept the private private. Like most people of that time and place, they did not hold hands, hug, or kiss in front of anybody, probably not even in front of other family members. Still, maybe there was a cook or a nurse who comforted Richárd and Róbert when their sister and mother died. Maybe they were held, served extra helpings of poppy seed noodles and plum dumplings. Maybe a loving aunt folded them into her lap and held them in her rocking chair. But maybe their grandfather Adolf or their father József put a stop to such nonsense, thinking this would only make the boys "soft."

Sigmund Freud was thirty-seven years old then and was already delivering lectures on his theories to small audiences every Saturday evening at the lecture hall of the University of Vienna's psychiatric clinic. His psychoanalysis was hardly mainstream, and besides, Adolf would have had nothing to do with all that basking in one's own melancholia. Not when there were lessons to be memorized, work to be done, money to be made, land to be acquired. Later, Freud would remark that everyone's notion of God is based on his unconscious notion of his father.

It is late in the day, and the sun is going down. Back when Richárd was growing up, it was believed that sunshine killed germs. The nurses for the Engel de Jánosi children were instructed to take the children for several walks during the daytime, and the older ones often went up to the hills, in the Mecsek Mountains.

James looks out the window, maybe to see if there really are gangs of Roma, who, like the walking dead, descend on the town at nightfall. A boy and a girl lean against the building across the street, making out. "Unbelievable," he moans.

We decide there is not enough time to visit *Jánosipuszta*. Not today. Renáta reassures that we will be back home before dark. We can come back to Komló to visit *Jánosipuszta* another day. But I am so overwhelmed with the Adolf room, I am hardly concerned with *Jánosipuszta.*

James detours back into the rooms with ancient rocks and coins.

Before we leave, the director of the museum ceremoniously presents me with a dark blue book in Hungarian, the history of the Engel de Jánosi family. I thank her and kiss her back and forth on her cheeks three times. I already have four copies of this book, but what I really want are copies of Richárd's pictures in the glass case. It feels strange to ask the museum's director for copies of family photographs. I give her my card. She says she'll have to see about it. I never hear from her again.

The museum director leads us to the art gallery where there is a show of abstract art. Renáta translates—the paintings are all by the Engel de Jánosi relative we have not met, the artist Anna Stein, who lives in Paris and who grew up in *Jánosipuszta.* Anna will be coming to Pécs for the plaque ceremony, the plaque that has not yet been made and a ceremony that keeps getting postponed. I try to study the abstract gold, yellow and red canvases, most of them faces of a woman. But I cannot focus on these paintings. I return to Adolf's room and stand before the glass case below the certificates of nobility. I stare at the picture of Richárd.

After our visit to Komló, Renáta's former students, the boys on the bus, email the lyrics to the Pink Pitbull song called "Adolf," which Renáta translates. I search the lyrics for secret clues:

Uncle Adolf Jánosi-Engel built a coal mine for us
He came to us in the southwest bringing culture thus
Miners in plastic caps marched on the stones
They broke down the coal walls as if breaking bones.

Adolf Jánosi-Engel
You did not hesitate,
Come and build a new mine
And bring culture again.

October
What Does This Mean, *Good? Nice?*

he woman from the Immigration and Naturalization Office calls
my office at the university and asks me to come as soon as I can.
This is regarding my case and there is not much time. She speaks to
me in English. They hope I still have my case number. This is the
best way they are able to proceed. The woman on the phone is saying
that I need to bring with me please the original copy of my marriage
certificate.

She says my copies are useless. She wants original documents.

We thought we came prepared. I have a *copy* of our marriage
certificate, copies of our birth certificates, health and insurance
papers. My mother even convinced me to bring copies of baptism
records. "They will want to see that you are all Christian," she said.

My mother was right. About everything. I'm certain they want
proof that Pat and I are Christian and that we were married in a
Christian ceremony. We were, in fact, married in a Catholic church,
with three priests present. One of the priests was Pat's uncle. Pat grew
up serving as an altar boy, for God's sake. For years, I played bad
guitar at Sunday morning mass at my Catholic church. Now I wish
he and I had sealed the deal under a *Chuppah* and saved a shard of the
stomped-on wine glass. I'd run with it all the way through the rain
to the Immigration and Naturalization Office and wield that Jewish
chunk of glass at that porn star's neck.

"*Sajnálom,* I'm so sorry," I say, when I finally get to the offices and
to the woman requesting our original marriage certificate. "*De nem
értem.* I don't understand." Anger is making my Hungarian better.

The woman official says that her boss insists. They need official
documentation. A copy of the marriage certificate is not good
enough. They must have the original. Today the woman official is
wearing practical brown pumps.

At this point I'm sure she knows exactly why I've come to Pécs, that I am here to research my murdered relative Richárd, that in the course of my findings, I've uncovered other murdered relatives, their homes and properties conviscated, and that I've realized just how complicit, how utterly guilty the city of Pécs and the entire country of Hungary was at the tail end of World War II. Maybe still is. Governments lie. I am a threat.

I stand and stare at this woman requesting my original marriage certificate, daring her to kick me out of this office, this city, this country, this place that was once the home of my ancestors. I would love to get back to the United States, to my parents, and to our home. They need us. They want us. I think of home, where I am mostly happy and comfortable and nobody questions *why* or *if* I should be there. I consider our pretty, magnolia-decorated Marriage Certificate in my locked file cabinet in my locked office back in Indiana.

I take a deep breath. "*Sajnálom,*" I say. So sorry. I tell her that I did not bring our original marriage certificate to Hungary. I brought a *copy*, as suggested by the Fulbright offices in Washington. I pause at the word *Washington*.

"I'm afraid that a copy will have to suffice. *Sajnálom.*"

I add that my husband and I have been married for eighteen years and that we have a son, James. Our union is legitimate, to say the least. I wait and watch the woman official disappear behind the row of glass windows and into one of the many back rooms.

I finally sit down and look out at the rain, waiting. I turn to stare back at one of the overhead cameras. Mentally I am packing my bags.

Why did Peter Engel and his wife, Marie, even bother with this place? Why didn't Peter just say, *Screw this, honey. Forget Pécs, let's go back to Bonyhád*. At least there, we can live in peace. Why did he even *want* to live in this city where he was obviously not wanted?

All my life, I thought my mother was just paranoid.

The woman official returns with her "boss," whom I have never met. The boss woman is wearing a bulky wool suit cinched at the waist with a black leather belt. The boss asks if I could please arrange to get my marriage certificate here as soon as possible. I recognize the importance of remaining calm. I am an actress now, breathing down my anger. I am channeling every ancestor who has ever delt with an Eastern European Bureaucrat. I am terrible at chess, but I checkmate her dominatrix *modus operandi* by recalling my authority as a fiction writer.

I tell them that the original copy of the marriage certificate was destroyed in Hurricane Katrina. I am from Mississippi, as my passport states. My husband and I were married in Mississippi. We left the orginal marriage certificate there in my parents' home. I don't bother saying it was a vacation home. The boss woman asks me to contact the Mississippi archives to obtain a new copy. The room in the Naturalization Office suddenly narrows. I belong somewhere else, certainly not here. A gulf separates me from this boss woman. I think of Richárd. I think, *I dare you. I dare you to kick out another Engel de Jánosi.*

"I will certainly see what I can do," I say. "But so much was destroyed in the hurricane." Surely they read about it or heard? I pause to let them ponder all that was lost, all that was destroyed for me and for my family.

I get up to leave, shaking the water off my thin raincoat. Let that soak in. I thank them again for their time, assuring them that I will see what I can do, knowing I have no intention of ever tracking down the original marriage certificate. I will spend the remainer of my time here hunting for documents concerning the dead, not searching for any certificates for me, the living.

When I leave their offices, I meet up with Pat and James at the Kafka Kafé for dinner. Most of the cafés in Pécs know us to be "the Americans," so they automatically give us their English translated menus. When I join them at their table, I read over the menu, consider the "Chicken in Sesame Coat in Saladnest" but order "Pork Pieces on a Haystack of Sticks" because it sounds less cozy and pleasingly aggressive.

I explain to Pat and James about the Naturalization offices and we try and laugh about the boss woman. I tell them we might be going home earlier than planned.

"You shouldn't have lied," Pat says.

"Yeah, Mom. That wasn't a good idea."

The "sticks" in my haystacks are thin, crisp French fries and they are delicious. Pat watches James count out the forints for the waiter. It's Wednesday night and the Hungarian band starts playing jazz, music that might lead us to freedom.

My cousin Peter in New York writes that he called and suggested to the mayor of Pécs that it might be simpler to cancel the plaque ceremony and just change the name of the road that used to be named for Adolf. When the Germans occupied Pécs, they renamed the road, because the road was named after a Jew. Then, when the Soviets occupied Pécs, they didn't restore the name because Adolf was, after all, a capitalist. Peter jokes that Adolf's legacy continues to lose in a country that always loses.

The mayor of Pécs says they cannot possibly change a street name, because this would mean that all the maps of Pécs would have to be reprinted and Pécs cannot afford to reprint maps. The mayor reschedules the plaque ceremony to sometime in October.

Pat and I conduct a workshop about cover letters and resume-writing at The American Corner in Pécs. Sponsored by the American State Department, the American Corner offices are in a lovely old building a few blocks away from our apartment, and we visit once a week to chat with the two friendly women directors and to lead English discussion groups to help Hungarians improve their English, an easy, volunteer job. James uses the American Corner library to check out magazines and books in English.

I arrive early to return *Popular Mechanics*. Outside, I pass Secret Service men in black suits next to a black limo marked with little Hungarian and American flags. Inside, I chat with my students from the university about that day's reading quiz, which they call a reading check. They all look past me as the U.S. ambassador to Hungary whooshes into the room.

Dressed in a navy blue pant suit, Eleni Tsakopoulos Kounalakis is an authoritative, well-spoken, young businesswoman from San Francisco. We first met Ambassador Kounalakis in Budapest back in August when she hosted a Fulbright gathering. She knew me by name and she was familiar with my research project and where we would be living. I am deeply impressed by this woman who is very put-together in her stylish suits and pulled-back hair. I did not know about her visit to the American Corner.

I reach to shake her hand, but she hugs me.

"How's the research going with your family?" she asks.

"Sometimes it can be frustrating," I stammer. "There might be a plaque ceremony to honor one of my relatives. That means a lot."

"No one has been here from your family for such a long time." She's addressing the room now, which has suddenly become populated with students and staff. "And now *you're* here."

I am not sure at all if being in Pécs is a good or a bad thing. It just *is*. If I had not come, what difference would it really make? My mother never went back to Vienna to visit her parents' graves. She focused on her own living family. That doesn't mean she doesn't care about her parents. Whenever my father visited his parents in Mississippi, it was agony because they always asked him why he didn't visit more.

Ambassador Kounalakis turns to the others in the room and explains my research project. She talks about Adolf and the Engel de Jánosi family, and she astonishes me by telling everyone about the upcoming plaque ceremony and the importance of recognizing history—the good and the bad. She talks about the Greek word *catharsis*, and, being Greek herself, how important that word is to her. The ambassador turns back to me and says that she hopes to be back in November, and, if she is, she will try and make it to the plaque ceremony.

After the ambassador leaves, I am speechless. Did she cross some lines of diplomacy with her talk about catharsis? Pat arrives, and at that moment, he is the sturdy, steady ship to my tiny tugboat. Together, we go upstairs to a larger room full of Hungarians. There he begins to instruct them on how to write a cover letter and a resume. He has handouts, bless him.

He stresses the importance of verbs and clarity. *Clarity, clarity,* he says. He goes over a real cover letter on the white board. He pronounces his words carefully and people appreciate this. He goes through the sample resume from one of the participants and he begins cutting adjectives and adverbs, explaining the one-page resume, impatient bosses in the 21st century, and the value of getting to the point.

The Hungarians in the room groan with every cut.

One woman raises her hand and stands when she speaks. "From an early age we Hungarians are told to write with more adjectives and adverbs. We learn to love the sound of ourselves."

Pat and I both love Hungarian sentences in translation, and how some Hungarians make connections in strange and interesting ways. In an early writing assignment, I challenged students to write about themselves in third person. Zita wrote, "She can neither sleep nor eat, and then she walks by those confectionary shop windows with anguish. Every now and then she wants to run away, go out to the world, explore it, find out what it is; otherwise, she feels like hiding underneath the blanket all through the day. Her hair and eyes are brown."

Most of my students have learned English by reading Victorian British novels. Many write *nay* for *no*. They are British-inspired when they write sentences such as, "Speaking thusly, he pushed himself onto his feet with a grunt."

Katalin wrote, "She likes her eyes, not the dark circles that make her a fake junkie, but her *eyes*. They are not the kind of pale blue eyes that Lou Reed sang of. There is no sour desperateness or sad pain in them, but the challenging passion and trusting willingness that someone can never get past."

When I hand their papers back, several students come in groups to my office, wanting to know why I've made so many marks and comments in the margins.

"What does this mean, *Good? Nice?*" one young woman asks. "Can you explain the difference?"

I tell them I am responding to their writing as a reader would, as an editor, as their teacher.

"Our teachers here never say such things to us," the young woman says without smiling. "This makes me want to continue."

My students are bright, but then, there are so many who simply disappear. One girl tells me she has to miss class for one month out of the three because she has to go to Australia to be with her sister. "Will that affect my grade?" she asks. Another student says she has to miss two weeks because she is going to London to visit her boyfriend. Another misses a month to get married. Three others miss the semester entirely, but appear, surprisingly, to take the final.

When I ask my colleague about these disappearances, he explains it this way: Hungarian students sometimes take up to ten years to graduate because they can. In addition, students can take and fail a class up to three times until they pass. The government pays for their education and would rather they stay in school than join the work force because there are no jobs. If they went looking for jobs, the number of people out of work would increase.

After the cover letter and resume talk, Pat and I meet up with James for dinner at a café in the square. We order the "hand of pork" and James explains what he learned about Hungarian rules of etiquette. Men open doors for women, but men go first into a pub or a bar because they take the first slap, fist, hit, or knife. "The man's supposed to see if there are bottles flying or if there's a fight," he explains.

When the pork chops and spinach arrive, we watch the two older Hungarian men sitting on a bench, staring at the new water feature in the square, changing lights from blue to green to red to yellow in front of the expensive McDonald's, which serves fries on trendy black porcelain plates.

That evening James and I Skype with my parents and tell them everything couldn't be better. They have adjusted their laptop so we can see that my father's feathery white hair is gone. They both look exhausted, and, too tired to talk, they just want to hear our stories. James tells his grandfather about the nobility documents and the Engel de Jánosi family crest.

"It was his businesses, especially the coal mining, that got him the certificate of nobility," James says.

Virtually bald, my father forces a smile. He likes to see James figuring this out on his own—the pay-off to work and discipline. "John McMullan came over from Dublin with a cypress trunk."

James interrupts, "With only the tools of his trade," in an iambic pentameter way. It's like the beginning of a song or an epic poem they've both memorized. They're talking about James' research on my father's ancestor, John McMullan, who sewed sails for ships, then headed to The New World himself. He joined the Continental Army in 1776, and, as family legend has it, he met George Washington at Valley Forge, where, apparently, Washington needed a tailor.

"So, John had these tools of his trade in the army?" James says. "Armed with a needle and thread? Ready, aim, sew!"

"That'll be enough out of you," my father says, smiling for real.

"We get it, we get it, you two, but the American work ethic doesn't always work out," my mother says. "Besides, we were discussing *my* family!"

My mother sips coffee, still in her housecoat; she has not brushed her hair. We all settle around these family facts, knowing we're just accidents of birth anyway, and we come from a world that no longer exists.

My father disappears from the laptop screen and James leaves too. My mother leans in. "I've lost my ring," she says. I think I hear her voice cracking, or is that some cable under the ocean crackling? "I can't find it anywhere. I wish you were here to help me look for it."

I know she's talking about the one thing her grandmother, my great-grandmother Marie left her—the family ring, the one with the Engel de Jánosi crest on it, used to seal envelopes with melted wax, the one she hoped to give to me. It was blue and had the Engel angel engraved in it, her wings spread wide. My mother loved that ring, and always carefully took it off at night and put it in her jewelry case.

"I wrapped it in a Kleenex so that I *wouldn't* lose it," she says with tears in her eyes. She is tired. "I think I might have accidentally thrown it out. I'm sick about it."

"Don't worry," I tell her. "It'll turn up." I'm really telling myself this. I loved that ring.

Soon after the ambassador's visit to Pécs, I receive an email from the mayor's office saying that he is working on the plaque ceremony and if there is anything at all he can do to make my family's stay in Pécs more comfortable, to let him know. I consider siccing the mayor on the woman official porn star and her boss at The Immigration and Naturalization Office, but I decide to see how things play out without pulling strings.

That weekend we all attend the city's *pálinka* festival. Some call the fiery Hungarian brandy their own central heating system. I surprise myself, drinking more than one shot. James eats what he says is a wonderful pork dish.

That night James vomits over and over while Pat and I take turns holding his head. I brought our only son to this country and now he is poisoned by the food. This is all my fault.

"Do you think someone did this on purpose?"

Pat and James look at me like I'm crazy. I sound like my mother. Maybe I *am* going crazy here. Our neighbor, The Maestro, bangs on the wall. I can't help myself. I bang back. *Fuck The Maestro.*

The following morning, James stays in his room. He organizes his foreign currency, stacking the Euros here, the Forints there. We walk together to the American Corner library, where he checks out a book. Then he spends the afternoon in our apartment on the sofa reading Franz Kafka's *The Trial.*

A Bridge of Tolerance

When Richárd's father József was young, he practiced for hours on a silent piano his father, Adolf, built for him. At the age of ten, József was finally allowed to play a real piano, performing for audiences in Pécs. He had only to hear a tune once, and he was able to repeat it, note for note. After a recital, when he discovered the boy's name was *Engel*, The Lord of Wahnfried supposedly said to József, "Are you really an angel? Have you been sent from heaven?"

József did not want to work in his father's lumber business. He wanted to play the piano. As a reward for completing his Matura, or final exams, Adolf let József study the piano at the Viennese Conservatorium in Vienna. With his father's backing, József was able to live comfortably while he was a student. Once, József played in a concert, and, afterwards, Franz Liszt rose from his seat and kissed József on the forehead. For a week, József did not wash his forehead.

When the time came, Adolf took the train North to Vienna to fetch József. József pleaded with his father, saying he wanted to stay and continue his musical studies. Adolf arranged to meet József's teacher, Robert Fuchs.

"Can you guarantee that my son will have a brilliant virtuoso career?" Adolf apparently asked.

Herr Professor Fuchs acknowledged József's musical talent, but said that there was no "guarantee" when it came to art. Besides, Adolf didn't think being a musician was a decent profession.

József went back to Pécs and went to work with his father at Adolf Engel & Sons.

"First you work in the family business, then you can play," Adolf supposedly said.

In Pécs, József eventually fell in love with his first cousin, Róza Justus, which was still not uncommon in small Hungarian towns, where wealthy families such as Adolf's took their queues from

European royalty, such as the Habsburgs, who often married from within to keep the titles, money, and business in the family.

As he worked with his father in the lumber business, József continued to play his silent piano in trains on business trips. He helped establish a music society in Pécs and a symphony orchestra, the same symphony orchestra which our current neighbor, that late-to-bed-goer, The Maestro conducts. József also wrote essays about his love of music and Judaism.

József had two musical idols: Giacomo Meyerbeer and Richard Wagner. In 1850 Meyerbeer's Judaism emerged as an issue when Richard Wagner wrote the essay *"Das Judenthum in der Musik"* or "Judaism in Music" denouncing Meyerbeer and his Jewish "commercial" approach to opera, claiming that Wagner's own vision was the *real* art. The essay was a personal attack made worse because Meyerbeer and Wagner were friends. Meyerbeer gave Wagner his first big break, encouraging the production of *Rienzi* in Dresden. Wagner used a pseudonym, but most of his readers knew who wrote the article.

It is impossible to read Wagner's angry attack and *not* see his obsessive hate toward Jewishness and Jewish artists. Wagner claimed he wrote the essay to, "explain to ourselves the involuntary repellence possessed for us by the nature and personality of the Jews, so as to vindicate that instinctive dislike which we plainly recognize as stronger and more overpowering than our conscious zeal to rid ourselves thereof."

Wagner wrote that Jews were unable to speak European languages properly and that Jewish speech took the character of an "intolerably jumbled blabber," a "creaking, squeaking, buzzing snuffle," incapable of expressing true passion. This, he wrote, debars them from any possibility of creating song or music. "Although the peculiarities of the Jewish mode of speaking and singing come out the most glaringly in the commoner class of Jew, who has remained faithful to his fathers' stock, and though the cultured son of Jewry takes untold pains to strip them off, nevertheless they show an impertinent obstinacy in cleaving to him." According to Wagner, the only way a

Jewish musician could possibly redeem himself was to convert, and even then it was too late.

Virtually the only response to Wagner's 1850 article were a few letters of complaint from professors at the Leipzig Conservatory, the musical elite. But no one read those letters.

Wagner's campaign against Meyerbeer prompted the decline of Meyerbeer's popularity, especially after his death in 1864. Wagner's attacks were also a significant milestone in the growth of German anti-Semitism. Who can forget that Hitler's favorite composer was Wagner?

After Meyerbeer's death, Wagner reissued his essay *"Das Judenthum in der Musik"* or "Judaism in Music" in 1868, in an extended form, with a far more explicit attack on Meyerbeer. The 1868 version was published under Wagner's own name, and because Wagner had a bigger reputation at this point, the piece was widely publicized and reached more readers. One of those readers was József Engel de Jánosi in Pécs, Hungary.

József wrote his own article, *"Das Judentum in der Musik; eine Abwehr"* or "Judaism in Music; A Defense." In his article, József says he writes against the musician Richard Wagner, not as the musical József Engel but rather the Jew József Engel against the Christian Richard Wagner. József defends Meyerbeer, who had also been József's friend, but, more importantly, József chastises Wagner for his attack on all Jews. József's article against Wagner's anti-Semitism was published and republished between 1869 and 1882 and drew forth numerous replies. One came from Richard Wagner.

József and Richard Wagner formed a pen-pal friendship, and from all the consequent family accounts, they became very close. József traveled frequently to Bayreuth in Germany where Wagner lived. Family lore has it that when Wagner greeted József saying in German, "Herr Engel, did you come from heaven to see me?" József replied, "No, Herr Wagner, I came from Pécs."

I email a librarian at the Wagner archives in Bayreuth, Germany, and she locates one of József's visiting cards. On this card Richard Wagner invites József to the dress rehearsal of Tannhäuser. The librarian thinks there might be more coorespondence. József saved all of Wagner's letters, keeping them locked in a safe inside Adolf Engel & Sons in Pécs. When the Nazis occupied Pécs in 1944, they found these letters from Richard Wagner to József Engel.

They burned them along with other letters, documents, deeds, and everything else in the safe.

József had other famous friends with whom he enjoyed traveling and spending long weekends, namely, the Russian novelist, Ivan Turgenev. József met Turgenev in Carlsbad and many articles about the meeting and budding friendship between the "Hungarian lumber baron" and the Russian writer appeared in Pécs newspapers. Dressed alike in their grey day suits, these two bearded men took long walks in Carlsbad. József most likely told Turgenev all his troubles with his workers, the agonizing pull of his own musical interests, taking care of the family business, the frustrations of working with his father and with provincial Hungarians, often uncultured and anti-Semitic local magistrates.

Later, József wrote about his friendship with Turgenev to family members. A 1976 article with the headline *125 évvel ezelőttszületett jánosi Engel József, Turgenyev levele a Pécsi Naplóban A "szürke cilinderes" mecénás"* or *Born 125 years ago, József Engel de Jánosi, Turgenev's letter in the Journal to patron of Pécs* appeared in the Pécs newspaper cites one of the many letters from Turgenev to József.

W. Somerset Maugham wrote in his memoir *The Summing Up,* "Turgenev stated that he could not create a character at all unless as a starting point he could fix his imagination on a living person." József and Ivan talked a great deal about families, fathers, and sons, long before Turgenev wrote his novel, *Fathers and Sons.*

While József managed *Jánosipuszta* and the lumber company in Pécs, József's father Adolf was in the process of setting up his growing business in Vienna, working with my tall, beardless great grandfather, Mortiz, in the parquet floor factory there.

Workers processed the logs in the Pécs factory, cutting and curing them. Then they loaded these planks of lumber onto a train headed for Vienna, where workers there designed and cut the wood into parquet flooring pieces. Working in tandem, the Hungarian Engels stayed together with the Austrian Engels, becoming much like the floors they cured, cut, and pieced together.

Three months before József's first son was born, a fourteen-year-old Christian girl named Eszter disappeared in a small village northeast of Pécs. Eszter's mother jumped to the conclusion that Eszter had been kidnapped and murdered by local Jews, and she began her own investigation. She gave a five-year-old boy, the son of the synagogue sexton, sweets, and the boy supposedly told her a Jewish man cut off Eszter's head, and his father, the sexton, served Eszter's blood on a plate to him and to his fourteen-year-old brother. The criminal court in the county seat ordered a formal investigation and reports of "the Tiszaeszlár trial" appeared in Hungarian newspapers and in the national press.

Hungarians and Europeans began talking about the strange and mysterious ceremonies of Jews. Word spread that Jews needed Christian blood for ritual ceremonies.

Thirteen accused Jewish men were eventually found not-guilty, but the damage was done. Twenty-one years *before* Captain Alfred Dreyfus of Alsatian Jewish descent was falsely charged and sentenced to life imprisonment for treason in France, the Tiszaeszlár blood libel trial in Hungary had everything to do with anti-Semitic politics of the time, and helped politicians establish Hungary's first National Anti-Semitic Party, which won sixteen seats to the Hungarian parliament during the 1884 election.

This was the Hungary into which Richárd was born.

On July 31, 1882, while people in Hungary were still engrossed in the Tiszaeszlár trial, József's wife Rózika gave birth to their firstborn. They did not name him Ivan, for József's friend, Turgenev. They did not name him Adolf or Peter or Abraham, after József's "fathers," nor did they give this baby a Jewish name. They named him Richárd. The Germans didn't rename him as the archivist at Yad Vashem supposed. József named his first son after his anti-Semitic friend, Richard Wagner.

Maybe József thought he was building a bridge of tolerance. Maybe he was getting back at Wagner, or making a point—the Jew-hater was now connected to the Jew. Or maybe József was simply trying to protect his son with a Christian name. Regardless, even after Wagner died, the angel from Pécs continued to visit Wagner's widow, Cosima, in Bayreuth, bringing her the best fruit grown on the Jánosi estate.

Like Sunburned Figures

It is October 23, a national holiday in Hungary to honor the Hungarian martyrs in the 1956 Revolution. Because we were not here in March for the 1848 Revolution Memorial Day, my university colleague Gabi is making today a two-for-one Memorial day to honor *all* the martyrs in *both* revolutions.

Gabi begins the holiday "celebrating" Hungarian martyrs by taking us on a tour of the gardens in Pécs. Gabi has close-cropped hair, rosy cheeks and beautiful translucent skin. She walks with energy in hiking boots, jeans, a simple sweater and a moss green scarf wrapped several times round her neck.

We begin at the fountain near our apartment on Jókai Square and walk through Széchenyi Square, passing the Mosque of Pasha Gazi Kassim, built between 1543-1546 when the Turks took Pécs. The site of a cat-and-mouse game of religious occupation, the mosque was first built on top of St. Bartholomew's, a 13th-century Gothic church. But then, when the Turks were expelled from the city, the Jesuits took it back, later adding the unfortunate concrete addition. Now the building has a green domed "mosque" roof, on top of which is the Islamic half moon stuck through with a crucifix. Inside, there is a Muslim side with passages from the Koran written on the wall, and a Catholic side with an altar. We've seen all this, unofficially. It's nice to have a guide who knows the dates.

We pass the bishop's library where Richárd's grandfather, Adolf, schooled himself and kept warm. The building was recently renovated into a city museum, and inside are photographs, papers, books and seals, many of which once belonged to the Engel de Jánosi family. Zoli took me there. The director served us warm spiced wine, and said that I was welcome here any time. I pause outside the doors, but Gabi is not interested in going inside. Gabi has never asked why I've come to Pécs, nor do I offer to tell her. At the university, I get the feeling that most of the faculty don't have much to say about 1944 or the Jews of Pécs. They would rather discuss Communism.

We walk past the Cathedral with its five spires, which dates back to 1040, after Hungary's first king, St. Stephen, founded the Ecclesiastical Diocese of Pécs in 1009. We hike through a shady, grassy park towards the Northern Wall Promenade, cross the street, and head up a steep hill towards Aradi vétanúk útja, just outside the western wall of Pécs, a street lined with a row of stone busts chiseled with various shaped mustaches.

Gabi says the really rich people live above this city wall, some in the tall houses on this steep street. But "rich" in Hungary really means middle-*classish* for an American. Like most of Hungary, Pécs is in the middle of an economic crisis. The town is heavily in debt. To save money, they lit fewer fire works on St. Stephen's Day.

Garlanded with wilted flowers, the stone busts of dead Hungarian Revolutionary martyrs line most every village street in Hungary, and every year citizens and school children "celebrate" their martyrdom by wreathing these statues with flowers and recalling how exactly the martyrs lived and died. Most every hero of Hungary has been put to death.

Gabi pulls out a notebook and reads, "And the question for today is: What does it do to the mind of a nation to be around so many martyrs, men who have been brutally murdered defending their own country?"

She pauses in front of each bust, glances through her notebook, and tells the stories of each martyr after they were arrested by Austrian soldiers. One was reading a French text on building sturdy fortresses before the soldiers took him out to shoot him. Another was playing the flute. Some were Hungarian noblemen, some spoke no Hungarian, some were bourgeois, and one was an Austrian aristocrat.

Pat wipes away what looks like a tear on one of the busts, the one with Kaiser Wilhelm whiskers. He takes his own glasses off and cleans them on his shirttail. The day before, at the ANK school during a ceremony remembering the 1956 Revolutionary Martyrs, a teacher leaned over and whispered to Pat, "You did not come. We waited and America did not come to help us."

In 1956, the Hungarians in Budapest who protested and fought against their communist Russian occupiers had hoped that America would swoop in and help, as they had helped the Allies during World War II, but America did not come and help Hungary. Hungarians still remember this.

"I hate the Habsburgs. I really do," Gabi says. "They were all scoundrels, and Marie Theresa? Just a hag. A horrible hag."

I am certainly no big fan of Marie Theresa, who once said, in German, "The Jews are worse than the bubonic plague." She enforced edicts, banning Jews from Vienna and Prague. But Gabi goes on, as though this hate for Vienna has been building inside her for hundreds of years. Gabi can't stand Vienna with all of its huge monuments to all of those horrible people, the Habsburgs. She hates the way Austrians remember their own history. Here Austrians are identical with the Habsburgs. I wonder if Gabi knows my mother is Austrian. I wonder if Gabi resents me for this. I also wonder if I'm getting more and more paranoid living in Hungary.

My grandfather was a monarchist and so is my mother, still, even though she's all for democracy. They swooned over everything Habsburg and they were proud to know many of them. My mother still keeps a framed family photograph, signed by her friend, the last Habsburg prince. I want to defend Austria, but I really can't. Hitler marched into Vienna with such ease, and then came the round-ups. Austria betrayed my mother and her family, so why should I defend Austria?

Gabi reads out the thirteen curses for the Habsburgs, all of which seem to involve suicide, infertility, or murder. She concludes with the killing of "Sisi" or Empress Elisabeth of Austria, when the anarchist Luigi Lucheni stabbed a pointed nail file into her heart, and then the assassination of Ferdinand, both of which, from Gabi's telling, seem to have been natural consequences of being a Habsburg.

"I thought Ferdinand was a nice guy, the one who was going to help the Serbs with laws and things," James says.

"No," Gabi says. "He was a Habsburg. He was not a nice man." Gabi's specialty is the 19th century. She loves Herman Melville and Thomas Jefferson.

"But that's not what I read in my World War I book," James says. "He was going to help out."

Gabi shakes her head. "No," she says.

James had a rough week. In history, his teacher asked him if he was a racist. The class was discussing civil rights in America. Most Hungarians know a lot about American slavery. Until 1990, during Hungary's most recent occupation, the Soviets were keen to translate and teach anti-American propaganda, so, naturally, America's history of slavery and civil rights issues became a genre in and of itself.

"My best friend is black," he said.

"That's what they all say," she said in front of the class.

After a school lunch of cabbage, noodles, cottage cheese and jam, James has taken to bribing a music teacher with 150 forints to unlock the music room so he can bang on a drum kit. He says it calms him. For an hour he drums with The White Stripes, Arcade Fire or Vampire Weekend playing on his IPhone.

James watches Gabi carefully, then shrugs. "Maybe Ferdinand wasn't going to help out. I only read the one book." James is learning diplomacy. That and the value of a bribe.

Gabi leads us to the final bust as we finish our tour of the thirteen martyrs. There is a great deal of information in Hungary about the 1848 revolution and the 1956 revolution. In fact, when the Hungarians I know speak of suffering, they do not talk about World War II. They say the era of Russian occupation was by far the worst and most horrendous time in Hungarian history. Never mind the thousands of Jews the Hungarians arrested, harassed, then sent away to be murdered. The killing was unseen. Evidently, the Holocaust is a chapter of history that has not been fully explored in Hungary. Or maybe it's just ignored. Where's the soul-searching? This is a country that is more often on the wrong side of history, and I wonder why Gabi doesn't have that question in her notebook: Why?

It's clear that Pécs would rather forget what happened in 1944, or at least, move on. They are more inclined, even eager to recall and commemorate the years of Soviet occupation. That was an evil done *to* them. Hungary was the victim. Most of my students at the University of Pécs are very familiar with Hungary's history, but not so very familiar with Hungary's history with the Jews. The overall feeling is that there was World War II with the Germans occupying Hungary and now both the Germans and the Jews are gone. End of story. The Holocaust is mostly a German debt, not really a Hungarian one.

These same students know so many details about battles in Rome, Africa, Europe, and the Middle East. They even know a good deal about particular battles fought in Mississippi during the American Civil War. They are astounded by the existence of the Ku Klux Klan.

"How can such hate be possible?" one student asks one day during class. "How can one group of people hate another entire group of people?"

"Really?" I want to say. "*You're* asking *me* that?"

In my Contemporary American Literature class, one student asks the meaning of a jeweler's loop, mentioned in Philip Roth's *Everyman*.

"It's a Jewish traditional custom," another student informs her.

I explain to the class the definition of a jeweler's loop, a monocle for jewelers. I force myself to understand that their eyes only see the *jew* in the word *jeweler*.

All of Hungary *could* take a page out of Germany's playbook, fess up, and apologize more publically and adequately for their role in the Holocaust. And like Germany, Hungary could require that every student visit a concentration camp. Then again, maybe Hungarians have been too influenced by all the years with Germans, communism, and propaganda. Nostalgia trumps truth when it comes to history. I doubt anyone will face Hungary's recent dark past squarely, discuss it, or teach it. Is *selective* memorializing also a part of a country's character? What about remembering accurately?

Gabi leads us through hidden gardens. We trespass through quiet paths between Roman walls, and pop out on Ferencesek utcája across from the Polo Outlet where there is a sign that reads *20% off, 30% off, 40% off!* A blind man with a voice like James Taylor's plays his guitar and sings Hungarian songs. Three unsmiling students walk with signs offering free hugs.

The streets of Pécs are lined with wonderful old houses, untouched by invasions or war. They've thought of everything to protect these homes. Spikes on the roofs keep the snow from sliding down and the spikes above the windows prevent the pigeons from settling. Gabi says that, legally, the views and the historic houses of Pécs are protected, sometimes even the insides of these homes are "protected." We peek into the open window of one of these homes. A cat sits on an old wooden table licking its paws.

We pass what were once Turkish baths. The baths have now become a place for the homeless to sleep. Besides the coffee, there is not much effort to preserve what is left of the Turkish invasions, a culture and its remnants now irrelevant here. Pécs is a Christian town with barely a Jew or a Muslim.

We stop at The Mosque of Jakovali Hassan, one of the best-preserved Turkish monuments in Hungary, mostly funded with money from Turkey. It is open and quiet with the mirrors and the glossy floor. A handsome heavy-lidded young man takes our forints, without looking Gabi or me in the eye. He tells us about the five pillars of Islam, the minaret, and the Madrassah.

We look at maps of the Hungarian towns the Turks took and occupied, until they reached Pécs. We stare at the colourful whirling dervish costumes, the drums, the plates of fasting, the ancient Koran and prayer beads, and tiny silver coins.

"I would have lost these for sure," James says, leaning in to get a closer look at the coins.

We walk through the museum, and then get to the mosque itself, which is charming, clean, and well preserved. The little garden outside is lovely in the dimming light and oncoming cool of the evening. We take turns touching the 15th century minaret.

"Isn't it wonderful to touch stones so old," Gabi says.

I think of the muddy red paint chips I've slipped off Peter's former home. I'm even glad for the bits of plaster that came off too.

We thank Gabi for everything and ask her out for dinner. We three like eating and drinking with our new Hungarian students and friends. Sometimes, we meet up in "ruin pubs," pubs set inside what are the ruins of old buildings. The saying goes, Hungarians fight by the sword and make peace by the glass. At table, drinking, our friends talk, telling complicated stories, waving their hands to rouse up their particular version of the past. When food arrives, we all hunker down and eat what, to us, is often unidentifiable. Most of our Hungarian friends eat as though this might very well be their last meal. We learn that it is customary to eat everything on your plate, but you should also leave some food in the serving bowl. If you eat everything, your hostess will be shamed, as though she has not prepared enough. She will then push more food on you, and it's rude to refuse. Inevitably, we leave a Hungarian table having eaten too much.

"I'm Orthorexic." Gabi explains she has a fear of eating anything bad for her. She doesn't go to restaurants except when "forced" at academic conferences. She says she has other fears as well, like getting kidnapped and carved up. She says that ten years ago, you couldn't walk alone in a park in Istanbul because someone would gas you, steal your kidney and you'd wake up dizzy and with a wound. "It's not like in China where they kidnap you and you wake up in a *room*."

Later, Gabi sends a wonderful recipe for mushrooms and pasta and she has us over for dinner with her family for "cabbage night," and we eat three different dishes of cabbage. It is one of the best meals we have in Pécs.

When we get to our apartment after the tour, Pat and I drink Pécs rosé, eat almonds, and cook a chicken and rice dinner in our two pots. Someone in our building is making cabbage. Again. The Maestro's boy next door practices his scales on the piano. Again.

We talk about Gabi's question of the day. What does it do to the mind of a nation to be around so many martyrs? James thinks that maybe this makes Hungary less sure of itself—whatever they do, they will be "put down." This may account for the doomed and gloomy attitude some Hungarians have. *Whatever we do, it won't make a damned bit of difference. Might as well have another Pálinka.*

James puts his napkin over his head, ties it under his chin, and makes a comically sad face. "Jó," he says.

Sometimes it seems ridiculous, maybe even a little depressing and cruel, dragging my husband and son all the way to Pécs to piece together a dead relative's life, a relative no one has properly grieved.

What does it do to the mind of a family to know of so many victims like Richárd, and to know that a city and a country betrayed its own? Will I ever be able to trust Pécs, or, for that matter, Hungary?

Will I eventually resent Hungarians as my mother resents Austrians? And what about the rest of Europe? Most countries gave their Jews up for dead. How should the children, the grandchildren, and the great-grandchildren of Jewish survivors know or "appreciate" these countries?

Someone unlocks a door in the hallway. Outside in the street, we hear Hungarian children talking. The Maestro's boy plays "Happy Birthday" on the piano. Birds roost in the courtyard tree.

I listen very carefully. The birds seem to be saying *Lead me. Lead me.*

Later that night, after dinner, a cold wind blows through the apartment as we sleep, kicking up papers and slamming doors.

They come to me in dreams, all of them. Richárd and the other Engel de Jánosi's, like sunburned figures behind closed eyes.

Amour in The Broken Castle

"*Sajnálom. So sorry,*" the woman behind the desk says. "*But the castle is broken.*"

James and I are at the new Information Center on Széchenyi Square in Pécs, asking for information about *Jánosipuszta.*

"Broken?" James says. "What does that mean?"

The woman stares at him. I know what she's thinking. *Children should be seen and not heard.*

She ignores him, then turns to me and explains she is so tired. She gives me a coupon to a spa, a place to "take in" the sulfuric waters. Then she says she has to go to lunch. There is no one else there in the office who can help. *Sajnálom.* So sorry.

"Well, *that* was Kafkaesque," James says, after she's gone.

Renáta and Zoli offer to drive us, and, so, one sunny Saturday morning, we set out for the outskirts of Komló, to *Jánosipuszta.* As Komló grew, it absorbed the tiny town of Jánosi. We pass a place called Dirt Park, which has tracks for motorcycle riders to ride fast. Not much further, there's a sculpture of Lenin, his nose missing. Zoli says there are still foxes in the woods. Plenty of deer too.

The long dirt road through the woods is exactly like the dirt road I rode as a girl in Mississippi as my father drove to the annual family reunion place, called Spring Lake, an unpainted, three-story clapboard house where family gathered. It was a hunting lodge, too, where uncles shot deer and made Brunswick stew, cooking in cast iron pots over open fires.

Jánosipuszta is a big symmetrical stucco building with a small front door. I picture it the way Adolf must have seen it: the house can easily be divided into four private residences for the four families of Adolf's sons. It's more lodge than castle and sits close to the road, looming over a bus stop with a rusty corrugated tin roof.

The four sons, who were all partners in the family business by then, were unanimously opposed to Adolf buying *Jánosipuszta*. They were also against the whole coal-mining venture. They believed that Komló would be a burden on the family finances.

But Adolf saw that his family was splintering apart. By 1900, there was a clear geographical divide among his sons. There were those who stayed behind in Hungary to take care of the lumber factory. The Hungarian Engels were the musically-minded József and his mustached sons Richárd and Róbert. The other Hungarian Engels were those who took care of the farm outside Pécs, in Ocsárd, my cousin Peter's family. Then there were The Austrian Engels, my mother's side of the family. Their task was to run the parquet floor factory in Vienna, which polished, finished and pieced together the rough lumber coming in from Hungary.

When Adolf bought *Jánosipuszta* in 1880 from the Duke, Alfred Montenuovo, he might very well have conjured up that line from Exodus 32:6, "And the people sat down to eat and drink, and rose up to play." Relatives from both Austria and Hungary gathered here. Richárd came for meals, family visits, and, for a while, he lived here and took care of his father, József. My great-grandfather, Moritz, came with his son, my mother's father Friedrich. When Moritz died, Friedrich traveled alone. My mother never saw *Jánosipuszta*.

As we get out of the car, we can hear the motorcycles at Dirt Park. A black dog trots over.

"*Nyugi, nyugi*," Zoli says to the dog.

A few steps and we're inside the unlocked house, which has the feel of a run-down school. It's a shell, a carcass torn open. The brick has been hammered and shattered, the copper wiring all pulled out and pawned. Zoli says people are still coming here and picking away at the inner walls. Once again, I find myself looking for evidence of Richárd.

Jánosipuszta was finished in 1900, the year of the great Paris Exposition, when the Austrian army won a prize for most elegant uniform and Adolf won a gold medal for his lumber business. The Hungarian King himself decorated Adolf with the Golden Cross of Merit.

Towards the end of his life, Adolf's son, József, preferred living at *Jánosipuszta* rather than in Pécs. Richárd made sure his father was comfortable there too.

The Austrian families rarely came. By 1938, they stopped coming altogether. They were either in hiding or leaving Europe. After the brief German occupation in 1944, the Soviets turned *Jánosipuszta* into a home for old people, then into an orphanage.

Abandoned now, everything in the house has been stripped and stolen. Zoli says the roof looks to have been repaired in the 1940's. The imported brick is still original.

I picture a time when the parquet floors glistened. We walk slowly and carefully through the gutted, vacant rooms smelling clay and mold. Plaster and debris dust the two front rooms. I imagine this place made prettier with paint, beautiful furniture, potted plants and a few good rugs. All the front rooms open up to balconies. Upstairs, there is a charming side balcony with ruined wrought iron. Surely along the fence, they grew roses or bushes of lavender—the fragrance penetrating the house, always a bundle in a vase or basket.

We walk through more empty, shattered rooms. So many rooms. I step over a doll's torn off arm, then look past the vines growing up through the bare window casings and imagine them all here. Aunts, uncles, cousins. All the Engels. Us then. Us now.

I can almost hear the swish of long skirts on the parquet floors of these empty rooms and the uninterrupted ticking of a grandfather clock. Are they still here, where Adolf meant for them to gather as a family? Have they come home?

Outside the black walnut trees still grow, the lilacs and the climbing roses. I imagine the heavy oak furniture, a couch draped with a Turkish rug, an elderly relative putting away his copy of *Le Figaro* on a rococo table, lighting a cigar, removing his pince-nez, a sure sign of his good spirits. Or perhaps there was a lighter touch—simple, reed armchairs lined with soft lambskins. Adolf's daughters dressed in black moiré silk dresses, their thick, perfumed hair pinned up with jeweled roses, gather here in this room, passing trays of tea, Kosher plum brandy or Tokay wine and red Russian caviar. They bring with them their scent of bath salts and Caron perfume. Nearby, their husbands sit at a card table playing Tarock, commenting on the new way a son has trimmed his hair and beard.

I breathe in the oak, carefully polished with beeswax, for as Adolf often told his sons and his daughters, the value of old oak lies in its color: ashen grey. The wrong polish can make it look too dark and shiny.

Perhaps József is at the upright piano, playing Schubert or Wagner. A lorgnette lies on a table, the one an uncle once used to better see the pretty young actresses on stage in Vienna. József is pleased. While Róbert was away in Germany studying law, József arranged his son's marriage to Marianne Krausz. The young girl is not as enthusiastic as Róbert clearly is. Still, Marianne's mother, a strong-willed woman has told Marianne that even if she does not love Róbert now, feelings will come later. Or, they might not. No matter. Theirs is a good financial match. And so József plays on.

Perhaps the Pécs side of the family sit there on their divans, dreading the arrival of their Viennese aunts, uncles and cousins. The rift has already started—the ones in Hungary are made to feel like "country cousins," and those in Vienna are thought to be haughty and showy, maybe even a little flashy, coming only to visit for short periods, with their fancy suitcases, their tennis rackets, their Secession hairstyles and their colorful shawls, as though they were going out not to visit family, but to view the animals at Schönbrunn. Friedrich, the great professor, never bothers bringing his wife, the Catholic from Paris. He hasn't even introduced his only daughter to her own family. Who *does* this? What kind of man *does* this? Is he or is he not an Engel? Keeping his only daughter away from her *family.* Is he ashamed? Is he renouncing them all—his family? His Hungarian past? His Jewishness? Who does he think he is?

I am Friedrich's granddaughter, not a historian, but a fiction writer, something Adolf would have frowned upon. Foolish work, Adolf would have said. Still, I know that history is written from what is found; and, what is *not* discovered, what is *not* saved is lost and forgotten. These lost stories are the stories that attract me the most. There is so little information about Richárd. Here in *Jánosipuszta*, where I know he spent so much time, I *will* Richárd back to life.

Almost unnoticed, he stands there, tucked away by the window in broadcloth trousers. His temples are not yet greying. He returned from Munich some time ago, with his degree in engineering. His father said the family business needed an engineer.

Richárd has told his father József about the girl he would like to marry. Clearly, he's in love. But she's Catholic. József forbids the marriage. He tells Richárd to quit the girl. Now he must focus on his work. And then there is Róbert, and *his* upcoming marriage to Marianne Krausz.

József continues to play the piano while Richárd stands at the window, looking out. He lights a cigarette. Maybe now he tells himself he is nothing like his father, will be nothing like any of them. He considers small differences. He wears Western-styled tweed suits, shirts and ties while his father still wears tails. He wears a brushed felt bowler hat. His father still wears his top hat, even for walks. The differences will grow. For now, Richárd would not marry the Catholic woman. He would make his own arrangements, find love his own way.

Outside the window, the lawn is yellow from the heat, and the hawthorn and rosebushes are in their last bloom. He can hear the music of cutlery on plates and he smells Sunday dinner cooking from the kitchen—a caraway soup, chicken stew, pasta with curd and bacon, and later the inevitable ripe cheeses and pastries. Or perhaps they will be served a "themed" dinner, which his uncle Moritz writes about in one of his plays. Everything is red, the color of love: they start with the Hungarian drink *egri bikavér*, "bull's blood"; then tomato soup, shrimp and lobster served at the same time, English filets with red cabbage and beets, a fourth course of chicken-fricassé with *choux-rouges*, a *soufflé aux framboises*, and finally strawberries, fresh cherries from the south, and other items the color of *amour*, all of which Richárd prepares to choke down.

He wears the signet ring with the family crest. It's too big, fitting his finger clumsily. He would prefer to go off on his own. People say that about him. He is not inclined to relinquish his privacy. The Germans have a word for it—*alterstil*, "the style of old age when artists live more in themselves than in the world."

Before dinner, he turns to join the family in the front room, looking around, considering the wealth of his life. Does he think of this time, this place, or does he think of his future? Does he look past the room at a table with wine bottles and peeled fruit? Can he see everything before him? Is he reminded of the word *Jánosi,* which means *God is gracious*? Does he consider parables from the Talmud and wonder, *if we are not the chosen, how is it that it can be this good?*

He sits, crossing his legs, and, ignoring everyone, picks up Balzac, Ibsen, or Turgenev's *Sketches From a Hunter's Album,* and begins to turn the pages.

In my mind Richárd knew what he had, but I also realize that the only Richárd I know is the Richárd I've imagined. I cannot presume to become Richárd's first person, but his "I" is a part of me now, just as all our relatives somehow are becoming a part of us.

They were monarchists. All the Engels were, for, with a monarchy, there was stability. They were appalled by clueless would-be leaders, drunk with their own authority, inevitable embarrassments for their countries. Even if the Austro-Hungarian Empire had a weak King, there was always the hope that the weak one would die, and then there would come a known, well-mannered, educated man, for it was almost always, a man.

"This place is creepy," James says.

"It could be cleaned up," Renáta says. "What do you say? Should we all go in together and buy it?"

I swallow hard. I wasn't even supposed to know about this place.

Outside, as we step out from the broken castle, the black dog trots over. Pat and James join me to noogy noogy with the dog.

It occurs to Zoli that the mayor of Komló should meet me. He calls him on his cell phone and sets it up. Within minutes, we drive to a Komló country restaurant, where we sit at a table drinking pálinka with the mayor.

He has dark hair, dark eyes and he says he is very happy to meet us. When Renáta says *Jánosipuszta,* the mayor shakes his head sadly, staring down at the restaurant's linoleum floor.

"*Nem,*" he says. No.

He says it's a shame what's happened. He says he wishes Komló could afford to keep up the place. He tells us all about his economically depressed town with the closed mines and no jobs and nothing much on the horizon. He says if we are interested in buying *Jánosipuszta*, we *could* apply for help from the EU. However, the time for compensating Hungarian victims of World War II or the Holocaust has passed.

"You can no longer get a free T.V. or a check advanced for your mortgage or even your rent," he says in Hungarian. "You can no longer buy back your own property."

Part of me hoped that my mother might still be a partial owner of this place. Isn't it every child's dream to bring gifts back to the parent? And what if my mother and Peter and Anna and any other living Engel still legally owns *Jánosipuszta*? What if?

After 1990 and the change of the regime, restitution laws were put in place, but these laws had a time limit. If the original owner could prove she really was the owner of the property, she could get back the property or get a certificate for which she could buy what was now state property.

With his sad eyes, the mayor is apologetic and embarrassed, as though he really does want to say, *Here, have another drink, and here's a coupon to buy back the family's property.*

We put on our coats. We've had a window into Richárd's once beautiful life. But that's all over now. The castle is broken, the town is in ruins, and the mayor has all but given up. We thank him. He thanks us. We take pictures, pretending to be happy.

*My grandfather, Friedrich, my great grandfather, Moritz,
and my great uncle Rudolph Engel de Jánosi, Vienna, Austria*

Part III

Austria-Hungary 1845–1945

Transactions

Permanent Residence is printed in bold on Yad Vashem's Page of Testimony, but I don't know which house or estate Richárd called home. Adolf bought houses and real estate as though he were making up for his father's loss when he didn't pick up the wheat on Yom Kippur. In his lifetime, Peter's son, Adolf owned over twenty-five homes and seven vast estates.

Residence has more meaning than mere house. More than bricks and mortar, the Engel "residences" were *homes*. Say *home* enough, and it sounds like *womb,* and the mystic syllable *om.* For an Engel, home was everything—life, happiness, security, safety, permanence, and *legitimacy*. Whenever and wherever Adolf sought a new home, he staked his claim. He might as well have planted his own Engel flag with the family crest there at the center.

As the Habsburgs marched south to Hungary in earlier centuries to reinforce their claims on the Empire, Adolf headed north to Vienna to expand his own Empire. In his memoir, *...aber ein stolzer Bettler*, my grandfather, Friedrich, wrote that Adolf and his gardener took a train from Pécs to Vienna and walked the streets of the fashionable district, Döbling, not far from his lumber factory. He knew about a "little palace" for sale.

Stephan Baravička built the Baravička Palace for the Crown Prince of the Monarchy, Grand Duke Rudolf. But when Prince Rudolf came for the final inspection, a north wind sent a smokey scent from an insecticide factory nearby into an open window, and Prince Rudolf refused the purchase. Years later in 1889, Prince Rudolf shot himself and his mistress, Mary Vetsera, in another palace, Mayerling, the Imperial Hunting lodge, while Stephan Baravička died penniless at eighty-four.

There was no foul insecticide scent the day Adolf and his gardner inspected the place, which was painted a light, Schönbrunn yellow. The long windows were topped with what looked like eyebrows.

While his gardener carried sleeping bags through the empty rooms, Adolf admired the long, wide ground floor, and the two upper floors, each about fifty-five meters long with inlaid Baroque floors and views of the Viennese Woods and the rising grape hills of Nußdorf and Grinzing.

That night Adolf and his gardener slept in their sleeping bags in one of the empty rooms. According to Hungarian peasant custom, if you sleep overnight in a house, you seize possession of the house. Adolf first possessed the house as a Hungarian before he bought the house, legally. He called it the *Hofzeile*, and the family would always refer to the *Hofzeile* as their little palace. This is where my mother grew up.

While Adolf lived at the *Hofzeile,* he continued to make trips by train to *Jánosipuszta*, but, as he grew older, those trips south to Pécs became less and less frequent. The *Hofzeile* was Adolf's final acquisition and it was to be the most lavish of all his homes.

In the front garden, he had his gardener put up statues decorated with golden inscriptions: Zrinyi, Ruediger von Starhemberg, Field Marshall Radetzky, Kaiser Joseph II and two busts of Franz Joseph— one young, one older. Later he had a change of heart and he ordered his gardner to turn the pedestals around with new inscriptions— Zrinyi became King David; Ruediger, King Solomon. When he walked his grandson Friedrich through this garden, Adolf insisted Friedrich take off his hat in front of every statue.

Adolf's gardener cultivated gardens with fruit trees, adding more and more fruit trees, saying he would never enjoy their fruits, but at least his grandchildren, his great-grandchildren, and his great-great grandchildren would. Behind the *Hofzeile* was a wall and a two-story building nicknamed the "Devil's Castle" because, it was said, Kaiserin Maria Theresa received her lovers there, with a noticeable preference for Hungarian bodyguards.

Already Adolf's daughters Helene, Louise, and Marianne had married well and moved away. Bertha remained in Pécs with her husband in Loránt Palace. Adolf's sons Alexander and Moritz married, and they all lived with Adolf and Anna in the *Hofzeile* while they worked with Adolf, managing the factory there in Vienna.

Alexander and Moritz returned often to *Jánosipuszta* for family gatherings and to discuss family business. The members of Adolf's family would never be without a home or without property, not in his lifetime, not as he had been when he was a young boy after his father Peter died.

A year after Adolf's youngest son, Moritz married, his wife Marie gave birth to a son, Friedrich. A year later, in 1894, Marie gave birth to another son, Rudolf. In 1896, came Magdalena or Madeleine, whom they nicknamed Magda.

Moritz made it clear to his sons Friedrich and Rudolph that they would not have to take over the family business if they did not wish to do so. They could be academics if they wanted, and they would certainly study at the university. He told them if they lived modestly, they would be financially secure always. Moritz never defined *modestly*.

In the conversations I recall with my great-grandmother, Marie, theater meant a great deal to her husband, Moritz, but not very much to her. Marie did not speak of Moritz much at all when I knew her. She talked about swimming, walking, sailing, playing tennis, and climbing mountains. She liked physical activity and she appreciated her health, which was exceptional. When she lived in Vienna she selected herbs from the garden and brewed her own teas. She also served her children spinach the night before school tests.

When she lived at the *Hofzeile*, Marie often loaded her two sons into the family wagon to drive to the Viennese Woods or to the Klosterneuburg Meadows to swim in the Danube. Magda was born with a heart defect, so Marie arranged other activities for Magda at home.

The role of women was changing then, especially in cosmopolitan cities such as Vienna. In November 1905, women's suffrage was granted in Austria, making them much more progressive than other countries. In December of the same year, Austrian Bertha von Suttner won the Nobel Peace Prize. Meanwhile, in newspapers, women could read about how to practice the "necessary exercises" ten minutes a day for a well modeled pair of arms. Walking outdoors was encouraged.

"Be out in fresh air but keep the air from your face," one columnist wrote in German in the daily paper *Die Zeit* in 1905. "Wear veils, use powder and protect the skin with a layer of good cold cream. The hair should hang loosely. Like the body, it needs fresh air and freedom at least twice a day for a quarter of an hour at a time."

When the *Teufelsburg* or Devil's Castle behind the *Hofzeile* crumbled beyond repair, Marie had it torn down and replaced with a tennis court. Marie loved tennis and read about tennis player May Stutton, who shocked Wimbleton with her short, loose-fitting tennis dresses while most women played sports in whalebone corsets. Winters, Marie had the tennis court flooded and made into an ice skating rink.

Marie arranged for dancing classes at the *Hofzeile*, careful never to overheat Magda. There were five male Engel de Jánosi dancers, all cousins: Friedrich, Rudolph, and Alexandor's sons Hans, Stefan, and Karl. Marie invited her friends' children to come most Sunday afternoons. The children danced with the children of those in attendance: Gustav Mahler and his sister Justi who was married to Arnold Rose. The young conductor Bruno Walter came too, along with Julius Bittner, and Sigmund Freud with his daughters, Sophie, and Magda's best friend, Anna. Most Sunday afternoons, over seventy people came to the *Hofzeile* to dance. Friedrich claimed that the friendliest was Gustav Mahler, who never stood to the side like the other parents. Herr Mahler danced with the children.

The dances led to theater productions, and the theater led to telepathy. Bruno Walter was an especially impassioned devotee of "spiritism." During one of these spiritualist get-togethers, Moritz was told by telepathy to kiss Mahler's sister. And he did.

Moritz had a reputation of being easy-going, which some saw as lazy. Tall, elegantly dressed, Moritz cut a dashing figure. According to Friedrich, he made an impression on women whenever he entered the Bosendorfer in Vienna or Café Central, where he liked to sit Sunday mornings, reading the *New Free Press*, smoking ceremoniously and slowly Figaro cigarettes with a gold holder.

In his memoir, Friedrich recalls that Moritz was not interested in politics, but he appreciated more than anything, loyalty to country.

He recalls Moritz saying more than once, "If an ordinance required that every Austrian was to wear black and yellow stockings, then I would still today go on the street with black and yellow stockings." Moritz said his greatest wish was that his children grow up to become useful members of society.

While Moritz traveled for both business and pleasure, Marie handled most of the family's business. During Moritz's "business" trips to Munich, he visited his friend, Henrik Ibsen. They usually met in the Café Luitpold. Ibsen sat there with a stack of newspapers, searching for material for a new play. The two stayed talking over coffee for hours, and they took long walks. Ibsen visited the *Hofzeile* in Vienna, too, enjoying the fruit gardens and Sunday dances.

Moritz was captivated by his friend's take on life and money. "Money may be the husk of many things but not the kernel," Ibsen wrote. "It brings you food, but not appetite; medicine, but not health; acquaintance, but not friends; servants, but not loyalty; days of joy, but not peace or happiness."

Mortiz took to wearing his dark suits until they were threadbare.

It is difficult to tell if Moritz enjoyed living with his parents while he and Adolf worked together in the lumber business. According to my grandfather Friedrich, his father Moritz was not "predestined by his inclinations for the career of a wood industrialist." Moritz loved the theater and he loved to write and to teach. He did not lead an extravagant life. He dressed and ate simply, trained to do so by his father. Years later, Moritz taught with joy and energy courses on wood technology at the Institute for World Trade in Vienna and he wrote detailed books, all for little compensation. Moritz was never inclined to make *more* money.

Much later, after we leave Hungary, I attend a funeral in New York, and there meet a distant Engel de Jánosi relative who found in his attic all the books his father saved from his father. His father never told him anything about being Jewish or being an Engel de Jánosi, but he collected and saved everything written by an Engel de Jánosi. This relative knows me through my grandfather's books. He also has the only copy of my great-grandfather Moritz's published play, *Transactions*.

Transactions takes place in a grand home, a hunting lodge like *Jánosipuszta*, situated outside a small Hungarian town like Pécs. The head of the family, Anton Sturmer gives long-winded speeches and spends every waking minute thinking about money, building, and investments.

At one point in the play, the real estate agent, Rosenhügel tells the university professor Warneck of his problems working with the ambitious and very successful builder Anton Sturmer:

Rosenhügel. In business too he was always so impatient. Everything took too long for him. Before a building even had a roof on it he had to have the enforcements all squared away, and his manic work habits hardly left him any time to live.

Warneck. But therein also lies the secret to his speedy success: intensive, unflagging industriousness. He has a bit of the genius in his blood, as well as a bit of the American . . .

Transactions is a family drama, involving unhappy marriages and partnerships, afternoons spent hunting, playing Tarot cards, discussing gout, land dealings, drinking the local Tokay wine. It wants to be *A Doll's House* but it isn't.

In 1884, Ibsen wrote a play set in a small, provincial town, where the cultured serve the best Hungarian wine, Tokay. Hjalmar Ekdal, a photographer with a big ego is married to a strong, unimaginative woman who, at one point, admits that she is the "better business man." Ekdal lives with his crazy father, who lost his fortune in a timber trade with a wealthy merchant in town. Ekdal's daughter is going blind as a result of a sexually transmitted disease because of her mother's previous relations with the wealthy merchant. The play is called *Wild Ducks*.

Ibsen invited Moritz to the Viennese premiere of *Wild Ducks* in the Volkstheater. They sat together in the author's box, and, years later, Moritz talked about how, when the public yelled accusations towards their box, Ibsen simply stepped up to the railing, bowed, and thanked them.

Moritz never traveled to his lumber company's production points to see the oak harvests in Croatia, Slavonia or Siebenbürgen as his father Adolf had. Moritz left the hands-on business of lumber production to his brother, József, in Pécs, preferring the city life in Bavaria and Munich, and checking in at the Hotel Four Seasons. He took his son Friedrich on these business trips. They especially liked the Munich Festivals.

On a snowy January evening after a light supper, Adolf sat down in a chair in his sitting room at the *Hofzeile*, facing the garden. He often did so. On this particular evening, he might have gotten up and squinted out the window to have a closer look at the snow piling up on the statues placed all around the perimeter of the garden, the ones he first named for various Habsburgs, then re-named for his Old Testament heroes.

He was reading a book by C. Joseph von Bretton, *Practical Comments on Silk Growth,* which gave him an idea. Silk-making. He would bring in mulberry trees and plant them in his vineyard in Vienna, and on the other estates in his own Austro-Hungarian empire: Jánosi, Felsomindszent, Szatina, Simonfa, Oscárd, and Pazdany. He had already completed his brief autobiography for his children. When he died, there would be no one to have claims on him, for he owed nothing, and for this he was grateful. He wrote, "I love life, do not fear death, and I am always ready to give account to the eternal judge."

Perhaps Adolf went to his desk that cold night, to go over his ledgers, his ink pen poised over each line item while he sat in his study facing south. On his desk, was his inheritance—Peter's prayer book. Hanging on the wall behind him, the framed tablet with a short history of the first Jewish synagogue built in Pécs, inside his father's home.

Adolf died the night of January 10, 1903 at the *Hofzeile*. He was eighty-three years old. He died in the same Viennese neighborhood where his idol, Istvan Széchenyi, another Hungarian died.

After his father died, Moritz spent most evenings playing Tarot cards with his mother, Anna, who was going blind. Anna occupied the ground floor of the *Hofzeile*. Neither Moritz nor Marie nor the other Engel de Jánosi's at the *Hofzeile* took much notice of the news reports sweeping into Vienna. They were busy with the factory and with their studies.

While Moritz read plays by Ibsen, and articles about the free trade zones of the Austrian Hungarian Monarchy, his son, Friedrich, studied law at the University of Vienna. As Friedrich wrote years later in his memoirs, "it was 1912 and there were no problems." Anything felt possible. Even though the *Academe des Sciences* in Paris voted against her membership because she was a woman, Marie Curie won the Nobel Prize.

None of them could have known that first one war, and then another would change all of this.

The day Moritz's mother, Anna Engel de Jánosi died, Franz Ferdinand was assassinated, and World War I was declared.

And so, while the whole Empire was distracted with news of their assassinated heir, while stock markets fell, and armies mobilized, and more than a few Austrian citizens packed to leave what appeared to be their dying empire, the Engel de Jánosis went to the Jewish cemetery at the top of the hill in Döbling, and mourned their own, more personal loss.

Before 1914, the family hardly ever discussed politics, but after 1914, Friedrich remembers hearing his parents complain that, "things were getting worse and worse" and that business was bad. At some point during this time, the family's finances tightened. Everything that happened before the war became as trivial and valueless as the Austrian currency.

Moritz and Marie's daughter, Magda married Wilhelm Schiller, but her heart stopped suddenly one day and she died on December 6, 1919. She was twenty-three years old.

Some time later, Moritz sent his son Friedrich to France on business for the lumber company, and there Friedrich saw a woman walking over a bridge near her aunt's villa just outside Paris. Carlette had "gold hair" and she wore a light blue summer dress with polka dots. Later, he wrote in his memoir that he was "seized" with real passion. "I would have to do everything I could to receive her 'yes.'"

Friedrich had an income now from the Lombard Bank, the bank that now owned their home, the *Hofzeile*. He had, at this point, earned three PhDs, and, while he continued to study, he also wrote, and lectured at the University of Vienna for a minimal salary. His father Moritz continued to tell him not to worry about money.

Carlette said "yes" and married Friedrich. They moved to the *Hofzeile* in Vienna.

Carlette's parents visited often. Her father had transferred the family fortune to Austria to help "poor Austria," but now the money was worthless. He remained trustee of the family's milling business in Vienna.

Friedrich was never close to his father-in law, but he liked Carlette's mother, Rose, who he says was always in a splendid mood. He said that she was a great bridge player, had a seductive laugh, and was a "big success" in Viennese society.

In 1924, the Lombard Bank filed for bankruptcy. Friedrich lost his job, but it hardly mattered to him. He was deep into researching a book about social problems of the Italian renaissance. The Rockefeller Foundation offered him a grant to continue his research and write in the United States.

Moritz urged him to take the offer, and Friedrich and Carlette made plans to go.

It was sunny on May 5, 1924, the day Moritz's appendix burst. He was sixty-five years old and he had serious financial troubles. Friedrich recalled his father lying in bed that day, making figures with his fingers in the air.

Moritz died and was buried on May 7 next to his mother and father in the Döbling cemetery in Vienna.

Friedrich wrote that all they had left to eat were the apples from the garden, and for every meal they ate baked apples. Adolf Engel & Son's shrank to six workers. The machinery was out-dated. Friedrich's first thought was to rent the factory to Moritz's brother, Alexander, who still lived with them in the *Hofzeile*. But his uncle Alexander's offer was so low, Friedrich refused. He called the Rockefeller

Foundation, and, with great regret, passed on the grant. He proposed his colleague and friend from *The Geistkreis* or "Mind Circle," an informal group of academics who met regularly at the university. Erik Voegelin accepted the post.

Friedrich had never set foot inside his father's lumber factory. He knew nothing about the family business when he and his wife, Carlette, took control of the company. They came up with a routine, which he recorded in his memoir:

8-9:00 a.m. Factory
11-1:00 Friedrich at archives
1:00-2:30 Lunch
2:30-4:40 Friedrich at archives
5-7:00 p.m. Factory
Saturday morning: Café with Carlette to do a weekly balance for salaries.
Saturday afternoon: Throw discus on the tennis court with trainer, archives, symphony.
Sunday: Chamber music at the *Hofzeile*

At that time, the social democrats were in control of Vienna's politics. They were building apartments—huge complexes such as the Karl Marx Hof—all for "the working people." Vienna's skyline was changing, and, all at once, there came a renewed demand for oak floors or "common parquet."

Friedrich got a loan from his mother, Marie, to update the factory. He hired up to 100 workers. Soon, Adolf Engel & Sons was back up and running.

By the winter of 1928, Carlette was expecting and became sick with the measles. They spent time in Baden to recover. On a warm day in July 1929, Carlette gave birth to my mother, in the newly renovated Rudolfiner Hospital, just up the street from the *Hofzeile*.

Years later, when she was ten, my mother, Madeleine, held her imaginary friend's hand, and together, they jumped and jumped on the stacked lumber, humming songs. Madeleine was an only child, and her father, Friedrich, gave her this imaginary friend beside her. He'd named her Magda after his sister.

Madeleine was often lonely, but she and Magda loved these piles of planks. Sometimes they played a game of hopscotch, and other times they just sat on the wood, breathing in its oak scent. The lumber came from far away forests Madeleine had never seen, a place in Hungary called Pécs.

When they grew tired, Madeleine took Magda inside the family's parquet floor factory, where they breathed in more fresh smells of cut wood. The two walked hand-in-hand, watching the strong craftsmen sawing the wood into pieces that looked like big jigsaw puzzle pieces. In buildings all around Vienna, the men knelt down as if in prayer, fitting the pieces back together in their own, better way, and, in this way, the cut wood was made whole again, looking like mosaics in art books her mother showed her.

Hand-in-hand, the two girls watched the grandmother Marie at one desk, and the mother Carlette at another desk, both of them talking on two phones at once, the receivers shaped like black tulips held to their ears.

Neither Madeleine nor her friend Magda knew then that Carlette was on the phone making arrangements to obtain transport documents to get out of Austria.

That same year, American movie goers watched a new movie about a brave young girl named Dorothy who tries to make her way home from a faraway land. "The Wizard of Oz" was released a month before Germany invaded Poland. No place like home.

Occupying Forces

We meet Renáta and Zoli in front of the Post Office Building in Pécs, and without a word, we climb into the back seat of their car. Zoli keeps the car running while Renáta hands over a thick brown envelope. We feel like undercover spies. Renáta has translated more articles about Richárd. Once the exchange is made, we think our visit is over, but no. Zoli wants to take us to Villány on a Hungarian wine tour.

Zoli drives thirty minutes into the country until we reach a village with wine bars lining the main street. We four sit and share dark bread smeared with goose fat, sprinkled with paprika and chopped red onions, and we wash it all down with Hungarian rosé. We have a whole new appreciation for paprika, which we now know should look nothing like the tasteless brown powder in our spice cabinet back in Indiana. Hungarian paprika is neon red and can be sweet, spicy, or smokey. We even read that goose fat is *good* for you. We have more of the good dark bread as we celebrate Renáta's dogged, indispensible work, which will allow me to further piece together what I can about Richárd's life during World War I.

After we return home, my laptop rings in the middle of the night. We have never received a Skype call before, and all three of us rush downstairs, worrying that it's bad news from home. The woman's shakey voice sounds like my mother's. "This is Stein Anna," she says. Her accent is French. "I understand you want to know about Richárd, yes? He was my uncle."

Stein, Anna or Anna Stein is my artist "cousin" living in Paris. We saw her paintings at the museum in Komló. My cousin Peter gave her my number.

"You want to know? I tell you."

She does not press the button that shows her face. She remains a shadowy figure. Pat and James go back to bed, while I get out my notebook.

Over the next several weeks Anna calls at night by Skype to tell me about her great uncle Richárd, and about Richárd's brother, her grandfather, Róbert.

In 1914 when World War I began, Richárd was thirty-two. His brother Róbert was thirty-one years old. They both signed up to defend the Austro-Hungarian Empire. My grandfather Friedrich was twenty-one, and his brother Rudolph, nineteen. They too signed up to fight and defend the Empire. Most of the Engel de Jánosi men served during World War I.

Friedrich and Rudolph served in the cavalry, a fashionable and expensive arm of service. They supplied their own uniforms, equipment, and horses. When they left their home in Vienna, their long swords dragged across the polished parquet floors of the *Hofzeile*. Their mother, Marie, was too sad to be angry with them for the scratches.

Those in Pécs who served were given hero farewells by the brass band in town. Ladies saw their men off at the train station, some throwing bouquets of flowers.

Marianne helped Róbert pack. Róbert said goodbye to Marianne and their now four-year-old daughter, Rózsika. After both Róbert and Richárd said goodbye to their father, József, they went to the cemetery in Pécs to the graves of their mother and their sister, Natalie. They prayed and said goodbye to their dead. Then they reported for duty at the army barracks near the train station in Pécs.

In Pécs, the artist, Tivadar Kosztka Csontváry, painted and drew scenes of soldiers heading off to war at this time. In these paintings, soldiers line up and march toward blurry mountains. In one painting, two soldiers stand in the middle of a winding road looking straight at the viewer. They are not smiling.

Róbert and Richárd left Pécs by train on March 28, 1915 at 10:00 on a Sunday morning. The following morning, they were on separate trains, and by 5:00 that afternoon Róbert was celebrating Passover at the local synagogue in Satoraljaujhely Ujhelyi, near the Slovakian border in northern Hungary.

In his 1915 *Hadinapló*, or military diary, Róbert wrote about his routines such as going to the blacksmiths, honoring the birthdays of both his living and his dead family members, and praying on high holy days. He complains about the rain and the blizzards, the conditions, his exhausted soldiers, the despair, and all the paper work involved in his job as an army administrator.

Richárd and Róbert never fought side by side, but Róbert thought of his older brother. He wrote,

31/07/1916. Monday: I worked a little. I remember that today is my brother Richárd's 34th birthday, I wish for the next birthday we will be already at home in peace. 23-week-long rain. Terribly worn out men.

Róbert also thought often of his wife, Marianne, referring to her as his "dear sweetheart." He writes that she is such a "soft, elegant, and wonderful woman."

Róbert wrote about the period between May 1915 and February 1917, when he fought on the Russian front and later on the Romanian front. The "Great War" was to be the last "old-fashioned" war, where soldiers like Richárd and Róbert's cousin, Paul, returned home scarred by saber cuts. Sundays there were cease-fires, and Hungarian and Russian officers even met to play bridge. Mondays they returned to shooting and killing each other.

Throughout the two years they were away fighting, neither Richárd nor Róbert were spared the rough army life, marching with the other soldiers in the cold of winter, before their winter uniforms arrived. Their Viennese cousins, Friedrich and Rudolf, fought on the Russian and the Italian fronts.

These four cousins learned one of the first rules of soldiering: eat everything you get when you get it, because you don't know if you'll get anything again. In his later years, when I knew him, Friedrich suffered daily, blaming his stomach ulcers on the horsemeat he ate in World War I.

An artillery officer on the Galician and Italian fronts, Friedrich said he was bored waiting in the trenches, so he studied philosophy. He already had one Ph.D. in law and another in history from the

University of Vienna. Once, he shot and hit the thread of an enemy's spy balloon, bringing it downs. He received the silver medal for bravery.

Friedrich's brother Rudolf was stationed on the Russian front, where he was shot and killed. Whenever my great-grandmother, Marie, spoke of Rudolph, her eyes watered. Each and every time she said his name. She told me once she never recovered from the death of her youngest son. Her favorite son.

During their time at war, Róbert, Richárd and Friedrich witnessed political and socio-economic tides turning and the end of an established order. In Russia they saw street demonstrations. Peasants seized land from their landlords. Troops refused to fire at starving crowds. Nicolas II abdicated. Even though the Habsburgs were still figureheads, and Franz Joseph was still technically the Emperor, The Rule of One was vanishing fast in Western Europe. In 1917, the Russian Revolution overthrew the Romanov Dynasty and the Germans put Lenin on a train to Moscow — their way of getting rid of a troublemaker.

Richárd and Róbert served as officers in the army until they were both absolved from army service in 1917. They were needed to run the family business in Pécs. Several other Engel de Jánosi men made their way back home from the war as well. Paul Engel de Jánosi returned to Budapest having been a prisoner of war in Siberia for four years.

When Friedrich returned to Vienna, Schönbrunn Palace was a welfare center where women lined up for bread. Workers at Adolf Engel & Sons swept up the sawdust to mix into their bread and stews. Some ate their pets. The monarchy was over, and all the suffering and warring amounted to nothing. Most of the young men coming home were no longer young—in age or in spirit. Dismayed soldiers or prisoners of war returned often six years older with little to no financial help from the country for which they fought. Not everyone received war disability pensions. The saying went: "in Austria all roads are crooked." The Austrian author Stefan Zweig wrote that on trains, you could hear tired, angry soldiers returning from the front, talking about Jews and Serbian "trash." There was not enough coal for the trains in Austria to run on time either. In Austria, money saved up by three generations became worthless in a mere two weeks. Families were swindled out of land, houses, businesses and property that had been theirs for hundreds of years. People learned new words for stealing. *Commandeering. Expropriating. Reclamation.*

Yet, some Viennese, fearing this changing world, continued to play the Radetzky march, "God Save the Kaiser."

When Richárd and Róbert returned to Pécs they found a devastated economy governed by Hungarian Communists hoping to separate Hungary from Austria and the rest of Europe.

At the Komló museum in one of the glass cases, there is a black and white picture of Róbert and Marianne together again in their salon at the Wedgwood blue house on Rákóczi út. Róbert stands touching the back of the chair in which Marianne sits near a table strewn with flowers in the shape of a heart and a heart-shaped card. It is their wedding anniversary. He is smiling. She is not.

While Róbert was away at war, Marianne cared for their daughter Rózsa, their house in Pécs, managed the servants, and spent time doing charity work and other 'womanly pursuits' such as playing music, sewing and visiting friends. She fell in love with a man from Üszög named Imre Grosz. Years later, Marianne wrote that she did not care for Róbert when their families arranged their marriage and she still did not care for him after she married. She said she never did fall in love with Róbert the way her mother promised she would. When Róbert came back home from the war, Marianne realized she could not stand to stay in a loveless marriage.

She wanted a divorce. Róbert was devastated. Marianne said she couldn't live in Pécs any more either. She wanted to live in Budapest with the man she loved.

József stepped in to advise Róbert. They would not stand for Marianne's complaints or her behavior and insisted that Róbert put Marianne on house arrest. Locked inside, for a year Marianne was not allowed to leave the Wedgwood blue house near the factory on Rákóczi út.

At this time, Richárd and Róbert spoke less and less to each other. Even when they were eating at the same table in Pécs with their father

József, or at *Jánosipuszta* with the extended family, they would not speak to each other. If one had something to say, he would say it through someone else. For instance, Róbert would say to his father, "Father, please tell Richárd . . ." even though Richárd would be sitting across the table from Róbert.

Something had changed between the brothers when they returned to Pécs after their service in the military. When they returned, their father clarified their roles and status in the family business and this may have stirred up animosity, jealousy, or rivalry. They might have suffered from post-traumatic stress having been in constant battles for the last two years abroad. Or maybe, the unsettling issue of Marianne came between the brothers.

Maybe Richárd was disappointed that Róbert had fallen into the family's tight grip. Maybe Róbert was disappointed in himself. Maybe they were both ashamed: two years of leading others into battle, they were now just followers.

A parallel universe grew between the unwillingness to fall in line within the Engel de Jánosi households and what was going on in Hungary. The collapsing monarchy was bringing independence and chaos both to the Engel de Jánosi households and to Hungary.

In Hungary people were looking for people to blame. Surely the Jews created this mess. Before the war, the accepted Hungarian criterion for anti-Semitism was a kind of joke: Do they "hate Jews more than necessary?" Even if you didn't *hate* Jews, it was prudent to *pretend* to hate Jews. During the war, there was a tendency to blame Jews for the collapsing monarchy and the resulting chaos. But after the war? Anti-Semitism flourished.

Early in the morning on May 20, 1918 a group of battle-weary soldiers and disaffected privates in the Sixth Imperial and Royal Infantry Regiment, soldiers who had witnessed the beginnings of the Russian Revolution, swarmed onto the parade grounds in Pécs shouting demands to end this miserable war. Many shouted praises for Hungary's enemy country, Serbia, less than forty miles away. One group of soldiers stormed the duty officer's room and ordered him to hand over the keys to the munitions supply and to the treasury. The duty officer shot at the soldiers. The soldiers bayoneted him to death.

By mid-afternoon, 1500 armed men took over the army barracks, arrested their officers, occupied buildings, and set up armed patrols around town. Pécs was littered with dead and wounded men.

Trains brought in more troops from both Budapest and Serbia, leaving the city at loose ends throughout that spring and summer. In October 1918, Hungarian soldiers and workers revolted in Budapest, bringing to power the liberal-radical politician Mihaly Karoly. On November 14, 1918 the Serbian Army crossed the Drava River and into Baranya, entering Pécs.

Bertha and Leopold fled Pécs for the *Hofzeile* in Vienna. The Serbian army commandeered Loránt Palace as their headquarters. The Serbians were primarily interested in the coal and the coal mines in the Baranya territory. Pécs was the only industrial town in Hungary surrounded by mines, and by then, sixty-six-year old József was living on the estate in Jánosi, running one of the largest coalmines in Hungary.

It is very possible that József told Róbert's wife, Marianne, he was taking her with him to the *Hofzeile* for her own protection.

"You'll be safer with me," he might have said when he came to fetch her in Pécs. *It will be for the best.* Whatever he said, József put his sons Richárd and Róbert in charge of Adolf Engel & Sons, the coal mines, and *Jánosipuszta*. Then he and Marianne took the train to Vienna, not to the *Hofzeile* in Döbling, but to the Rudolfiner Hospital. József institutionalized Marianne. For surely she was insane. Why else would a woman consider divorcing an Engel?

In Pécs, Richárd grew frustrated with the Serbian occupation, especially with the increasing mis-treatment of Jews. In March 1919, Mihaly Karoly's rule as president gave way to the Bolshevik-inspired Council Republic under Béla Kun and a communist-led coalition. News of the change was slow to travel. They never got word in Pécs.

According to newspaper reports at that time, Richárd came forward as president and representative of the Jewish community. He made a speech in front of the house his uncle built. A crowd gathered near Loránt Palace in Széchenyi Square as Richárd protested the

Serbian treatment of Jews. According to all accounts, Richárd was the only Jew who protested.

The Serbian army arrested Richárd on the spot, and imprisoned him in Loránt Palace, the family home, the former "Rat Fortress". Imprisoned, Richárd began a political fast.

After the first, the second, and then the third day, Richárd continued to refuse food. No one else seemed to be following his example, and there was only a one paragraph mention of Richárd's protest in the local newspaper during those days. Did being there, in his family's home give him strength? Did he stare down at those fitted parquet floors made up of wood from all over Hungary, Moravia, Serbia, Croatia and wonder how or if these countries and his family would ever be pieced back together again?

Richárd was used to religious fasts, but those never lasted over twenty-four hours.

While Richárd was held in Loránt Palace, and Marianne was locked up in Rudolfiner Hospital in Vienna, József wrote "The Merchant of Rome or Shylock's Original Figure" to contradict Shakespeare's "Merchant of Venice" in order to make the merchant "friendlier" to Jews. At the end of his preface, József writes, "May this work fulfill the task meant for it and lower the Shylock figure to the same level of meaning, which the witches and aerial spirits of Shakespeare deserve."

Richárd fasted approximately four days until the Serbian army finally released him, unharmed. There is no mention of why the Serbians freed Richárd, and it is unclear if his fast did any good. Richárd's protest was mentioned in the book, *Kempelen Béla: Hungarian Jewish Families.* (Makkabi. Budapest, 1939). "*Richárd, a kommunizmus után felekezete védelme miatt fogságot szenvedett.*" *Richard suffered imprisonment after the Communist period because of his defense of his faith.*

From the asylum, Marianne wrote to her brothers who were still living in Pécs. She wrote that she was growing more and more depressed. She told them she was not insane, but in the insane hospital, she would become insane, and that surely she would take her own life.

"Please," she wrote. "Come and free me."

Marianne's two brothers did finally take the train to Vienna and rescue Marianne. She refused to return to Pécs with them. She took the train to Budapest, instead.

Bela Kun's communist coalition lasted until August, when Kun's government resigned under the leadership of Miklós Horthy. Meanwhile, the victorious wartime allied powers put pressure on Hungary for border revisions.

Hungary lost 70% of its territory and half its population to neighboring countries as a result of the Treaty of Trianon, which leads many to still say or at least think: Hungary is a country surrounded by itself. In 1920, Miklós Horthy signed that God-awful deal, but some Hungarians blamed Jews, not Horthy.

Gangs of Hungarians, most directed by Miklós Horthy, travelled the countryside, dragging out Jewish families and beating them to death. There were lynchings. Over 10,000 Jews lost their lives on the battlefield during World War I defending their homeland and Empire, and now, they faced murderous, destructive anti-Semitism from their own countrymen. Was this period, known as The White Terror, the beginning of Hungary's ethnic cleansing? Part of it? Regardless, Richárd, Róbert and others in the Engel family managed to survive. Again.

Miklós Horthy devoted the next quarter century trying to get back that 70% of the country he signed away. His "colleague," Hitler promised to get him those lost territories, which of course led Hungary into a second world war and another blood bath.

József left the *Hofzeile* and returned to Pécs, without Marianne. Róbert signed the divorce papers, the first recorded divorce in Pécs. Marianne married Imre Grosz in Budapest, then moved to Üszög, where they remained for some time.

József sold the Komló coal mines and a portion of the lands in the village of Jánosi to what was left of the "empire" before all Hungarian property was nationalized. Even though he sold the mines at a low price, with the family's approval, the sale prevented the family from being forced to hand over the mines for free.

On October 12, 1921, Miklós Horthy visited Pécs and his men forced any and all remaining Serbians soldiers back into Serbia. Dressed in his World War I military uniform, Horthy made a speech where Richárd had made his speech protesting the Serbian treatment of Jews.

William Butler Yeats' new poem, "The Second Coming", was circulating in various countries, defining the era. "Things fall apart; the centre cannot hold;/Mere anarchy is loosed upon the world . . ."

There in the middle of Széchenyi Square, in front of the Loránt Palace, Horthy stood. At the end of his speech, someone took a picture of him talking to a man who was wearing the traditional native costume of a white shirt, black vest and black boots. The man is seated on a white horse. Behind Horthy, at the top of the makeshift wooden steps, stands a balding, grey-haired man dressed in a dark suit with a dark overcoat, holding a black top hat. The man stands next to a little girl, dressed in traditional Hungarian costume. The man is not smiling and he is not watching the exchange between the man on the white horse and Horthy. He is looking beyond them, beyond the crowd of soldiers and bureaucrats. This man is József.

At the paprika festival in Szeged, Pat finishes his bowl of Fisherman's Soup, looks at a map, and shows us how close we are to Serbia. The Fulbright gathering is winding down in Szeged and we all have our fat envelopes stuffed with forints, which we will use for food and rent. We find out about how other Fulbright projects are coming along. No one has quit, but many have fallen ill or have been slowed down. In Szeged we visit cemeteries and crumbling synagoues.

With another family, we slip away for a day to "picnic in Serbia."

Pat drives our tin can of a rental car to Subotica, Serbia, and, as soon as we cross the Hungarian border, the green road line on the rented GPS screen stops. Even though it has the word *global* on it, the GPS doesn't go into Serbia, stopping exactly at the border. On the other side of the road, there are more cars filled with people going into Hungary.

I've brought our passports but the border guards don't bother checking them and everyone's smiling. We open the car windows and smell apples apples apples.

Subotica once was a part of Hungary. In 1918 at the end of World War I, Subotica became a part of the newly created state of Yugoslavia. Then after Horthy signed the Treaty of Trianon in 1920, Subotica belonged to Vojvodina, which later became a province of Serbia.

Pat parks the tin can and we meet up with the other family. We use the clean restrooms in the McDonald's—we're American, it's still a McDonald's, and I feel that using the restrooms without buying so much as a French fry is perfectly acceptable.

We walk around the town's open market and peruse a long table of used paperback books. Nora Roberts in Serbian alongside Stephen King, James Joyce, George Orwell, and Fyodor Dostoevsky. James stops at one of the stalls to have a good look at old Serbian currency.

I recall the lovely novel *Skylark*, written by Dezső Kosztolányi, who was from Subotica. I search for his name on signs and notice how everything looks exactly as it does in Hungary, only here, the roads are worse, the buildings more cracked and beyond repair.

We walk the long stretch between rows of trees and happen upon the bust for Dezső Kosztolányi. I retell his story of a middle-aged couple living in a dead-end town, at the end of the century with their unintelligent, unattractive, unimaginative, unmarried daughter, Skylark, who goes away for one week, changing their lives forever.

"Is every story about these places so depressing?" James asks.

We head for the marketplace where we see people leaving with baskets of produce. We splurge on fresh apples, figs, dried dates and apricots. We stop and have a snack at a wonderful neighbourhood coffee shop and sit and stare at the rows of beautiful old crumbling buildings, looking like so many painted sand castles. Any minute, with the next wave, they will collapse.

We say goodbye to our friends, squeeze back into the tin can and head back towards Hungary. The line of cars at the border is breathtaking, and we sit parked in the middle of the road. After an hour, we watch men from other cars get out and wander around.

At the border, guards carefully read our passports. It occurs to me then that our passports might not have that magical stamp from the Immigration and Naturalization Office. When we left Hungary, we never thought that we might not be able to get back in.

The guards check the trunk of our tin can. They are looking for weapons. We look at the other open trunks. Most people have bushels of apples. The car in the lane next to ours gets checked, then approved, and begins to move. A man I think looks a great deal like Richárd sits in the back seat. It looks as though he is tapping his wrist watch, waving us to *Get a move on.*

Where They Burn Books

When József traveled from *Jánosipuszta* to Pécs, he stayed with Richárd on Rákóczi út, taking long walks every day around town, his fingers playing imaginary piano keys on his gold-tipped cane. Pécs was not a modern city then. Wagons loaded with wares clogged the streets and small carts stood in front of shops, while men loaded and unloaded boxes of oranges, lemons, and figs. Salesclerks wearing identical caps greeted József. The trolley road along Király utca in the midst of crowds. Automobiles, telephones, and radios were rare. There were electric streetcars, but the street lamps were not yet electrified. Every evening at dusk, men lit the street's gaslights. A heavy rain would often snuff them out.

On Sundays, József usually traveled back to *Jánosipuszta*, to play Tarok with the pastor of the Catholic Church. József took his duties as owner of *Jánosipuszta* and the parsonage seriously.

His younger son, Róbert met and married his second wife, a widow named Erna Erdősi-Baiersdorf from Vienna. She had no children. Erna sculpted prehistoric animals and humans for displays in natural history museums in Pécs and in Vienna.

Bertha and Leopold had returned to Loránt Palace, but Leopold died shortly after in 1922. He was seventy-six years old. Bertha lost her hearing and used a long black hearing horn for the rest of her life. My cousin Peter recalls Bertha as a big, cheerful woman dressed in black moiré that rustled over her parquet floors. She often pointed out to anyone who listened that the Engel de Jánosi women were blessed and cursed with their bountiful hips.

In 1931, József fell passionately in love with an attractive blond woman from Pécs. She was fifty and Christian. He was eighty. József lavished her with gifts. He began legal preparations to change his will so that she would receive the oak forests surrounding *Jánosipuszta*. Richárd intervened.

Richárd's father had not allowed Richárd to marry the Christian woman in Germany. Was Richárd simply looking out for his father and the family's holdings when he stopped his father from willing the *Jánosi* forests to this Christian woman who visited him from Pécs? Or maybe, Richárd's intervention was simply revenge.

József did not alter his will. The Christian woman stopped visiting him at *Jánosipuszta*.

From that time on, Richárd spent more time at *Jánosipuszta*, taking care of his father. József only had running water in one bathroom far away from the bedrooms and living rooms. He could hear the water running in the pipes and the noise disturbed him. Guests used chamber pots and a butler provided pitchers of warm water.

On May 10, 1933 students and leading Nazi party members at universities across Germany burned books they associated with an "un-German spirit." Enthusiastic crowds threw books by Bertolt Brecht and Thomas Mann into a giant bonfire. Other books by well-known intellectuals, scientists and cultural figures, many of whom were Jewish went into the fire. The largest of these book bonfires occurred in Berlin, where some 40,000 people gathered to hear a speech by the new propaganda minister. In his speech, the propaganda minister announced that, "Jewish intellectualism is dead" and he endorsed the students' "right to clean up the debris of the past." The new propaganda minister was a slight, mousy-looking man named Joseph Goebbels.

József Engel de Jánosi was eighty-two years old when he read that his own book, *Merchant of Rome,* was among the volumes publically burned in Leipzig. Maybe he wondered where this would lead. Maybe he was outraged. He might even have been proud that he was included alongside Albert Einstein, Sigmund Freud, Theodor Hertzl, Stefan Zweig, and the nineteenth century Jewish poet Heinrich Heine, whom József's friend, Richard Wagner, had railed against once upon a time. In 1822, Heine wrote, "Where they burn books, they will, in the end, burn human beings too."

Where Mountains Fall into the Sea

The plaque is ready, but the mayor of Pécs is not.

The Adolf Engel de Jánosi plaque ceremony is controversial for Mayor Zsolt Páva and he does not want or need *any* controversy. It is election year. And already Mayor Páva has had difficulties at the municipality.

Mayor Páva is not a party man and it appears necessary to be affiliated with the current party in Hungary to win elections. It would be beneficial for Mayor Páva to align himself with Prime Minister Viktor Orbán, but he does not. Mayor Páva has very little support from the "ruling party" in Budapest, the right wing, anti-Semitic party. The far right has taken over parliament, and the far right leans more and more towards the old, Nationalistic, anti-Semitic, Fascist ways.

My university friends explain it this way: Hungarians look East towards Russia because Russia is *known*. Students wear a popular t-shirt that reads: *No Order, New Order, Dis-Order.*

In emails and over the phone, Mayor Páva promises Peter there *will* be a plaque ceremony for the Engels of Pécs. But in the months we have been here, the plaque ceremony has been cancelled so many times, I seriously wonder if it will ever take place at all. Peter asks if there is anything *I* can do.

Really, what can I do? I find myself staring out windows, wondering *How did we get here again?* Was this an accident, a coincidence, or a conspiracy? I want to tell Peter not to bother booking plane tickets. Most likely, there will be no ceremony for Adolf. Hungary is not ready to celebrate a capitalist or a Jew.

I still can't get into the antique shop.

The hall monitor at the ANK continues to detain James at the door in the morning.

We still haven't received official clearance from The Immigration and Naturalization Office.

At the university, after class one day, I return the chalk, the classroom keys and the boom box to Bea. Already, I am so far along in the American Southern Literature class, I'm playing Johnny Cash and Elvis. "Folsom Prison Blues" is the students' entrance song and "Hound Dog" is their exit. Pat and I are in the midst of planning an end-of-the-semester "Southern Night" featuring Pat's jambalaya and a screening and discussion of the movie, "To Kill a Mockingbird."

Pat is working with a Hungarian chef gathering ingredients, using the jambalaya recipe he "borrowed" from the chefs at Galatoire's in New Orleans. Finding shrimp and Andouille sausage is proving to be a challenge, and Pat discovered that spicy Hungarian celery bulbs are not at all the same as American celery. The "Cabbage Ladies" at the market guide him to alternative produce.

Bea reminds me there is still no word about our visas from the Immigration and Naturalization Office. I shake my head and shrug to act as if I no longer care. Standing there in Bea's small office, my colleague László tells me he found out that the plaque has been ready for some time. The plaque designer is letting everybody know that it is "high time, no, past time to honor the Engel de Jánosi's."

Bea listens to László's update. Later, after I've left the office, Bea asks László about my "famous family," about why I *really* came to Pécs, and if I came just to get back the Engel properties.

At the end of October, the mayoral reelection is held and Zsolt Páva wins. We receive word that the plaque ceremony is set for November.

My cousin Peter emails me a photograph a friend of his once bought at an antique store in Pécs. I wonder if the photograph is a thank-you for providing more plaque information. The black and white picture has that steam punk look of Victorian men looking towards the future and the next best invention. Seven dapper men wearing hiking suits and black bowler hats sit on a pile of rocks looking off to the distance. The caption: *Engel Besteigüng des Vesùr May 9 1883.*

Three of the men have their walking sticks, one has a folded black umbrella, another has what looks to be a new traveling jug and a folding telescope. They all have beards. These are not heavy-set, robust Hungarians or be-ringleted, orthodox Jews. They are fit, well-dressed, tall, handsome men out on a hike, seated only for the moment, for the photographer.

"Mountains or water?" That's what my great-grandmother asked me once when I visited her in Washington, D.C. "Which do you prefer, hiking in the mountains or swimming in the sea?" I was ten and I'd never even seen a mountain. Then again, I'd never been in a "sea" either—just the Mississippi Gulf. "Swimming," I said. "In the sea."

"The trick is to find places where the mountains fall into the sea." She winked.

With that wink, I felt she was giving me the magic formula to happiness. But *Where do such places exist?*

Most of the Engel de Jánosi family, I discovered, liked the mountains *and* the sea. Flat country makes them melancholy.

In the black and white photograph, the handsome young Moritz poses relaxed, legs crossed, with his full, neatly-trimmed beard and mustache. He's in his dark country walking suit and tie. Coat buttoned.

Cousin Eùdward Jùstùs sits beside Moritz. Their good friend Mórné Krausz is there too. Later there will be an arranged marriage between the Engels and the Krausz family. Mórné's sister, Marianne will marry Moritz' nephew, Róbert. It will be considered an excellent match.

These men have evidently just hiked up a steep mountain, on top of which they can rest and regard the fine views all around. From there they must feel on top of the world. Everything is going their way.

Kristallnacht

Changes happen slowly, and, if you aren't paying attention, unnoticeably.

Each time a new law is made and announced, they think, *just wait. It's too crazy. This will all blow over.*

At the university in Vienna, Friedrich spoke with his colleagues about how other countries saw the ridiculous nature of this tyrant, a fool with bad hair, a loudmouth who couldn't even get into art school.

Hungarian relatives felt the same. What was happening in the rest of Europe would never happen in Hungary, definintely not in Pécs. They were so far south, history barely touched them. They were Jewish, yes, but veterans were protected. Hadn't the Engel de Jánosi men just fought for their country and their empire? That *had* to count for something. Besides, Hungary would never turn her back on her own people. And they were Hungarians, were they not?

In 1935, when she was with her parents in Rome for a semester, my mother, with her dark hair parted neatly in the middle and plaited in two long shiny braids, was eager to please her teachers. She wrote a paper praising Mussolini's invasion into Ethiopia. She received high marks, though her teacher thought her Italian needed improvement.

In 1936, Mussolini allied with the failed painter and former wallpaper hanger from Austria, the so-called loser, Adolf Hitler. The same year, Richard Strauss's opera "The Silent Woman" was canceled after two performances in Vienna because Stefan Zweig, a Jew, had written the libretto. During the 1936 Summer Olympics in Berlin, Hungary won sixteen medals. Six medalist winners were Jewish, and one, the Jewish Hungarian wrestler Károly Kárpáti, pinned a German directly in front of Hitler.

In the spring of 1938, Hitler marched into Vienna while Friedrich was researching the Diplomacy of the Vatican in Rome. Pope Pius XII remained silent on the issue of anti-Semitism and Hitler. Friedrich converted to Catholicism.

In his memoirs Friedrich said he converted because he felt a love and preference for Catholicism. His second wife, Christiane, once told me that my grandfather was "born with Jesus in his heart."

In 1938 a new anti-Jewish law, Act XV, came into effect in Hungary. This law was designed to limit the number of Jewish lawyers, doctors, engineers, journalists and actors in Hungary. The act stipulated that Jews could only be admitted to these local chambers when the ratio of Jews in that chamber was below twenty percent. This anti-Semitic act openly violated Act VII of 1867, which granted Jews emancipation from such laws. Approximately five thousand Hungarian Jews converted to Christianity after the passing of Act XV, the first anti-Jewish law.

At that time all official documents, including passports, listed the holder's religion. In 1938, my cousin Peter's father, Paul Engel de Jánosi, his wife Kitty, and their children Peter and Clarissa converted to Roman Catholicism. The rabbi of the synagogue in Pécs, Rabbi Wallenstein, told Peter that he was glad only because Peter's great-grandfather Adolf was not alive to know about their conversion.

Some members of the Engel de Jánosi family began to quietly prepare their way for emigration, transferring considerable amounts of money to banks in Switzerland. Paul and Kitty, moved their furniture and silver into homes of friends for safekeeping.

That year, the American automobile maker Henry Ford wrote that Jews were the great threat to the Anglo Saxon race and that they were, in fact, the world's foremost problem. He was awarded the Nazi Eagle.

One day in March 1938, while her parents were in Rome and she was at home with her grandmother, my mother, Madeleine, went to the dentist's office to have a cavity filled. She was nine years old. The dentist was a thin man in a white coat and he smelled of peppermint. His nurse smiled and showed my mother the button to push whenever the pain became unbearable. The button stopped the drill. They did not yet have Novocain.

Just as the dentist began drilling, my mother heard shouting and motorcars outside on the street. The dentist stopped drilling and he and the nurse went over to the open window. A band played. My mother got out of her chair to see what was happening.

She saw the motorcar with the white flag first. My mother thinks he came by in a tank and that he was standing. She recalls that he was short and not at all intimidating, waving to the crowd, with his drooping hair and the fat black caterpillar over his upper lip, a little mustache. My mother's mouth was stuffed with cotton as she watched the crowd throwing flowers at Hitler and his Nazis marching alongside the cars in their brown and black uniforms and jackboots.

"Perish the Jews!" People shouted in German. "Down with the Catholics! *Ein Volk, ein Reich, ein Furhrer.*"

Airplanes passed overhead and dropped German leaflets that read: *The Jews are behind Everything* and *Nazi Germany welcomes Nazi Austria*.

Relieved with the respite from the dentist's drill, my mother clapped and waved along with the nurse standing there at the window.

On November 9, 1938 people throughout Germany and Austria went through towns with sledgehammers destroying Jewish homes, businesses, hospitals and temples. They killed at least ninety-one Jews. Authorities did not arrest the people who looted and murdered. Instead they arrested thirty thousand Jews, sending them to concentration camps.

The gangs burned over one thousand synagogues, ninety-five in Vienna alone. They destroyed or damaged seven thousand Jewish businesses, including the largest synagogue in Vienna designed by Ludwig Förster, the architect who had worked with Moritz on the Loránt Palace on Széchenyi square in Pécs. All but the foundation of the Förster synagogue was completely destroyed. The night would be known as *Kristallnacht*, Crystal Night, or Night of Broken Glass.

Friedrich and Carlette were in Rome having dinner with a friend at the German Embassy. Their friend told them not to return to Vienna. He said what had happened in Germany was nothing compared to what would happen in Austria. If they stayed in Rome, they would be protected by the German Embassy.

They agreed with their friend. It *was* dangerous. But their daughter, my mother, Madeleine was still in Vienna. Friedrich's mother was there too, and she was Jewish.

On the night train, heading into Vienna, Carlette said to Friedrich, "Now we are entering Austria. When and how will we leave it again?"

Soon after, Carlette's brother, René Kalmus, came to the *Hofzeile* and told his sister they had to get out of Austria altogether.

"Now," he said. *Maintenant.* He was appalled and furious that Friedrich had not made any arrangements for them. "He's not even thinking about you or his daughter. You both need to leave." In my mind, René told his sister to leave Friedrich behind that night.

Neither René nor his wife were Jewish but they had secured an apartment in Switzerland and were leaving as soon as they could.

"Join us there," he said. "You and Madeleine are in danger."

Carlette told René that Friedrich was the most in danger. Even though, according to Nazi "law" the mother was the carrier of the "Jewish gene," it mattered that the father was Jewish as well.

My mother remembers hearing her uncle that day, the day he came to convince his sister to leave. She said she saw him hold Carlette's arms and say to her, in French, that they all had to leave, that nobody was safe, not her, not her daughter, not Friedrich or anybody else in the family.

Maybe Friedrich felt that he and his family were exempt from all that was happening. Maybe because he was an Engel de Janósi, or maybe he felt irreproachable, untouchable because he had three PhDs or because he was the *Herr professor* or *Herr doktor* in the exclusive academic world of the University of Vienna. Friedrich barely regarded himself as a Jew—so much so that he disassociated himself from other, practicing Jews such as the *Ostjuden*, who at that time were pouring into Western Europe to escape Russian pogroms. A close family friend and senior faculty member at the University of Vienna offered to collaborate on a book with Friedrich—a historical study of jokes told in each European country. Friedrich liked this project, but declined the offer to collaborate because he felt his colleague was "too Jewish" and he thought his association might harm his chances for promotion. The man who would have liked to work with Friedrich was Sigmund Freud.

Freud left Vienna on June 4, 1938 with his wife, his daughter, his wife's sister Minna, his personal doctor and his doctor's family, two housekeepers, and Jo-Fi, the dog. Freud's four sisters pleaded with their brother, Sigmund, to provide visas for them too, but Freud said he was unable. He just couldn't.

Freud's four sisters died in concentration camps.

My mother does not recall her parents coordinating anything with the Engel de Jánosi families in Hungary. It was nearly impossible to stay in touch with family in this new world. Carlette's brother had already left for Switzerland and she was focused on getting her immediate family out of Austria. She was on the phone constantly, or, she came home late in the evenings after standing in lines to get the proper papers and bribe the right bureaucrats. She wore her best suits, her best coat, and good shoes. She said it made a difference. She didn't know then, but dressed so well, she was sold three phony boat tickets to the United States.

Hitler had already moved into his rooms at the Hotel Imperial on the Ringstraße near the Opera. Nazi-German soldiers got busy confiscating Jewish property and took over Adolf Engel & Sons in Vienna.

In 1939 the Hungarian Parliament passed a second Jewish Law, Law IV that further reduced the economic participation of Hungarian Jews to five percent. 250,000 Hungarian Jews lost their source of income. They were a "threat to national economy and culture," "alien and destructive." The definition of a Jew was now a person who belonged to Judaism or to one of whose parents or two grandparents belong to the Jewish community, even if this person converted to Christianity. The act also authorized the Hungarian government to "promote emigration of Jews."

Jews whose ancestors settled in Hungary before January 1, 1849 were exempt, as were Jews who were Olympic champions, university professors, and war heroes. Richárd and most of the Engel de Jánosi family fell into this category, giving them all a false feeling of relief and hope. They paid more taxes and penalties, but otherwise, their every day lives were not affected by the new laws.

The system of exemption involved an enormous amount of bureaucracy and paperwork, most of it involving payoffs. But if you had the correct "immunity certificates" and papers, you could keep your home, your property and you did not have to wear the yellow star. However, once you were "tagged" a Jew, using your rations, you had to buy the correct shade of canary yellow fabric in order to make a yellow star six-by-six centimeters, which you had to stitch onto coats and jackets.

That year, Germany took Czechoslovakia. The British and the French prepared for war. When Nazi-Germany fired on Poland and tanks rolled across the border, World War II began. Even if they heard about what was happening in Poland, most family members in Pécs still felt immune. What happened to the Polish Jews could never happen to them, not in Hungary.

One night in 1939, Richárd's father, József sat up in his rooms at *Jánosipuszta* reading an article in his favoritie wood industrial journal concerning the particulars of the lumber business. József was eighty-eight years old and he had a bad cold. When he fell asleep that evening, he never woke up again.

After their father's death. Róbert continued to lead the company of Adolf Engel & Sons in Pécs while Richárd was mostly in charge of the large farm in *Jánosipuszta.*

In a file of old pictures, there is one black and white of a funeral scene, and I look at it more carefully, searching for clues. I recognize the Pécs Cemetery now, and I can name a good many faces in the crowd. Richárd and Róbert look like twins with their buzz cuts, their mustaches, and their sadness. Richárd stares down at his father's big black coffin just as it is being lowered into the ground, his face blank and pale, his mouth slightly open. He looks stunned.

Did Richárd and Róbert suspect that their old world was coming to a complete and definitive end? Even though they were not on speaking terms, they still sat down together at a dinner table, their bellies full, the fire crackling, the help clearing the dishes. They had all the time in the world to argue, apologize, and make amends.

They heard outlandish rumors of roundups going on in Germany, Austria, and elsewhere. Jews were being deported. No one believed it could be true. Who does this?

Two women wearing black stand on either side of Richárd. One is Erna, Róbert's second wife. The other is Marianne, Róbert's first wife, her face covered with a black lace veil.

Who is there for Richárd?

I learn about the love of Richárd's life years later after I write an opinion piece for *The Los Angeles Times*. In 2015, when Hungarian police sprayed crowds of Syrian migrants with water cannons, and Viktor Orbán announced to the world that his aim was "to keep Europe Christian," I felt compelled to write about the situation, bringing up Hungary's dark past.

After the piece is published, a woman named Darinka emails me from Slovenia, hoping I can provide her with any information about an unknown Engel de Jánosi, a man named Richárd. Darinka is researching her ex-husband's Slovenian family so that her son can know more. She writes that in the early 1900's, three sisters moved south of Slovenia. One of them Theresia, Vandur Dyhrn went to Pécs, Hungary around 1930 to live with the man she fell in love with, Richárd Engel de Jánosi.

She was 27 and Catholic. Neither Theresia nor Richárd was willing to change religions, so they lived together secretly in Pécs. They never married.

Darinka and I are both more than a little surprised. She has been researching Theresia and I have been researching Richárd, and in all this time, no one ever mentioned anything to us about about this secret love affair that lasted for almost fourteen years. Darinka is collecting photographs of the people from her genealogical tree for her son. Even though Theresia and Richárd were never married, Darinka feels that Richárd is like Theresia's husband and a part of the story—Theresia's story, her family's story, our story. She considers me her cousin.

I send her a photo of Richárd. She sends me a photo of Theresia and I can almost hear the *click* of a puzzle piece fitting. As soon as I see Darinka's photo, I recognize the thin, dark haired beauty at the funeral, standing beside Richárd.

The Proud Beggar

Friedrich's conversion to Catholicism and his links with the Vatican and with Pope Pius XII kept him and his family safe as late as 1939. But late one night in March, Nazi soldiers came to the *Hofzeile* to search their home. They looked through papers on Friedrich's desk, surveyed the art hanging on the walls, the furniture, the tapestries, the rugs. They made notes in ledgers. They spoke with Agnes, the housekeeper. Then they left.

On the night of April 1, 1939, Friedrich called for a taxi and left the *Hofzeile* alone. From the back, he turned around and watched his yellow palace get smaller and smaller.

At the train station, he bought a ticket to Switzerland. Inside the train, it grew darker that night at the border crossing. Thanks to his wife, Carlette, he had all his papers, none of which marked him as a Jew. He didn't have much money. After she discovered that first round of tickets were fake, Carlette spent the last of their cash on three more tickets. There was no way of knowing if they were real until they were used.

In his memoir, *…aber ein stolzer Bettler,* Friedrich writes: "When the train passed in the twilight before the Swiss border, I said to myself: 'So, and now I am a beggar. But in the dark, an unknown voice spoke: 'But a proud beggar.' At two o'clock in the afternoon I was in Zurich. All I had was six and a half Swiss Francs in my pocket. And the world was open to me."

For the rest of his life Friedrich told anyone who asked that he left Nazi-occupied Austria first, before his wife, daughter, and mother, because *he* was the most in danger, being both male and Jewish born.

After knowing my grandfather for only a brief time, and after reading his memoir and his other writings, I am convinced now that when he left Vienna, Friedrich Engel de Jánosi did not think about *who* he left behind so much as *what* he left behind. He described the house, the gardens, the manuscripts and his beloved primary documents in the university archives, all which he said he would sorely miss. He states clearly that he was the last Engel de Jánosi, when in fact he *knew* he was not. He left behind his mother, wife, and daughter, all of them Engel de Jánosis. And then there were the Hungarian Engel de Jánosis, his aunts, uncles, cousins still alive in Pécs and in other towns and villages in Hungary. He knew this. They were not dead, not yet anyway, but in his mind, they were.

Already, the historian was rewriting history.

My mother did not say goodbyes, even to her best friend because she left secretly. "Trust no one," her mother told her.

She only said goodbye to her grandmother, Marie, who promised to see her again.

My mother and Carlette left the *Hofzeile* by taxi on a cold spring night in late April 1939. My mother wore a dark blue coat several sizes too big. Her mother bought the coat big so that she could grow into it. My mother had the red measles, which had spread into her eyes. She said that even though she did not cry, there were still tears. Her mother wore good Italian shoes, a fox fur scarf and a hat with a black net covering her face. She told my mother not to look back, to never look back. My mother did as she was told.

When the train reached the first border crossing, the guards demanded to see their papers.

"*Sehr ansteckend!*" Very contagious!

Carlette insisted on keeping their cabin doors shut. She knew the Germans' fear of germs. The guards hesitated but they kept their distance. They asked that Carlette slide the papers under the door, which she did. They kept their gloves on, held the documents at the corners, quickly stamping them without checking for the word *Engel* or *Jude*.

Ancient tunnels supposedly dug during Roman times, ran beneath the *Hofzeile*, the gardens, and the street. Rumor had it that Marie Theresa used these tunnels to secret her Hungarian lovers to her house chambers. The Engel de Jánosi family used the tunnels to store wine and champagne. When the Nazis banged on the front door of the *Hofzeile*, and the housekeeper Agnes, let them in, my great-grandmother Marie used a hidden set of stairs leading to the tunnels to cross the streets underground to get to her sister's house in Grinzing.

Left alone in the house, Agnes the housekeeper had her pick of the family furniture, paintings, clothes, china, silver, and rugs. The Nazis looted the rest.

Marie stayed with her sister, Emma, who contacted Marie's friend and neighbor, the Austrian baron Ludwig Nathaniel von Rothschild, whose own Palais Rothschild down the street was being confiscated, plundered, or "Aryanised" by the Nazis. Even as Baron Rothschild was going through his own private and financial turmoil, he made arrangements for Marie. He contacted an orphanage he owned. The orphanage was used to the Baron's requests.

One early morning, before first light, an orphan girl led a horse and a hay wagon to Emma's house. The orphan girl delivered whatever produce she had buried under the hay, then instructed Marie to hide under the hay in her wagon. Marie and the orphan girl made their way out of occupied Vienna and into occupied Czechoslovakia.

Why bother searching for Jews in a territory they already occupied? That was Baron Rothschild's thinking.

Years later, Marie told me how the wagon's wood dug into her back, and how bumpy the ride had been. The orphan girl delivered Marie to a farmer and his wife who lived in the mountains. Baron Rothschild sent money to the farmer to keep Marie fed. My great-grandmother Marie stayed hidden there for five years.

Once, when she was out walking in the woods alone in the surrounding mountains, an SS officer passed and asked to see her papers. Marie told the officer she didn't have her papers. She was only out for a brief walk.

He looked at her for a long time.

"You have the bluest eyes I have ever seen," he said. "You cannot possibly be a Jewess."

When my great-grandmother, Marie, first told me this story, I fell in love with the way she said *Jewess*. Her blue eyes lit up. When my mother tells this same story, she whispers the punch line, as though *Jewess* was *cancer*.

After the war, Marie walked hundreds of miles to a Red Cross tent where she wrote to her son, Friedrich, who was by that time in Washington, D.C. teaching at Catholic University. Marie was seventy-five years old. With the help of the Red Cross, she travelled to Washington, and stayed with Friedrich, Carlette, and my mother.

My mother recalls those years of Marie pacing nervously in her rooms, her hard-heeled shoes clicking on the bare floors. One Christmas, when my mother and her parents returned from midnight mass, they saw their Christmas tree on the curb outside along with all their gifts.

Marie moved herself out of Friedrich's house and into the Lizner Home, a home for the elderly. She said she didn't want to be a burden. She preferred her independence. She might have moved there because she could no longer stand living with her converted son, Friedrich. The one who left her behind.

Growing up, I was one of the few to have a great-grandmother. She wrote me letters on the backs of paper placemats she saved after meals. She mailed scraps of fabric so I could make clothes for my Barbies and trolls. When we visited, she drank orange juice from tiny glasses and smiled with her whole face. She told me she talked to the birds, and every single day she walked. For her health, she said. She especially liked to walk near the river. She missed swimming in the sea.

She walked to the museums and she crossed the busy intersection of Wisconsin and Western Avenues in D.C. At the supermarket, she pushed her grocery cart with a list from her "younger" seventy and eighty-year old friends, who asked her to buy them fruit or little "tid-bits."

I sat next to my great-grandmother Marie in Washington, D.C. one April when she opened a happy birthday letter from Richard Nixon, congratulating her on turning 100. She puffed out her lips and said she wished the letter was from a President she liked. She told a nearby *Washington Star* reporter that her time hiding in Czechoslovakia had been excellent for her health because the mountain air was so good. She made no mention of any hardship or the fact that the farmer and his wife didn't like her, had, in fact, resented her presence and putting them in danger. Nor did my great-grandmother mention the fact that when she walked to find a Red Cross unit, she suffered frostbite and lost two toes. My great-grandmother made her hiding in Czechoslovakia during World War II sound like a vacation.

Before she died, she said that she had already taken up too much space and time. She asked to be cremated, her ashes sent back to Vienna. Her last words were, "I am going home." Hers was the first death I witnessed and it is one that stays with me.

In Döbling, Vienna, Marie's remains are with her husband Moritz's, and his parents' Adolf and Anna. They are all one burial plot away from Marie's friend, Theodor Herzl, the Austro-Hungarian writer and father of modern Zionism, which is the foundation of Israel, where I first learned of Richárd.

The Nazis never discovered the underground tunnels. Carlette used the last of their money to pay to ship their art, rugs, books and furniture to the United States, but the Germans claim the shipment could not be found. Neither my mother nor her parents ever received compensation. During the war, the *Hofzeile* was bombed and completely destroyed.

My mother spent part of the war in southern France, living with relatives from her mother's side of the family, relatives who were willing to hide all three of them.

Friedrich accepted a teaching post at King's College in Cambridge, England. But they couldn't all go. There was not enough room or money. At a train station in London, they split up.

Her parents took a train to Cambridge; my mother boarded a train alone, south to a place called Test Bourne. A family there agreed to take her in. She was twelve years old. She did not speak English and she was alone for the first time in her life. Her father gave her an English dictionary, which she began reading on the train to teach herself English.

This part of my mother's story astounds me. Her father left her a second time. Because of this, I tend to forgive her neediness, and her inability to say goodbye.

Half a year later, my mother finally boarded a train north to Cambridge to live with her parents. She recalls this as a happy time because they were together. Her mother was trying to learn how to cook. They ate a lot of baked apples.

Sigmund Freud was living in London by then, but Friedrich was not inclined to visit his old friend. Maybe he was embarrassed. In his final months, Freud wrote, "Banal but terrifying things happen in our lives. But then we forget them. Somehow though, they don't forget us. Memories lie buried, yet remain forceful enough to shape our lives. The act of forgetting is as strange and interesting as the power of remembering."

When the Johns Hopkins history department offered Friedrich a job, the three of them were able to obtain visas, and, together they traveled to New York and then on to Washington, D.C. Carlette got three part-time teaching jobs and enrolled my mother in Sacred Heart, one of the schools where Carlette taught.

None of them knew how to cook. Again, they ate baked apples, Campbell's tomato soup, and canned pumpkin, which they had never tasted. My mother read cookbooks.

In his *Remarks on the Austrian Resistance, 1938-1945* (Journal of Central European Affairs, July 1953), Friedrich Engel de Jánosi uses the word "Jew" once, and he writes mostly in the passive voice, as though he is some distant third-person, and not a member of a highly regarded, aristocratic Jewish family facing annihilation.

"The Austrian resistance movement has been criticized for having gone into full action only in the last stage of WWII when the outcome was already in clear sight. Such a charge may be countered by the statement that to some extent a similar attitude held true of many resistance groups, that geographically the situation of the Austrian fighters was a difficult one lacking . . . a frontier bordering on allied territory. Furthermore, immediately after the Anschluss the first wave of arrests brought to concentration camp and jails 76,000 people from Vienna alone; the well-prepared Gestapo took care to get hold in this way of all potential leaders of an opposition movement in addition to Jews and Communists."

Reading this passage, one would think this particular scholar, like many Hungarians, admired Hitler and the Nazis for their efficiency.

Maybe Friedrich was willing to forgive Hitler his hatred for the Jews because of Hitler's hostility to communism and socialism. Maybe he found Hitler palatable at the time because Hitler had, after all, crushed the German labor movement, and for that he and other property-owning industrialists were willing to forgive him anything. Maybe this attitude was what was behind Friedrich's comment when he said to my cousin Peter, "Hitler is good for business."

Surely Friedrich struggled to understand what was happening to him and to his family when he wrote, "It is when the powers come into conflict, when their task becomes manifestly 'to hold their own,' that the historic moment arrives. From the clash of opposing forces, new developments arise; to a large extent 'historical development . . . springs . . . from the political antagonism of nations.'"

Maybe Friedrich would have agreed with William Butler Yeats, who reasoned that only new life emerges out of violence. But then Friedrich wrote, "The individual is first of all the active man: In history man is simply what he does." *Man is simply what he does.* Friedrich wrote this after he left first, left his mother, his wife, and his daughter behind, never sure what would happen to them or if they would all be together again, or alive.

I visited the University of Vienna, a long time ago, right after college. I listened to one of my grandfather's former students explaining to one of his own students who Friedrich was. "He was Jewish," this man said in German. "He was a Bourgeois Jew. '*Engel*.'" This man's *Engel* was meant to explain it all. *Engel*, which of course means *angel*, but to most Europeans still means Jew. Never mind the books, the lectures, the mentoring, or the day-to-day teaching. Never mind that this particular former student was now a professor himself, sitting in what was once my grandfather's office. This 21st-century man, a former student who claimed he loved my grandfather, still identified Friedrich Engel de Jánosi with one word: *Juden*.

Richárd Engel de Jánosi
1882-1944

Part IV

Hungary 2010

November
Bring the Dead Back to Life

L ike the petals on Ezra Pound's wet black bough in his "Station at the Metro," Anna's smiling face is an apparition in this crowd at a coffee shop off Széchenyi Square. Both Peter and Anna are here for the Plaque ceremony. Besides my cousin Peter, Anna is the last living relative who can tell me about Richárd.

Even though I don't know what she looks like, I recognize her in her nubby bouclé pink jacket the color of Japanese cherry blossoms. In her seventies, she wears a long brown leather skirt and practical walking shoes. She has short blond-grey hair and vibrant blue eyes. We kiss three times. She carries a rabbit fur coat, which she carefully folds outside-in, protecting the fur. The lining is patched and hand stitched together, mended over and over. Her briefcase is a plastic zip lock bag. I can see business cards, papers, and notes.

When we sit down, we order coffee and Anna asks about my mother and my mother's father, Friedrich. She wants to get my relationship with her straight. For a moment, I worry that Anna thinks I'm lying. I tell her everything I can about the family tree that joins us.

Anna says Friedrich knew her mother, Rózsika, well and that he visited her in New York while she was a librarian at Columbia University.

"It's *fantastique* that I do not know your mother and she does not know me. *Fantastique.* After the war, we didn't have to hide anymore. But for some, when they came out of hiding, they remained in hiding." She shakes her head.

"My mother was never in hiding," I say. "She was Madeleine Engel de Jánosi right up until the day she married."

Anna reminds me that our cousin Peter cut the *Engel* off his name. "Why does he do this?" she asks. "Is he ashamed?" I tell Anna what Peter told me, that he leaves off the *Engel* from his *de Jánosi* because it was burdensome and complicated to write out and spell for people, especially Americans. Anna blows air through her lips, *puff,* and tells me her brother, Gábor, changed his last name, too, when he moved to America. He went from Stein, which is German for stone, to Szikla, which is Hungarian for rock. She explains that it's very Austro-Hungarian to do such things, very much an Engel de Jánosi trait to hide family origins.

I assure Anna that my mother simply did not know the Hungarian side still existed because her father never discussed them. For twenty-nine years she was an Engel de Jánosi living in Washington D.C. But Anna is right: it is *fantastique* that no one, not even Peter, told Anna about my mother or me, and that no one told us about Anna. And it is *fantastique* that no one found my mother.

"Your mother's generation was very angry," Anna says, angry.

Outside, a band warms up in the distance. It's afternoon and church bells ring.

"But *why* do you want to know about Richárd?" Anna asks. "He is not an important one. He was a quiet man."

He is not an important one.

I tell Anna about Yad Vashem. I don't use the word *mission*, but I tell her my mission. She considers what I have said.

"Have you seen it yet? Have you gone? It's horrifying. It's like a rape." She says she cannot talk about her former home, *Jánosipuszta.* "Over and over, the place was raped by pillaging wanderers. They took everything we had. Everything. And it was meant for *me.*"

Peter warned me about Anna. He said that she could be "difficult" and that she thinks she is the only rightful heir to anything that belonged to the Hungarian Engel de Jánosi family. But isn't she?

When she was growing up in Pécs, Anna says she liked to go downtown to watch her grandfather, Róbert, work at the family lumber factory, Adolf Engel & Sons. Sometimes Anna's Uncle Richárd would be there too. Anna loved the smell of the freshly cut logs brought in by train from Croatia and Moravia. Workers unloaded the timber—mostly oak—in the back of the factory, where the trains stopped. Then they cut and sawed the timber into rough planks. Anna especially liked to jump on the boards before they got loaded back on the train headed to Vienna.

Outside the café, zither music mixes with the low hum of the coffee crowd and the clicking heels of our waitress. We order more coffee and apple strudel.

"So," Anna says. "What shall we call each other?"

We decide on "cousin."

I compliment Anna on her English. Anna's primary languages are French and Hungarian. Peter told me that Anna's English is not very good, but I understand her.

"I remember him. Richárd. He was a very rigid person. His mother died of pneumonia when he was six years old. His father József never remarried." She doesn't say much more. I've noticed this characteristic among many of her generation who have gone through what she has. Who can blame her? I would probably be the same way. You lose everything, but what you have is information and memories; those are still yours and in your control. Why give what you have away to a so-called "cousin" from America?

"Richárd never married?" I ask after a long pause.

Anna shakes her head and tells me what I already know, that Richárd fell in love with a girl he wanted to marry, but she was a Christian and his father József forbade the marriage. On Richárd's Page of Testimony is the line: *First name of victim's spouse*: Never married, I will write.

Later, Anna will say *fantastique* once again, when I email her that Richard did in fact have a lover, Theresia, whom he kept secret and with whom he "lived" for over fourteen years.

"He was a very good engineer," Anna says. "But he was very unhappy." When Richárd returned home, Pécs was a sad, dark little country town. He settled in to live and take care of his father, whose health was failing.

When he comes to me here, in Pécs, he's serious, the furrows between his eyes deepening. In dreams he never smiles.

Anna tells me about her own difficult relationship with her mother, who never approved of Anna's first marriage or her second. "She didn't want I should be artist. She didn't want at all." Anna says her mother thought like Adolf—they didn't think women should read novels or be too devoted to anything but the family. A woman must always and only be a wife and mother.

"My mother told to everybody that I'm not a good mother, that I'm not a good woman so she was not happy with me. Not at all. And I was always running after her to make it better and better. You know? I was always running and running after her. I loved her so much. She loved me also but there was always something wrong with me. And you know in this family the woman was nothing."

Anna says the Engel de Jánosi's were "very highly cultivated people who lived like the Arabic people, closing the woman in the house, not to read, not to have jobs, not to go out."

As Anna looks through the papers from her plastic bag, she bites her nails.

She shows me a picture she drew of her father, a clock inside his head. She shows me a book of her gold sculptures, all with the face and hair of her mother. One female bust with her mother's faces in the back and front is called *Janus*.

Then she gives me a photograph of Richárd, the copy of which I saw in Komló. In this headshot, Richárd has the stiff bearing of a former officer, impeccably dressed in his suit and tie. She says I can keep the picture, and she has it marked on the back, *1938 Richárd.* She thinks it was taken in Dubrovnik, Croatia on holiday.

"This is the way I remember him," Anna says, sitting up straight in her chair. "Aristocratic, tall." She tells me Richárd kept to himself. He was not someone who "bloomed in the presence of others." He was not a social butterfly.

Anna gives me copies of other photographs—a group picture from her parents' wedding party—thirty-one people, all of whom Anna has named and identified, the dates of their deaths scribbled in black beneath their names. Most of them died at either Mauthausen, Bergen-Belson, or the Arrow Cross shot them into the Danube in Budapest during the 1944 siege. She shares more pictures and information, talking quickly and energetically, at once angry and excited to tell their stories. She has a beautiful ferocity. She looks at the pictures and says that there are so many people she would like to thank. She says she would like to make a list of all the people who helped save her family's lives.

When the strong lattes with whipped cream and strudel come, we put away the pictures and papers and Anna tells her story about how she became an artist.

After his divorce from Marianne, Róbert remarried Erna Erdősi-Baiersdorf and they never had children of their own. But Erna took to her step-granddaughter, Anna Stein, and taught her about painting and sculpting figures and about pre-history at a time when it was not fashionable for women to have extensive knowledge of such things. Her step grandmother, Erna was Anna's first art teacher.

In 1940, under Hungarian law, everyone had to register with the government. The Lists were starting. The registration information on file included not only current religious affiliation, but lineage so that they could immediately identify and locate Jews.

"They wanted to preserve us. To save us," Anna says. The day they converted to Catholicism, Anna says she was quite happy. She was six years old and she liked the nun's black habits. She says no one talked before, during, or after the ceremonies. "It was not a celebration."

Richárd never converted. He stopped speaking to his brother, Róbert, altogether. Richárd would never forgive his brother his conversion.

Róbert and Erna were obviously thinking about their family's future. Did the rest of the family consider meeting to discuss the future for all of them? Did they consider making plans? They were together then, why not stay together, or perhaps organize a planned separation and then come back together in some designated meeting place? They were so clever in everything—business, engineering, writing, music—why couldn't they be clever then? But this is not the right way to think. They are not to blame. They were the victims.

On August 8, 1941, another law passed through Hungarian parliament. In order to "defend the race," parliament prohibited marriage and sexual relations between Jews and non-Jews. *Jewish* was now defined in strictly racial terms.

On September 6, 1942, a fourth anti-Jewish law passed in the Hungarian parliament, banning Jews from owning and purchasing land. After this law passed, Anna says Róbert contracted TB and his health deteriorated. He died on July 30, 1943, one day before Richárd's 61st birthday. Anna says Róbert died of a broken heart.

Even though the Catholic diocese of Pécs forbids anyone born Jewish to be buried inside, Róbert is buried here, apart from the other Engels in the Jewish Cemetery in Pécs. Before he died, Róbert paid for two spaces in the crypt at the Catholic Church, also known as the Mosque of Gazi Kasim in Pécs.

Róbert's widow, Erna, continued to live in the Wedgewood blue house at 54 Rákóczi ut. He put the house in her name. Erna wanted to take on her husband's former role as director of Adolf Engel & Sons and to continue the business, but the company was not in Róbert's name. It was in the family's name, Adolf Engel & Sons, and, therefore, belonged to the next in line, or, to the co-family owner, Richárd. In October 1943 Erna Erdősi-Baiersdorf appealed, but in December she withdrew her appeal.

Richárd ran Adolf Engel and Sons.

By the spring of 1944 in Hungary, all Jewish men and women were ordered to report to the authorities. At one point, Richárd and each of my relatives held a notice, ordering them to report.

As the war came to Hungary, the Engel de Jánosi family grew further and further apart. No matter how close they lived to one another, they thought it was safer to stay apart. They barely communicated.

Every person they passed could either save them or doom them; arrest them or hide them. If Jews had not gotten out of the country by then, more and more disappeared on their way to school or work, on their way to soccer practice, or perhaps even while they were looking for mushrooms in the woods around the Mecsek Mountains. Family members who managed to survive were learning a trait they would teach generations of children: trust no one, assimilate, blend, fit in, and learn to keep secrets. Already they were turning into ghosts.

Anna says that a relative named George Justus left Pécs and went to Switzerland right after the war ended, around 1947. Just as Friedrich had, George claimed to be the last Engel de Jánosi alive in the family. George knew that family members had been depositing their savings in a bank in Switzerland. George also knew the bank number there and he withdrew all the money apparently taking what was meant for Anna's side of the family. This loss was made worse because George Justus, who owned a sunflower oil factory in Pécs, was a cousin. "I remember him," Anna says. "He was a fat man."

When I ask Anna if she considers herself Catholic, she says, "I'm not religious. That's not my job. But I do not hide from who or what I am." She says she's not a Zionist either. "I'm not nothing. *Rien.* This is my origin. So I'm not proud, I'm not ashamed. Even my son is not very interested in all these family things, but he knows what happened. We have always been Christian. For some Engels, once they became Christian, they want to forget all the rest. Then they have neurotic problems. They change their names, their religion, or both. They don't face these things."

By 1944, Anna and her family were on the move again. They couldn't afford to leave the country. They stayed together, traveling to the worst place for a Hungarian Jewish family to go in 1944: Budapest.

"In Budapest, during the siege, we were starving. We were, how do you say not to eat? We had nothing to eat. Nothing. Before the war, when I was a young girl I was anorexic. After the war, I forgot everything about anorexia. If you want to heal someone from anorexia, put her through war, and don't let her eat for days and days." Anna finishes her strudel.

She compares Hungarian Strudel with Viennese. I say I prefer Hungarian because there's more to it. After the apples and the honey, comes the sprinkling of poppyseeds, sultanas, chopped walnuts, and finally, the dusting of fine white powdered sugar. You don't get all that in Vienna, but it *will* be served on fine china with real silver and linen napkins. For this one moment, we both smile.

Anna puts her hand to her cheek as she chews. She says her teeth hurt and she needs to call her dentist in Paris. Because she went without food or proper nutrition for so long at a young age, Anna has a lot of problems with her teeth.

In April 1945, Anna and her family returned to Pécs. The trains were bad. It took three days just to get from Budapest to Pécs. People were starving in Budapest, but people in Pécs did not go hungry. Here, there was always produce, some smoked meat, and cabbage pickling in oak barrels.

"What happened to Erna? Róbert's wife?"

Anna finishes her coffee. Erna was arrested the summer of 1944. They transported her to Auschwitz. Later I make inquiries, and, according to the archives at Auschwitz, Erna was admitted July 7, 1944 and marked prisoner number 25086. On that day, she was not sent to the crematorium along with so many other Hungarians. On July 31, 1944, she was transferred from Auschwitz with a group of female prisoners.

Why Erna and these female prisoners were transferred is not known. During the evacuation and liquidation of KL Auschwitz, the German camp authorities destroyed almost all of the important documents, including prisoners' personal files. Erna and the other female prisoners were transferred five miles outside the picturesque town of Weimar, Germany, to Buchenwald concentration camp.

"And that's where she died?" The windows in the café are steamy.

Anna shakes her head. "She survived."

"Erna survived both Auschwitz and Buchenwald? How?"

"Art." Anna smiles. "She drew portraits of Nazi guards and made them look handsome." Word got around and other guards ordered Erna to sketch them. "She knew to portray them handsomely, even perhaps, heroically. And so, when she came back to Pécs, she had a full head of red hair," Anna says. Hardly anyone returning from the camps had hair.

I research Erna's story further. She was among those who General Patton's Third Army liberated. In 1945, when she was well and strong enough, Erna traveled back to the only home she knew—the Wedgewood blue house at 54 Rákóczi út in Pécs, Hungary, where everything inside was still there, unbroken and untouched.

Erna stayed in Pécs, living in the house on Rákóczi út with Marcel Stein, his wife Rózsika and their children Gábor and Anna. Erna asked the Steins to pay rent. Anna recalls a great deal of tension in the house. Pécs was occupied by the Russians then. Legally, Erna owned the house and Rózsika inherited the family lumber company, Adolf

Engel and Sons, but under Russian rule, they all knew their situation was precarious.

Erna requested permission to trade with firewood and building materials in order to operate the steam bath next door. She claimed that her late husband, Róbert, had the necessary permissions to all this, but "because of my deportation I was not in the situation to get the right papers after his death." She received permission to operate the steam bath, but her request to trade was denied.

For ten months, Erna ran the steam bath. During this time, she signed a document donating the house on Rákóczi út in Pécs to the Hungarian state so that it could be a natural history museum. Once her papers were in order, she left. She had saved enough money to move to Vancouver, Canada.

Through the years, the state took care of the house, first as a museum and then later for housing state bureacrats. Today it's an office for tax collectors. As a result, the house on Rákóczi út in Pécs is the best preserved of all of Adolf's properties.

Erna lived in Vancouver and wrote "The Method of Reconstructing Human and Animal Remains in Sculpture and in Paintings" for *Museum and Art Notes*, published by The Art, Historical and Scientific Association of Vancouver, Canada. Freed from Buchenwald concentration camp just four years before, she wrote, "To the reconstructionist, the work of resuscitating a world which has completely disappeared in the infinity of centuries or millennia is so beautiful a task not only from a scientific standpoint, but also from one of artistry, that it awakens the artist's fullest enthusiasm. For him there can be no aim more glorious than to conjure up a true picture of that life which roamed the face of the earth millions of years ago!"

After surviving Auschwitz and Buchenwald, Erna's work gave her joy and a reason to live. She writes: ". . . no reconstructionist may approach perfection until he has mastered all available knowledge relating to the animals . . . to their mode of living; to the era in which they lived and the general conditions which prevailed in that era . . . We must be careful too, that we do not represent a reptile with the eyes of a bird."

In Canada, she grew flowers, researched, and reconstructed skulls of native Indians. She spent her remaining years bringing the dead back to life. She was eighty-two when she died in 1971. Erna's name does not appear in the Book of Tears at the Pécs synagogue because she survived.

In the café, Anna looks exhausted. She wants to show me where she is staying in Pécs. She is proud of the deal she has gotten. Because she is a returning Pécs citizen, she stays at a hostel for free.

When Anna and her family left Pécs in 1948, the Soviets nationalized the family factory and claimed all the houses and property. They also required the Steins to pay compensation to 150 workers, which essentially, ruined the family financially.

Church bells are ringing. I ask Anna what sort of music she likes.

"Wagner," she says, wrapping a blue scarf around her neck. "I *love* anything by Wagner." She buttons up her fur coat, and together we walk towards her hotel.

"If I had stayed in Pécs, I would not be alive," she says. "Can you imagine? I was nine and my brother seven when we came back. We were the only Jewish children here."

As we pass the Mosque of Gazi Kasim, or Catholic Church on Széchenyi Square, Anna says she plans to visit the church where her grandfather, Róbert and her mother, Rózika are buried side by side. She will light a candle there and place a red rose on her mother's grave, for her 100th birthday, which is the following day, the day of the plaque ceremony. Rózsika means little rose.

We pass the big hotel in the center of town, where Peter is staying. Anna thinks that Peter should have included her more in the planning. Peter thinks that because he paid for the plaque, the planning is nobody else's business. These two cousins are among the last of the Engel de Jánosi's here to celebrate their great-great-grandfather and they are barely on speaking terms.

Anna urges me not to walk everywhere. "Your feet will get tired. You will get tired and you will lose time." She is a survivor, this woman. And she wants me to be one too.

The hostel is clean and well lit. Anna shows me where she will have breakfast with others in the morning and where she will read the paper near an open window. She shows me her tidy room, the stiffly made bed, and, as she brushes her shoes on the mat near the door, I notice the Turkish slippers with the pointed, curled-up toes. She says her husband, who is a Muslim from Algeria, gave these to her.

We kiss three times on the cheek and we hold each other for a long beat. "I struggled so with Adolf." Her breath smells of coffee and apples. Her eyes are so blue. "That is why there is something parallel between you and me. I make paintings and it is like a way to dreams. People are there with me like they are with you. I can see this. Richárd is with you. And we are in the same family. We have these same tendencies. But I never heard about you. Peter never spoke about you."

We both feel the closeness now, but I wonder briefly if Anna and I will ever really meet this way again.

On my way back to our apartment, I pass a girl singing in the square. An old man stands in front of her, and he is crying. He pulls forints from his pocket and puts these into the girl's zither box, then stands in front of her, and, still crying, he sings with her. I want to cry and sing too. I think of all the loss—the homes, the people, my relatives, all the connections never made. But then there is Erna with her red hair. She survived. And I know more about Richárd, and now I know Anna.

The old man cries and taps his cane, which is looped with two wreaths of sweet bread. The zither girl smiles and they continue to sing.

Feeling the Cold Badly

The following morning, before the plaque ceremony, Peter brings down a banana from the fruit basket I left with him in his hotel on Király utca. Peter says his doctor told him he needs more potassium.

"And more goose fat, if you can believe," he says, peeling the banana. We take a seat at the bistro table in front of the hotel where he and his wife, Monica, are staying. Peter waves down a waiter for coffees. "My doctor wants to know why my cholesterol levels are so good and I tell him I grew up in Hungary on goose fat. So he tells me to eat more goose fat."

Peter has thinning grey hair and wears a well-tailored grey suit with a red knit tie. He is eighty-two years old, and with his grey bushy eyebrows, he looks like my grandfather, Friedrich. He tells me he has been thinking of what to tell me because it is so difficult for him to recall. He says he and his sister both have "black-outs" of those years in hiding. But he remembers the day they took Richárd.

It was a chilly, sunny Sunday in Pécs. Sixteen-year-old Peter was in his apartment listening to his favorite aria "In Fernem Land" from Act III of Richard Wagner's "Lohengrin." Peter loved anything by Wagner.

He was finishing his final year at the Catholic gymnasium in Pécs. He had his own room with a washstand, basin, water pitcher, a hand-cranked record player and a few records of opera arias. He lived across the street from the villa where his family used to live. Peter's parents and his sister were in Budapest for the spring. Peter had just received the highest mark in his class for a favorable essay he wrote about Hitler. "It's a pity Peter's not a real German," Peter's teacher told Peter's father.

There was a knock on his door and Peter lifted the needle of his record player. Peter's father was there to check on Peter. They planned to meet with Richárd that day to go over family business. His father,

Paul was staying with Richárd a few blocks away. Together Peter and his father started down the stairs.

Just outside Peter's apartment house on Hunyadi út, five or six SS officers with the lightening-bolt symbols on their collars rode on army motorcycles around Széchenyi Square. Peter noticed they were riding their motorcycles on the right hand side of the road. Hungarians drove on the left side of the road.

"They confiscated the old-aged home in town and made it Gestapo headquarters," Peter's landlady said when they saw her outside on the sidewalk.

They watched the Germans riding their motorcycles. Pécs was their city now. They could ride the way they rode in Germany. The air smelled different somehow.

This was March 19, 1944.

It was a short walk from Széchenyi Square to Uncle Richárd's house. Neither Peter nor his father wore yellow stars. Peter says he doesn't recall ever wearing a yellow star.

During those past two years, Peter had come to know his uncle. Richárd talked to Peter as an adult. His uncle was slightly eccentric and perhaps lonely as a bachelor, but Peter thought Richárd was a nice man.

"He was probably gay," Peter says, sipping coffee. Peter never knew about Theresia.

Later, I find out that, at about this time, Theresia was begging Richárd to flee Hungary with her. They could go to the United States or England, she said. But he would not. He stayed.

Richárd was in charge of the family business at that time, even though there were tensions. Erna wanted to run the business, but everyone knew that wasn't going to happen.

Richárd did not hire a *stróman*, a straw-man or front person, as many other wealthy Jewish business owners did. He didn't convert to Catholicism or change his name either. He remained Engel de Jánosi, Richárd. Some would say this was honorable; others would say foolish. Most Jews at this time knew that lies kept you alive. Real names and papers got you killed.

The Jews of Pécs had already been marked and excluded months before. They were no longer allowed to shop in certain places at certain times. They were not entirely free to walk around, attend religious services or schools. They had to carry their papers with them. Ultimately, the Christians of Pécs had a choice. They could cooperate with the German Nazis and the Hungarian Arrow Cross, or they could resist. They could be rescuers, bystanders, or perpetrators. The Jews of Pécs had no choices. They could only be victims.

That spring day Peter and his father walked past the German soldiers on their motorbikes and past the synagogue Peter's great-grandfather Adolf had built. They crossed the street. Uncle Richárd lived next door to Adolf Engel & Sons, which was still the family lumber business. But on this spring day, lunch would be held at Erna's house, the Wedgewood blue house at 54 Rákóczi út. Uncle Richárd would be there, waiting for them. Surely there would be a lot of talk about lumber, parquet floors, the steam bath, and the future of the family business. Peter was not sure if he would see Erna, but no matter. He was anticipating lunch and that thick-cut dark bread smeared with goose fat, sprinkled with red onions and paprika.

As Peter and his father walked, they talked, going over their schedule to meet up with the rest of the family later that day. Peter's father put his hand on his son's shoulder to stop him.

A black car with swastikas on the doors pulled up in front of Uncle Richárd's house. "Turn around," Peter's father whispered to Peter in Hungarian. They turned, and headed back up the street towards Peter's apartment.

"Don't look back," Peter's father said.

Peter looked back. Three men in black uniforms with red swastikas on their armbands had his Uncle Richárd by the arm. Peter could hear the click of their boot heels on the cobblestone street as the men in black uniforms led Richárd into the back seat of the black car marked with swastikas. They shut the doors and then they drove away. This happened at approximately 1:00 in the afternoon.

Peter says he can still see those men taking his uncle now, as though it happened yesterday.

"*Turn around.* That's what my father said. *Don't look back.*" Peter allows his coffee cup to slide back into place on his saucer. The banana peel beside his plate blackens.

It happened sixty-six years ago. It doesn't matter that it happened before I was born. I am hearing what happened now, and I am witnessing the past in the present. It is wonderful and terrible to get these few facts; but the facts don't matter, because neither of us can save him.

Had Richárd ever considered hiding? Where do you hide in a small town? Who could he trust? He was an engineer. He must have known about the caves and tunnels below Pécs, unused since the Christians hid there during the Turkish occupation. If he had known that my great-grandmother, Marie, had escaped her home in Vienna using underground tunnels, could he have done the same to save himself? The year Richárd was arrested in 1944, the Catholic Church quietly commandeered these caves, not to help hide the Jewish families of Pécs, but to keep the Germans from taking their good wines and champagnes. The Catholic Church. Ever careful to save and protect *their* valuables.

Did Richárd know that it was too late the very moment they took him? Did he see Peter and his father walk away? Did he think there was a chance he could survive? He was clever. He was strong. He had experience in the military. He knew German. There was always a chance.

In March 1944, days after German troops occupied Pécs, and after they had taken Richárd, the mayor of Pécs signed an agreement with the Nazis and the Nazi-Hungarians, the Arrow Cross, to arrest all the Jews of Pécs. In his 1940 movie "The Great Dictator," Charlie Chaplin dubs the insane rulers the "Double Cross" party—a takedown of both the SS and the Arrow Cross.

Archived accounts at Yad Vashem tell the stories about what happened during those roundups all over Hungary. Neighbors turned against neighbors. Some were told they were being taken to a Ghetto, though most had no idea what that word meant. There is no Hungarian word for ghetto. Some were told they were being taken to Germany or Austria to work. They were allowed to carry 25 kilos.

Some carefully packed their belongings in suitcases. Some drained their Tokay wine. Some sewed diamonds in the hems of their skirts. Some had their children swallow family jewels wrapped in bread.

Why did Richárd get taken that day, before the roundups and before arrests were made "official" by the mayor of Pécs? Peter says Richárd was specifically arrested that day because he was outspoken in his politics and he was a prominent member of the Jewish community. He was also a wealthy landowner, who owned a profitable family business. He was the perfect Nazi catch and he was to be an example. He was taken together with a few others from Pécs, including Christians who openly opposed Nazis.

Peter waves down a waiter for more coffee.

He says that if he and his father had not stopped that day, turned around and left, they too would have been deported to a concentration camp. Peter's father left Richárd's house a mere fifteen minutes before the Nazis and Arrow Cross arrived. That evening, Peter and his father went to the train station. The Laktis barracks, where Richárd was held with other prisoners was right across the street from the train station in Pécs.

"I remember seeing the empty cattle cars there," Peter says. "But it was best not to ask questions." He stops talking as the waiter pours more coffee.

Why were they sending Jews to Poland? someone might have asked. A local guard might very well have let slip something about a 'final solution.'

Peter and his father boarded a train and left Pécs for Budapest without incident.

When the United States entered the war in 1941, the German government decided on a total solution, a final solution to the "Jewish question." Adolf Eichmann was chief of the SS appointed to "liquidate European Jewry." He was about forty years old, medium height, small face, thin lips. People said he looked like an office clerk and that the way he rapped out words sounded like the clatter of a machine gun. He had been in charge of the "actions" in Germany, Poland and Czechoslovakia. By 1944, Eichmann was in charge of ridding the newly occupied Hungary of all remaining Jews.

By then most of Europe knew it was a matter of time, but at this point, for Hitler and for the Nazis, it was more important to kill the Jews than to win the war. The largest remaining Jewish population in 1944 Europe was in Hungary. Both the Nazi-Germans and the Hungarian Arrow Cross dedicated those last months and days of the war not to win, but to murder.

It is well documented and overwhelmingly clear that by 1944 the world knew of the Holocaust and what exactly was happening in the concentration camps. But up until then, few of the Hungarian Engel de Jánosi family members hid, and very few left the country. Why? The question dogs me. When is it time to pull up stakes and get the hell out? What was it that my family believed or trusted in? Were they each looking for that one good Hungarian, that one good Nazi who would hide or save them?

Did they really think that humanity would never allow such evil to take place? Did they feel themselves to be special, different from all the others around them disappearing? Was that their thinking? That being an Engel, an angel, could save them?

According to Judit Molnár's article, "The Foundation and Activities of the Hungarian Jewish Council, March 20—July 7, 1944," as late as the spring of 1944 many Jews still did not believe the young people who risked their lives just to travel to the provinces, to warn Jewish people about what was happening.

"Leave," they said over and over, trying to get those doomed to deportation and elimination to escape or resettle in Israel. Too many Hungarian Jews were in a state of denial that they could not reckon with the power of another's evil imagination. It was simply too *fantastique*.

No wonder survivors and their offspring are paranoid now, after the fact. Fooled once, but never again. We will forever be on the lookout for signs or hints of trouble and hate. And now, all around, swastikas are popping up again.

By the time of the 1944 German occupation of Hungary, 63,000 Hungarian Jews had already been killed, but most Hungarians refused to believe the murdering was really taking place. Maybe Hungarian

Jews just didn't want to believe their country or countrymen, their neighbors and friends would betray them. Is that so foolish to think? Deported to a Camp? *Camp* sounded so playful. A summer camp. The expression *camp* comes from the German *Lager*. None of this *Lager* business made sense to a Hungarian, perhaps because there is no Hungarian word for *concentration camp*.

Like his first Serbian arrest in 1918, Richárd's second arrest was made in broad daylight. Everyone soon knew about it. Here was the president of the Jewish community and head of the most prominent Jewish family in Pécs. Richárd had a history of political protest. A Jew *and* a troublemaker.

"He saved us," Anna says. When her mother *knew* about Richárd's arrest, she did not waste any time leaving and going into hiding.

Peter says that when his father saw Richárd taken away, he finally realized that neither money nor the Engel de Jánosi name would save them or his children. These two relatives, my mother's "cousins" are alive because of Richárd's arrest. Other family members named Engel or those named Stein and Justus, those who ignored Richárd's arrest and stayed, some in an effort to reclaim property, were all eventually deported to concentration camps or labor camps, and, there, they were shot, hung, burned in the ovens, or died of exhaustion, starvation, or frostbite in death marches.

The day after Richárd was arrested, Theresia left Pécs. She returned home to Osijek, Croatia, where she lived with her sister and worked at the family's flower shop. Theresia told her sister she never wanted anyone again after Richárd. She died in 1979, unmarried and childless.

Erna stayed. For a few months, she tried to manage Adolf Engel & Sons after Richárd was taken away from Pécs. She did not flee, maybe because she *still* felt immune. She went into hiding with Christian friends in Pécs, but they reported her to the Arrow Cross. She was arrested in early July and held at the Laktis barracks, where Richárd had been held months before.

Did Richárd look back when they drove him away? Anybody with his ear to the ground, anybody who had been paying attention had at least a hint of what might lie ahead. When Richárd was finally forced to step into that car, that afternoon, surely he knew that he might never see his home or Pécs again.

Did he wonder about all that he and his family had given to the city of Pécs—the buildings, the parks, the swimming pools, the baths? How many forints and banknotes given to how many charities, churches, and city organizations? And there he was, getting kicked out of his own home because the mayor had signed the warrant for his arrest.

Hungarians didn't protest the arrests of 500,000 Jews that took place throughout the country in 1944. They have national holidays "honoring" the thirteen martyrs of the 1856 revolution and the martyrs of the 1956 revolution, but there is no "holiday" honoring the 500,000 martyrs of 1944. There was no 1944 revolution. In less than two months these 500,000 Hungarian citizens, were deported from their own country in more than 145 trains run by the Hungarian government and its national train corporation, MAV, both of them cooperating with the Nazis in the deportation. By the end of July 1944, the only Jewish community left in Hungary was in Budapest, the capital.

Peter says that many Hungarians gladly cooperated with the Germans, in part because of the long-standing, Hungarian anti-Semitism, and in part because of the opportunity to rob Jews of their possessions. The economy in Pécs was as bad then as it is now; there weren't many jobs, and there wasn't much money. Clearing out a huge portion of the population was only going to be popular because of the advantages for those left behind.

When the Jews of Pécs were arrested and rounded up, Hungarian Arrow Cross soldiers marched them through the main streets towards the train station. Crowds of townspeople lined the streets on the afternoon of March 19, 1944. Were these the same people who had cheered Richárd, tossing him roses when he went to war for them during World War I? Some of the townspeople hurled insults, others hurled stones, others were already inside the abandoned homes, making away with the loot, still others just watched the arrested Jewish families march past, moving towards the train station, their yellow stars stitched onto their coats.

By the time the town's Jews were marched off to their deaths, the people of Pécs barely took notice. If anything, thanks to their mayor who signed their arrest warrants and deportation papers, the rest of the people of Pécs may have quietly celebrated, for suddenly there were job openings and beautiful homes to occupy.

"They weren't *all* bad. Not *all* of them." Outside his hotel in Pécs now, Peter tries to defend Hungarians. "They hid me. They hid my sister." He shrugs.

Nazi soldiers and the Hungarian Arrow Cross held Richárd at the Laktis barracks near the train station in Pécs for approximately six weeks. At night, Richárd would have heard the deportation wagons screech, listened to the soldiers loading the wagons up with human cargo, closing the doors of the cattle wagons, nailing them shut.

People were forced to leave behind their carefully packed luggage. *We'll come for your things later,* the soldiers told them.

When it came time, Richárd too was put in a cattle wagon mashed together with eighty other people, an empty bucket serving as their toilet. No water. No food. The only light came through the cracks in the wood. Lying down was out of the question. Families were forced to separate. For most, the journey took about a week. Many died along the way. "In that cattle car. That's when I stopped talking to God," one Hungarian survivor said in his report for Yad Vashem.

It is said that when the Jews go into exile, the *Shekinah*, the divine presence, goes into exile, too — hovering over wherever they are, waiting for them to invite the sacred into their lives. This is one of the great gifts of diaspora, one that I hope Richárd held close: he was forced to travel into exile, but he would remain who he was.

Lajos Esztergár was the mayor of Pécs in 1944. He signed Richárd's death sentence. Soon after Richárd's arrest, on May 31, 1944, The Royal Court of Justice appointed a new company director of Adolf Engel & Sons: Antal Czizek. Lajos Esztergár signed the papers approving Czizek's appointment. The papers state that, "the Jew owners Adolf Engel & Sons can't lead the saw mill and the parquet company anymore because of 'other responsibilities.'"

Lajos Esztergár retired from his job as deputy mayor of Pécs in 1945, soon after World War II ended. He became a professor of law at the University of Pécs, developing an interest in child welfare. In 1949 the university fired him without pension. He was forced to leave his apartment. He was eighty-four when he died in 1978. His ashes are in the Catholic Church in Pécs alongside Richárd's brother, Róbert.

The former mayor's son, Paul Esztergár, does not return my emails or phone calls.

The destruction of the Jews in the country districts of Hungary was a simple business. The Germans made good use of their experience gained annihilating between three to four million Polish, German and Austrian Jews. Within two months, approximately half a million Hungarian Jews, about ninety-five per cent of the provincial Jewish population were arrested and sent to Auschwitz and other camps. Horthy issued an order to stop deportations, but only when the Jewish community in Budapest was all that was left. According to Hannah Arendt's 1963 coverage of the Eichmann trial in Tel Aviv, Israel, whenever Eichmann spoke of the deportations in Hungary, he said the Hungarian Gendarmerie was "more than eager" and "everything went like a dream."

There are no pock-marked buildings in Pécs, no streets or ancient edifices dotted with bullet holes or shell craters. There were no ceasefires at the end of the war in 1944 because there was no firing. Nobody protested or fought against the Nazi-Germans coming in and occupying this town. Pécs was and is much like Vienna: very few people resisted the Nazis or German occupation.

Home movies made from 1932 to 1944 in Pécs show silent, black and white parades, family picnics, running races, swimming meets, tennis matches, hikes up the familiar Mecsek Mountains, a new motor car driving through a town that looks as it looks today. In one old film, we see one shot of a few shiny black cars with swastikas on the sides and a clutch of Nazi soldiers admiring each others' boots.

And then, when the war was over, they just left. The Germans didn't even bother fighting the Russians for Pécs. And as soon as the

Germans left, Soviet tanks rolled in and occupied the town for the next forty-five years.

Some Hungarians still wonder to this day why the Americans didn't come and save them. Once at the American Corner, a friend told Pat that the Americans let them down after World War II and again in 1956. Good, I think. *Now you know what it feels like to be let down by a nation.*

The waiter brings Peter a bill for the coffee.

"Did my grandfather Friedrich ever try to help any of the family in Hungary?"

"We were all trying to save our own lives. We couldn't help each other." Peter picks up the black banana peel with his two fingers and drops it onto his tray.

After he and his father saw Richárd taken, his family spent the next eight months in hiding, sleeping where they could in Budapest apartments, eating what they found. Once, Peter's mother made a soup from a cow's udder. They survived the siege in Budapest, and in 1946, his family left for Vienna. Eventually, they all moved to the United States and reunited with family members from his mother's side. His father, Paul, never got over leaving Hungary or Pécs or living at Ócsárd, and caring for the farmhouse he had inherited. Paul told his son not to look back, but Paul spent the remainder of his life in exile, looking back, mulling over the past, growing more and more depressed. He died at Lenox Hill Hospital in November 1962. He was seventy years old.

"I met your mother once before she married, in Washington," Peter says, getting up from the table, helping me with my coat. The green Zolnay tiles in the hotel's entrance hall glisten. Someone is playing old *Yes* music inside.

"She doesn't remember, does she?" He smiles and shrugs. "Who knows?"

Peter retired from his work at the Ford Foundation. He spent a lifetime working and traveling, looking for who or what was left of the Engel de Jánosi family. He stayed in touch with my grandfather, Friedrich. I don't ask why he didn't stay in touch with my mother. Maybe he just didn't like her.

I thank Peter and say that I look forward to meeting up with him later for the plaque ceremony. We will walk together. For now, Pat and I have to make preparations for the gathering we've planned afterwards at our apartment. We need to get champagne. James has to clean his room. I want this to be a family reunion, a celebration, a homecoming for the few family members left.

As I go through the markets, I think of Richárd. Was Richárd thinking of his father when he was finally pushed at bayonet-point onto that cattle car in Pécs, one of the last trains headed to Mauthausen? Did he think of his grandfather, Adolf? Did he think he had failed, failed them all? Because who now would run the factory? The business? Who would take care of the houses?

In my dreams, Richárd is still boarding that train. Someone from the family comes to help, Friedrich or Marie. Or perhaps some deal will finally be made in Tel Aviv, or some influential man manages to stop the train, buy time and lives for so many bags of coffee beans. It's a trick I play on myself. After all, against all odds, I have found Peter and Anna. Maybe there are others. The records at Yad Vashem had Richárd's birth date wrong, maybe they missed something or someone else, too. There might still be a chance that Richárd even survived Mauthausen or hid in some other country the way Marie did. Maybe he married or even had a family.

It was spring when they took him. Hungarians say that you feel the cold badly in the spring.

In his account of the Hungarian Holocaust, *Kötéltánc*, which means *Rope Dance*, Sándor Krassó lists official announcements that appeared in the local paper, *Dunántúl,* between March 23 and July 6, 1944, the day 6,000 Jews were led to the main railroad station in Pécs where they were loaded in cattlecars and sent to Auschwitz.

March 31: "Jewish households cannot employ Christian servants....Jewish engineers, actors, lawyers must be removed from the professional associations."

April 1: "László Endre, administrative undersecretary of the Ministry of Interior, told the reporters of Esti Újság that the government decrees are only the beginning of the final solution of the

Jewish question. In the opinion of the Hungarian nation the Jewry is an undesirable element from moral, intellectual, and physical points of view. We must seek a solution that would exclude the Jewry from the life of the Hungarian nation."

April 5: "All Jews over the age of six must wear on the left side of their coats a canary-yellow six-pointed star."

April 6: "On Wednesday the cabinet made the decision to limit the free movement of Jews within the country."

April 9: "Jews by April 10 must report the details of their radios by registered mail."

April 15: "A Jew must declare all his assets on official forms. His assets cannot be sold, given to someone else, or pawned. He must separately declare real estate. A Jew cannot own stocks and cannot have more than 3,000 pengős in cash. Failure to follow this order may mean six months of incarceration."

April 18: "All Jewish white-collar employees must be dismissed."

April 19: "Ten people were charged for failure to wear the yellow star . . . one of them was interned."

April 21: "All Jewish merchants must shut down their stores."

April 23: "Jews can receive 300 grams of oil and 100 grams of beef or horse meat per month."

April 25: "Dismissed Jewish clerks cannot be employed by the same firm even as laborers."

April 27: "Jews cannot purchase lard."

April 30: "All Jews must turn in their bicycles to the Pécs police station within twenty-four hours."

May 4: "Within three days Jews must turn in their musical instruments and pieces of art, for example, pianos, violins, records, paintings, statues, ceramics."

May 6: [The authorities designated a certain part of town as the ghetto.] "Each room housed five people . . . . Out of the twenty Jewish doctors in town, five moved into the ghetto."

May 10: "Jews cannot take any valuables into the ghetto . . . They are allowed to take 50 kg total including bedding . . . Pécs Jews turned in 38 tons of lard, two tons of goose fat, and 60 kg of smoked meat . . . . Their radios must be turned in on May 11 and 12."

May 12: "The government commissioner in charge of the press ordered all forbidden Jewish books to be collected for 5 pengős per ton." [including works by such authors as Heinrich Heine, Martin Buber, Stephan Zweig, and, among Hungarians, Ferenc Molnár, Frigyes Karinthy, and Sándor Bródy]

May 18: "The City of Pécs offers for sale Angora rabbits turned in by the Jews." [On the same day there were four suicides by Jewish men and women.]

May 20: "The Pécs police authorities suspect that Jews are giving their jewelry and gold to Christians for safekeeping. All valuables of Jews belong to the state. Christians who harbor such goods will be severely punished. They can be interned."

May 21: "No Jew's book can be published . . . . Tens of thousands of Jewish books will be reduced to pulp . . . . We are making a reality of what Ottokár Prohászka and Lajos Méhely demanded."

June 11: "1,200 claims were received for Jewish houses and apartments."

July 2: "The Jewish ghetto will be closed. The Christian families can move back to their old apartments shortly."

July 6: [the day Pécs Jews boarded the box cars] "The ghetto is empty."

Survivors

At the corner of Munkácsy and Irgalmasok streets, we meet up with Peter, his wife Monica, Anna Stein, and Ilona, a retired physics teacher who lives in Budapest. Ilona is Peter and Anna's first cousin. During World War II, Ilona's brother Sandor survived a slave labor camp in Kőszeg, Hungary, but before the camp was liberated, he was forced to walk in a "death march" over the Alps to Ebensee, Austria. He died during the march on January 2, 1945.

The few remaining Engel de Jánosi family members walk through the center of Pécs towards the ceremony in front of the house on Rákóczi út. Peter wears the grey suit he wore that morning, and Monica looks chic in her black slacks and knit cape. Ilona wears a good dark skirt. Anna wears her leather skirt and pink jacket. Pat and James are tall and handsome in their blue blazers and pressed pants. I wear my one black traveling suit.

We walk on Irgalmasok utcája, one of the main thoroughfares. We are stepping in time. People see us. Some stop and stare. Once again, the Engel de Jánosi family, the "tolerated ones," walk through the town of Pécs. Do we *all* sense what's happening here? This was the walk Peter took with his father when he saw Richárd taken.

Off the square, an unsteady man lifts his bottle as we pass. I hold my arm up, thinking for a moment that he will throw the bottle. He licks his lips, and says something vulgar in Hungarian. Hungarian is a close relative to Finish, but the only word left in common with the Finnish is the word for *Drunkard. Iszákos.*

Men in uniform gather in front of the house at 54 Rákóczi ut. They are the band members tuning their instruments not German soldiers checking their rifles. The town and its mayor are not here to kick us out, but to honor Adolf. The mayor's office has built a steep wooden stage with steps, leading to the plaque, which is covered by a black cloth and which has already been fixed and hung. They've cleaned the sidewalks, but they didn't scrub off the *Need?* spray-painted in white on the house.

I wave to some students from the university and greet Christof Baiersdorf, who has driven down from Düsseldorf to videotape the event. I hug him as I would a relative. I hear Anna Stein say *Why is he here?* in English. She says Christof is not a blood relative. I want to say *there are so few of us, let's not be picky.*

"Here we go," Peter sighs as he and Monica step aside, distancing themselves from Anna.

Renáta has agreed to translate the speech I have prepared and she is nervous because she has to speak in front of a crowd. She wears a dark suit and a green Zsolnay necklace. We look like sisters.

Next door at the big shopping mall, there's a window display of mannequins wearing thong underwear and t-shirts that say *Totally Sexy Totally Glam.* We can smell falafels cooking at the stand down the street. The scent reminds me of Israel.

This moment means something different for each of us. I went looking for this one man, Richárd, and found Peter and Anna and other people I never heard anything about. Erna, Marianne, my own great-grandfather, Moritz. I found Christof, Renáta, and Zoli. Perhaps we all eventually return to our homelands to find what or who we've missed. Sometimes you have to hunt to find the connections. Sometimes the dead lead to the living.

So many of them were here, in this pink house, once painted Wedgewood blue. Adolf's son, József, lived here, then Róbert and his first wife, Marianne. Richárd and Róbert were born in this house, and Natalie died here. Then, after the divorce, Róbert lived here with Erna.

The covered plaque hangs a few feet away from the front door. I imagine Adolf passing through that door to visit his grandsons Richárd and Róbert. I picture Róbert locking this door, to keep his wayward wife, Marianne inside. Nazi soldiers banged on this door. This is where Richárd was born and this is where he was taken away.

I search for holes to the right of the door, looking for signs of a mezuzah. Did the family have one posted here, a parchment roll in a mother-of-pearl case containing a handwritten text of the "Sh'ma," the central Sabbath prayer? "Hear O Israel, the Lord our God, the Lord is one."

At which point exactly does the past give way to the present, and does time ever intersect? Through years of occupations, this house on Rákóczi út was forced to give way to new inhabitants. Just by being here, standing here in front of this house, we are bringing them all back, through memory.

"The strength of a nation lies in its memory," Benzion Dinur, Israeli Minister of Education wrote in 1956. "This is what distinguishes man. If we wish to live and if we wish to aspire life to our offspring, if we consider ourselves duty bound to pave a way to the future then first of all we must not forget."

Tall and dignified in his dark suit, his hair splashed with grey, the mayor of Pécs climbs the wooden steps, uncovers the marble plaque and hangs a wreath beneath it. Administrators in Hungary tend to have a soviet look with their man-bellies pouring over their belts. Zsolt Páva is fit. He waves and the band plays the sad anthem of Hungarian coal miners.

Mayor Zsolt Páva speaks while Renáta stands close, between me and James, whispering her translations into my ear. Pat takes pictures. The mayor says that Adolf Engel was a "man of such good" who did a great deal for the community. He built and he gave generously to charities still linked to his name. *Look over there a few meters away and see the Pécs Synagogue, one of the most beautiful buildings in the city, which he built 150 years ago. He is an example to the community, and because of his hard work and industriousness and because of the jobs he created, the city of Pécs experienced an economic boom.* The mayor adds that everyone here should use Adolf as an example. Even though everything was working against Adolf Engel, he prevailed. The mayor never once refers to Adolf as a Jew.

First they kill us, then they honor us.

Peter reads his speech in Hungarian. He thanks the mayor and the town and he talks about his love for Pécs. Everyone claps. When it is my turn, I say how my mother, Adolf's granddaughter wishes she could be here too. She thanks everyone. I read the rest of what my mother wrote:

"Thank you for celebrating the energy, ingenuity, courage and just plain guts of Adolph Engel de Jánosi. Thank you to my cousin Peter de Jánosi whose steadfast interest in our family history helped bring my daughter and our only grandson, back in touch with our Hungarian heritage — rounding out the memories of my childhood in Adolph Engel-Jánosi's
former Vienna home at *Hofzeile* 12. Memories of Adolph's parquet floor in the living room, the gardens, and of my father's, Friedrich Engel-Jánosi's final glance upward at our home before entering the taxi which
would take him to the train departing for Zurich, Switzerland in April 1939. My mother and I left the following week. My case of the red measles delayed our departure — nobody, including the Nazi border guards, dared to come near me."

As Renáta translates, I wonder about the Hungarian word for *guts*. My mother's speech is strange in some ways, but it's very much my mother, still defending her father's early departure. She calls Peter her cousin. A first. When Renáta finishes, she takes a deep breath. The crowd claps.

Anna Stein has no notecards, and as she begins, I can see from the reaction of the crowd, that hers is a very different speech. Peoples' eyes widen. They're whispering to each other. Her voice starts out calm but insistant. Then she rails.

"Whoa," James whispers. "What's she saying?"

Renáta translates Anna's Hungarian. Anna says there has been altogether too much thanking today, and she has no one to thank. She says she is here to *blame*—the mayor, the town, and all of Hungary for stealing the Engel de Jánosi land, businesses, and houses, especially this house right here, stolen from the Engel de Jánosi family. *She* is the rightful heiress, she says. *Not the town of Pécs and certainly not the mayor. All of this, all of it, it all belongs to her.*

Anna still sees this as highway robbery. How could she not? Later, she tells me she doesn't blame the people in Pécs. She loves them. Many are still her friends. Her feelings towards Hungary are like my mother's feelings towards Austria. They blame the country. Hungary and Austria's immoral roles in the Holocaust are unforgivable, and now it's too late, even for apologies.

I don't hear *Köszönöm,* thank you. When Anna stops speaking, the crowd claps lightly. The band plays the sad Coal Miner's song again.

A student, Bernadett, moves towards me, and whispers, "You know, your relative. She's angry, but she's right. Saying what she said in front of the mayor and all these people? That took a lot of balls." James guffaws.

Maybe Adolf would be proud of Anna. She was simply re-stating what her great-grandfather once said when he refused to thank the Viennese Court for passing a law that allowed Jews to own property. "When people have taken from me a natural right and have given it back again, I don't thank them for that."

Anna, Peter and my mother lost their homes and this loss has lodged inside of them forever. Each moved on in different ways. Because Anna stayed in Hungary during both the Nazi era and the Communist regime, she was the most affected. For her, to be happy and at peace must feel like a foreign language she once spoke as a child, but can no longer recall.

What can a town really do to apologize for its past sins? What can a mayor do? How do you make up for such grievous losses? Does grief have to be such a wasted, life-sucking emotion?

The plaque is nice, but anyone can take it down, and, once again, all signs of the Engels would vanish.

During the Soviet era, the villa where Peter and his family lived on Hunyadi út was divided up into five apartments. The Engel de Jánosi farm, which Peter's father managed in Ocsárd became a cooperative and then a community center. During the years of reparations, Peter sought compensation. He came away with approximately $200 a month to be paid out until his death. He also received the title to some property that was not Ócsárd, and, what he claimed, was a certain amount of satisfaction.

When Friedrich died, his second wife, Christiane, claimed the $100,000 he willed to my mother. She donated the money to Catholic Charities of Austria. Then, when Christiane died, the Austrian government claimed that money in addition to the $63,500 she willed to me. Peter wrote a letter saying he would mail jewelry she had willed to me, but he never mailed it and he never mentioned the jewelry again.

Any news or awareness about restitution from Austria came too late for my mother. She was taught and raised to think of the future, not the past. So she wasn't aware, wasn't paying attention, and then, time was up. Too late to claim anything.

How do you forgive a country? Or do you? Perhaps the question should be, when do you simply give up on your country, the country that formed you? United States Poet Laureate Natasha Trethewey, who writes about racism in her native Mississippi asks, "How do you *not* love the place that made you?" But all I'm thinking is, how do you stop from hating it?

I think of all the refugees then and now, risking their lives to flee their homes, their countries. And then there are those who risk their lives to stay, maybe because they love the familiar, their home, their country.

People gather for pictures. Anna will not have Christof Baiersdorf in the picture with us. She says he is not a relation, not an Engel de Jánosi. Christof rejoins the crowd on the sidewalk. Even when the man from the local paper tells us to, it's difficult for anyone to smile.

At one point in time Anna, Peter and my mother had everything, and then, all of it was taken away. Is there any relief in having survived? Or is there only sorrow, remorse, and maybe even a little guilt? It makes all the sense in the world now—forget your family name, heritage, seal, land, money, loyalty, duty. Say goodbye to all that. Free yourself.

Maybe they were right—Friedrich and all the other Engel de Jánosi's who got out and never told their children or grandchildren the whole truth. They didn't want to burden or overload us with family history. Too much baggage meant we wouldn't be able to move forward and into a bright future. Too much bitterness, anger, and sorrow leads us into that dark rabbit hole of despair. They didn't want to introduce us to their ghosts. But those ghosts find us anyway.

Sometimes, I Skype with my mother when she is alone. I read to her from the notes I take about Hungary, Pécs, and Richárd. Piece by piece I deliver the stories and history of her family. I am telling my own mother her family's historical roots. It feels rude. She might feel she no longer has secrets, secrets, which she came to love. A chord has been cut between us, but then, we've never been closer.

There are moments when my mother's memory begins to crack open further, as though the first truth of Richárd's existance begets other truths. She knows now why her father was so upset with her in 1956, the day of the Hungarian uprising right after students took control of the radio building in Budapest. That night, Friedrich came rushing home to the house my mother bought for him in Washington, D.C.

"He screamed and screamed at me," she tells me as we are Skyping one day. "I never saw him so upset. 'What have you done?'"

My mother assured her father she was not "working the Hungarian desk," but he never forgave her or The Agency for their failure to "save" Hungary.

"They knew but I didn't." During our call, she cries. "They wanted me to learn Hungarian. They said 'it will come naturally.' But I refused. I didn't know we had family there. If I had known, maybe things would have been different."

And now I've given my mother a new regret: because of her position at The Agency, she might have been able to make a difference in Hungary, could have possibly saved lives.

Part of me wants to turn my back on Europe and Hungary for good. I hear ancestral warnings: *Don't turn around. Don't look back.* Another part of me wants to move here, park myself and my family in one of Adolf's houses in Pécs, restore it and reclaim it as *home*.

We listen to the saw-toothed drone of an airplane overhead. Kicked out and almost obliterated, this family of Engels are practically shrapnel. But here in Pécs, I feel us molding back together.

People are leaving. Pat, James and I stay a little while longer in front of the house. I take a picture of James standing at the front door. When he was born we named him after my father and after Pat's father. We also stuck him with another formidable middle name: *Engel de Jánosi*. He looks small and serious now leaning against the doorframe of his great-great-great-grandfather's home, breathing in the moldy scent of thick Moravian oak, hopefully sensing all of the angels here with him.

At our apartment, Renáta and James make caviar sandwiches, arrange the cheese and honey cookies, and pour the Pécs champagne and Tokaji wine, Hungarian wine of kings.

Peter, Anna and Ilona step over the threshold of the apartment, and they each study the parquet floors. My mother does this too whenever she enters a new place with wooden floors. I find myself doing the same. We all inspect floors first, studying the wood's grain, luster, and pedigree.

"Not the best," Peter proclaims about our apartment's floors. "But adequate." Apparently, Adolf Engel & Sons produced thicker parquet.

Ilona wipes her feet over and over on the rug near the door, careful not to track in outside dirt. She keeps her hands folded, her gaze down. James offers her the tray of sandwiches and Pat pours her wine. She thanks them over and over. Peter whispers to me that Ilona has been through "so much."

I pour Christof Baiersdorf more Tokaji, noting that he is not wearing his skullcap, which he has taken to wearing more frequently. Christof was raised Catholic and only within the last five years discovered his Jewish roots. As we chat and Renáta translates, I ask Christof if he considers himself Catholic or Jewish. He shrugs and says in English, "I'm European."

Anna refuses to sit with Peter. She is angry with him for inviting Christof, whom she will not accept as an Engel de Jánosi.

"You said *thank you* to the mayor too many times," she tells me. "We have nothing to thank him for."

The following morning, Anna will wake us up with an early Skype call. She will apologize for her behavior, but she will tell me again how angry she is with Peter. She explains that once they were close, but not any more. "He feels now like a second Adolf. He's not a founder for any family. I have my life. He has his life. I have my family. He has his family. He has no authority over me." I recognize Anna's anger. It's my mother's anger, and sometimes mine too. Anger, another inheritance, another family trait, and, unlike the broad hips, this one will wear us all out.

James offers Anna the Tokaji. "I don't drink that," she tells him. "It's awful stuff, too sweet." She stays long enough for Pat's toast, a toast to the Engel de Jánosi family, even though the ones left are barely on speaking terms.

Living Family

The woman official at The Immigration and Naturalization Office leaves word with Bea at the university regarding our case. They request that I come with Pat and James to their offices as soon as possible. They hope I still have the case number. For the first time, the woman official requests that we *all* come, and that we all bring our passports. I am tempted to ask if I should also bring our packed luggage. Bea and I stare at each other. She says this is the first time she knows of such a thing.

That afternoon, after classes, I meet up with Pat and James at the Immigration and Naturalization Office.

"So, what's going to happen?" James asks.

"I'm not sure," I say. "I'm not even sure if this is a good idea."

I'm surprised when neither Pat nor James says anything to the contrary.

We sit in plastic chairs and wait for our numbers to be called. The office is busy and there is the smell of damp wool in the air. After thirty minutes, James slumps over. He snores. Two young women from Africa are ahead of us. Their Immigration and Naturalization Office official say they need their checkbooks because they have to check their bank accounts.

"There has to be enough money in order for you to stay," I hear the official say.

A man calls James' name, not his number. James jumps awake.

"It's OK," I say, not sure if it *is* OK.

James stands and goes before a man behind a sliding glass window. The man holds his hand up to me, signaling for me to sit back down.

"Passport," the man says. James presents his passport. The man behind the window tells him to stand back. I hold my breath and there is a flash. He takes James' picture. James waits for the picture to develop in a printer beside the man. The man behind the glass window flips through James' passport, finds an empty page, and carefully pastes James' picture alongside a red and blue certificate onto page twelve of his passport book.

"Cool," James says, running his fingers over the still-warm stamp. The man behind the sliding-glass window smiles. The seal is complete with a shiny silver emblem, the Hungarian seal and crown, a bull charging two stars, the date, and *Családi Együttélés*, Living Family, valid until December 23, the day we are scheduled to leave.

Pat is next. He follows the same procedure. He becomes Living Family as well.

They are safe. If the man doesn't stamp my passport, I will stay here. But Pat and James are safe and free to go. I realize how much I believe this to be true now and how comforting this fact is to me. They will be OK. I'll just have to take what comes. I am the official Engel de Jánosi, considered the Jewess. I can hear the way my great-grandmother said it, not the way my mother says it. It's more *jewel* than disease now.

I slip my passport under the glass window, ready for whatever comes next. The man flips through, finds a blank page, and stamps it, not with the word *zsidó* or Jew, but with the word *Hivatalos*, which means *Official*.

We are all valid until we leave. We are Living Family living in Pécs legally, officially. The feeling is palpable. But where are the woman official porn star and her boss woman? I want very badly to see them, maybe even, thank them, but I have a funny feeling that they are none too pleased about the final outcome. As the three of us step outside, it stops raining.

Broken Clouds and a Hatred for Hate

We take the train north to Budapest, travelling with our papers. I'm scheduled to talk to a group of writing students at Eötvös Loránd University during an evening journalism class. Ryan James, who teaches the class and writes all the Hungarian sections for Fodor's Travel Guides, offers us his place to stay in exchange.

We tour the parliament and stand in the room with empty desks made of beautiful wood cut from Hungarian forests. This is where the politicians, the decision makers sat then and now. This is where the laws got passed, and still get passed.

On April 1, 1944 administrative undersecretary of the Ministry of Interior, László Endre told reporters of *Esti Újság* that the government decrees were "only the beginning of the final solution of the Jewish question. In the opinion of the Hungarian nation the Jewry is an undesirable element from moral, intellectual, and physical points of view. We must seek a solution that would exclude the Jewry from the life of the Hungarian nation."

Recently, Prime Minister Viktor Orbán announced to the world that his aim was "to keep Europe Christian." Orbán also started a sham historical institute called "Veritas," which specializes in fake Hungarian History, especially the history of the Hungarian Holocaust. Under Orbán, "scholars" openly question the Holocaust and Hungary's undeniable role in it. Under Orbán, Hungary's largest circulation national daily, *Népszabadság* was shut down. Under Orbán, the Hungarian state granted the Knights Cross of the Order of Merit for "the promotion of universal human values," to Zsolt Bayer, a journalist who referred to Jews as "stinking excrement."

Orbán was the first European leader to show his support for Donald Trump. They tweet praises to each other. Orbán hailed Trump's inauguration as the "end of multilateralism," suggesting Hungary and others will no longer feel ashamed about putting their own interests before those of their neighbors and the wider good.

When Orbán tightened his control over the press and state finances, weakening Hungary's system of democratic checks and balances, and then passed a series of punitive media laws, silencing Hungary's free press, his visitor, Trump campaign advisor Newt Gingrich had nothing but praise.

Donald Trump's deputy assistant, former Breitbart editor, Sebastian Gorka appeared on a talk show and was asked about the White House leaving out mention of Jews in its Holocaust Remembrance Day statement. Gorka called the criticism "asinine." Before Trump hired him, Gorka served as an advisor to Viktor Orbán.

At Trump's inauguration, Gorka wore a jacket with a medal signifying a knightly order of merit founded in 1920 by Miklós Horthy, Hitler's ally who oversaw the deportataion of hundreds of thousands of Hungary's Jews, including my own family.

From these fine wooden desks, politicians still vote, deciding who are the real Hungarians, the Christian Hungarians. As we leave the parliament buildings, the weather turns and it begins to snow.

The following morning, I walk to the New York Café on Erzsébet körút to meet Gábor Schweitzer. There are no genders in Hungarian pronouns, and in our email correspondence, I never picked up any specific male cues. So, I try not to look surprised when "he" arrives. The "daughter" of the rabbi turns out to be a son.

"*Szia*," he says, apologizing for being late. It's Shabbat and he doesn't ride streetcars.

"*Szia*," I say back. Pronounced *See ya, Szia* is quicker than the more formal Hungarian greeting, *Jó napot kívánok*. Still, I never can get over how saying hello in Hungarian sounds so much like saying goodbye.

Outside it's getting colder. Inside, the café's windows are huge and drafty. At the turn of the century Budapest had about five hundred coffee houses and The New York Café was the most famous literary hangout for writers. During the 1956 uprising, a Russian tank bulldozed the building. After the collapse of socialism, an Italian Hotel chain bought the place and spent eighty million euros renovating the building into a luxury hotel with the Café on the ground floor. Gábor is a history professor in Budapest. He descends from a long line of well-known Hungarian Rabbis. His father, Dr. Joseph Schweitzer, is a retired chief Rabbi living in Budapest. Gábor's grandfather was chief Rabbi Albert Schweitzer, Richárd's Rabbi in Pécs. Albert Schweitzer was also with Richárd at Mauthausen.

"All my life I heard about Richárd," Gábor says as soon as we're seated.

"Really?" I take deep breaths to slow down.

We order lattes and they come on silver trays in tall glasses, with Seltzer water, and bites of brownies and caramel almond cake. Gábor talks about Judaism and the evolution of the less orthodox more Neologue Judaism in Pécs. Pécs was conservative but not orthodox. Gábor says they were not Neologues either. He tells me there was no Mikve in Pécs, no ritual bath for women and men. Pécs traditionally had troubles with water. The Danube is very far, which could be the reason Adolf thought to build the baths when he did. There were two swimming pools in Pécs when Gábor grew up there. He left Pécs in the late 1980's.

"The Engel de Jánosi's were the only wealthy, prestigious, and noble family in the region who kept the family business going until the Holocaust," he says. Gábor is the first Hungarian I have heard *say* this word *Holocaust*. There were three other families like the Engel de Jánosi's, but they went bankrupt in the second generation.

"When Róbert converted, it was a scandal," Gábor says, leaning forward. We are huddled now, digging into the conversation. He talks low, as though someone might hear us. At times we both look around to see if anyone is listening. It feels like a war is going on just outside, but it's only the sleet hitting the windows. "How could the son of József, a respected member of the Jewish community in Pécs, president of the Jewish community convert—how? Róbert wrote and gave lectures on Jewish topics. How could he convert? His wife, Erna converted too. She was fifty-five years old." Gábor tells me his grandmother went to Auschwitz with Erna. His grandmother was in her forties then. He doesn't think they knew each other.

Gábor and I are about the same age and about the same height. We could be brother and sister, but Gábor's eyes are more hooded and sad. Our relatives struggled together and died together. Some survived. Doesn't that bond us for life? Doesn't that make us both a *kind* of relative?

He says that Richárd was one of the prominent members arrested in the earliest roundup. Then Gábor tells me what his father and grandfather told him, that Richárd's heroic death was really tragic, because most of the men who were taken to Mauthausen survived.

"Heroic? Why heroic?"

"Didn't you know?" he says. "Richárd fasted. He starved himself to death."

I lean back. It's colder and colder inside the café. My eyes are watery and puffy, my nose runny. I don't have a cold, but I'm *leaking* emotion, as though I just learned about a close relative's death. Gábor smiles so that his eyes crinkle the way mine do and my mother's.

"People tell me sometimes, 'You are so sensitive.'" He shakes his head, gives me his napkin, and finishes his water. "Meaning, you are acting like a Jew."

"People described Richárd in this way," I say. "They say he was sensitive." I wipe my eyes with the café napkin. Many of my students tell me, jokingly, that artists need drugs, cigarettes and alcohol because they are so sensitive and they need ways to take the edge off reality. "Your grandfather told you Richárd starved himself?"

"My grandfather told my father. I did not know my grandfather."

After his liberation from Mauthausen, Gábor's grandfather, Rabbi Schweitzer, ate food too quickly and became ill. This was not uncommon. In *The War: A Memoir*, Marguerite Duras wrote about her husband returning from Bergen-Belsen. "If he had eaten when he got back from camp his stomach would have been lacerated by the weight of the food, or else the weight would have pressed on the heart, which had grown enormous in the cave of his emaciation ... It was a tricky balance: to eat was to die, but they could not go on not eating without dying."

As Rabbi Schweitzer lay sick from eating, he told everything he could about his experience at Mauthausen camp to his son, who wrote it all down. He talked about everything that had happened and about Richárd's fast. After Rabbi Schweitzer died, his son took his notes and wrote and lectured throughout Hungary about the history of the Jews in Pécs.

"But how did your father survive?"

"He was a slave worker and because of this he lived," Gábor says.

In 1939, before World War II came to Hungary, Jewish men had to join the Hungarian army, not as soldiers, but as laborers. They were forced to work hard labor in Hungary, but their chances of survival were higher.

The British and the Americans bombed Pécs' airport, but the civilian and non-civilian population did not suffer during the war years. Pécs was liberated in November 1944. After the war, after all the murdering, seven hundred Jews came to Pécs. Most of them were survivors from the fifty-one-day siege in Budapest. They heard there was food in Pécs. The Jewish school, which Adolf had built, turned into a Jewish Youth hostel for orphaned young people.

"Lots of lonely Jews came to Pécs to live," he says. "Some stayed. The majority moved away and settled in the United States or in Israel."

"Why do you stay in Hungary?" I wince at my own question. This is a question Northerners ask Mississippians all the time. In a television interview William F. Buckley once asked Eudora Welty how she could live in such a racist place as Jackson, Mississippi. In the final scene of William Faulkner's novel, *Absalom, Absalom,* when Shreve and Quentin are in their dorm room at Harvard, Shreve asks Quentin, "Tell about the South. What do they do there? How do they live there? Why do they?"

What I really want to ask Gábor is *How can you stand to remain in a country that betrayed us?*

Gábor shakes his head. "When you are a Jew and you don't live in Israel, you are never really home. Here? Everyday life is horrible. It's true. The politics now are horrible. It's terrible to listen to the news or read the papers. But to live here, to walk these streets and to look at these buildings and know the history, I wouldn't want to live any other place. This is where I am from. This is where my people are from."

Hungary is a part of who Gábor is. And even *I* realize the importance of his being here. Otherwise, they will have won. "It's a miracle that after seventy years, after the Holocaust, there is still a Jewish community here in Budapest."

We have been at the café all morning. Outside, the sleet has turned back to snow and it's coming down in clumps. I have made plans to meet up with Pat and James for goulash where our friend, Blase, a fellow Fulbrighter, wants us to meet his new Hungarian girlfriend. Afterwards, we will head back to where we're staying on Dohàny utca. The building is in the heart of the city in the old Jewish section, and we look for gold street stones, markers for where people were taken away and deported. Here, in this bruised city, there are still buildings pockmarked with bullet holes, and I take strange comfort in these visual reminders of the past.

Out on the street, tourists look up at the buildings, then back at their maps. Right around the corner is the Dohány Street Synagogue, designed by Ludwig Förster, the architect who worked with Moritz on the Lóránt Palace in Pécs. Förster's synagogue in Vienna was destroyed during *Kristallnacht,* The Night of Broken Glass, and his Budapest synagogue was damaged along with sixty per cent of the houses during World War II. Since then, Budapest's largest synagogue in Europe underwent a reconstruction funded by Toni Curtis, Estée Lauder, and other American Hungarians. Near the synagogue stands a memorial monument of a weeping willow with the names of Holocaust families. There is also a memorial in Budapest to those murdered by the Arrow Cross on the spot: empty bronze shoes line the banks of the river. The shoes are heartbreaking.

It's difficult to get a clear sense of Budapest from any one point. You mostly see the city's skyline from the river, not from a car or a bus. It's an old city and outsiders used to approach from the river, not from the road. Budapest's skyline is intricate, voluptuously baroque, and more than a little absurd.

For a long time, when I first learned about our family's sad history, I had a terrible, consoling hatred for hate that felt almost as gratifying as believing in God. I had no idea if I needed to be forgiven or if I needed to forgive. There were and there still are times when I honestly thought, how could anyone still live in Germany or Hungary? I stood with Elie Wiesel in his pre-forgiving stage: to flat out forgive all the family's murderers was to forget the lives lost. I will not forget those lives. I will not forget Richárd. Now I wonder if it's necessary to feel this hatred in order to remember.

Outside on the sidewalk Gábor and I say goodbye in a proper Hungarian way—three alternating air kisses on the cheek. Snow dusts his hair and eyelashes. I want to ask him so much more. I want to hug him as my brother. But that would be unseemly and make him uncomfortable. It *is* Shabbat, after all. I want to follow him, even walk three paces behind him. But that too would be altogether creepy and strange.

There is a story about a Hungarian poet who was in a labor camp. An officer says, "It's a shame they made them wear that armband with the star." To which the poet says, "There is no difference between they and we, between they and them, between you and me. We are we. We are Hungarians. There is no difference. There are no differences."

Pull on your gloves and tighten your scarf, I direct myelf. The snow is falling heavier now, and I consider the morning forecast for all of Hungary: *Broken Clouds.* Gábor and I begin to walk in opposite directions. From across the street we both turn at the same time and wave. We say *Hallo.* In Hungarian, *Hallo* is the simplest way to say goodbye.

Kaddish for Engel, 64240

At the Keleti train station in Budapest, people carry wicker baskets with food, bottled water, and big bunches of flowers cut from their gardens to give to a relative or friend. They wear old-fashioned, practical hats and boots, many of them old people without teeth, sitting, wrapped up babushka-style.

Traveling through Hungary and into Austria, Pat, James and I sit beside families eating cold roasted chicken and pork sausages, hardboiled eggs, cheese, bread, and drinking their homemade wines and *Pálinka*. We pass through granite tunnels and buildings covered with graffiti.

During the war, most of the deportation trains, including the one carrying Richárd, stopped in Vienna. Perhaps that's why there was a rumor often circulated among prisoners that they were being taken there to clear rubble. When the trains stopped, most Viennese pretended not to notice the loaded trains. Some slipped the prisoners bread wrapped in paper. When our train stops in Vienna, most of the women are Schiele-thin in their tall boots and geometric eyeglasses, and, even if their hair is dirty, they look sophisticated.

On this October day, church steeples dot the town bathed in yellow sunshine. Was Richárd able to look through the slits of his cattle car at this luxuriant countryside, in this particular section of Europe, still relatively untouched by war? Did he see Linz and these churches and wonder how this war, his arrest, these deportations, all of *this* could have happened to him and to the world?

From all accounts the deportation trains moved slowly. Stopping every five hundred paces or so, these cattle cars often stayed stalled on the dark railroad bed. The prisoners inside stood waiting, perhaps standing on one leg at a time. If they could, they took the opportunity to get rid of those who had died. Some officers allowed prisoners to throw their dead alongside the tracks, where stray dogs and foxes went after the corpses. Some women smeared their faces with lumps of coal to look wrinkled and ugly so as not to get raped by Germans. Some women colored their cheeks with pinpricks of blood to look healthy in order to be allowed to live. Nobody knew the rules of this new game.

Most of the passengers get off our train in Linz. The provincial capital of Austria in 1931, Linz was the Austrian Nazi Party headquarters. The young in this area were among the first to join the Nazi party. According to Rudolf A. Haunschmied's *St. Georgen Gusen Mauthausen,* fewer older farmers were Nazis "because of their strong faith in God." One woman said, "the young people believed in Hitler's promises that there would be oranges and work and money. They thought they would get a better position if they joined the Nazis." In 2009, Linz was voted a European Cultural Capital.

The train starts moving again and soon enough we pass cheap new houses, factories painted Habsburg yellow, a group of multi-colored houses shaped like barns with satellite dishes and plastic lawn chairs, the big stores Bau Maxx, Höfe, Dona Park, and finally, we see a quarry near the train station and truck loads of granite. In the 1920's, laborers marched in *Holzschuhe* or wooden clogs every day to work in the quarries. The area is now only famous for its *history* of granite quarries. Nowadays, the stone industry has almost disappeared. The quarries around Mauthausen stopped functioning in the late 1980s and early 1990s.

The trainman shouts when he announces *MautHAUSEN,* emphasizing *hausen,* a word, which could translate to mean *live* or *wreak havoc.* The camp is a four-kilometer walk from the train station, and, even though the original prisoners walked, I don't want to be exhausted when I get there. I consider what Anna Stein said about saving our strength. We order a cab.

A heavy-set woman cabdriver drives a clean new Mercedes. Her skinny boyfriend is in the passenger seat, along for the ride. The radio is on loud. It feels a little like swearing when I say the word, so when I say it, I whisper, *Mauthausen.*

"Concentration camp?" she says loudly.

"*Ja,*" I say.

Her boyfriend says something in German, playing on the word *concentration*. They laugh. "Concentration camp," the woman repeats. She drives, and they continue talking and laughing loudly.

Elie Wiesel once wrote, "I cry out with all my heart against forgiveness, against forgetting, against silence. Every Jew, somewhere in his being, should set apart a zone of hate—healthy, viril hate—for what the German personifies, and for what persists in the German. To do otherwise would be a betrayal of the dead." But Wiesel, who returned to Germany on a visit in 1962, found it difficult to sustain such hate.

Vormarkstrasse, Poshmarkstrassee. Our cabbie drives along the water of the baby Danube and through the yellow town. Red-faced men in outdoor cafes eat *wurst* and laugh on the wooden seats. The bright red geraniums in the window planters are in full bloom. In this area in upper Austria, Mauthausen served as a satellite labor and transit camp for Auschwitz. It's a lovely little town, impossible not to hate.

According to weather records, it was raining that day, the day he got off the train. Forsythia and pink hyacinths were just beginning to bloom in the woods.

Richárd and the others had received little food in the cattle cars. The SS forced them to walk the three miles in the cold rain from the train station, through the middle of the town and up the steep hill. After five years, the townspeople had gotten used to seeing prisoners coming off the trains. They yelled and kicked at them. They threw stones. Mauthausen is a quarry town. There are plenty of granite stones.

People living in Mauthausen claimed they didn't know what was going on at the camp. But they knew. Everyone knew what was going on up the hill in the biggest building for miles. Hardly hidden, it sits massive on top of a steep hill like some medieval fortress.

The town prospered during the war with the addition of a concentration camp. Back then, the big new camp meant jobs for local merchants, private business owners and those involved in supplying and constructing the camp. The SS families who moved here hired domestic servants from the town. When the SS soldiers could no longer keep up with the number of dead bodies, they outsourced their work to the townspeople.

The town's air reeked of death then.

We drive on through beautiful woods, up a long hill, past bare, plowed fields. And then we see the grey granite walls and the gate of the camp, so solid, well constructed, and carefully built. A woman in a red jogging suit fast-walks around the outer walls, getting her exercise.

There is a strange, mineral scent in the air. As soon as we enter the compound surrounded by all the granite walls, the day turns colorless, shadowless. It's neither warm nor cold, though we shiver in our coats.

Inside the gates, we are nearing the end of a long journey that began at Yad Vashem in Israel when the archivist said, "You are the first to ask about him. You are responsible now. *You must remember him in order to honor him.*"

The place is all grey. Walking up to the gate, it is hard to think because there really is no logic to what happened here. The stones are dripping white, as if the walls are crying stalactites.

Signs direct us towards the modern stone and glass offices of the museum's entrance. When I explain why we're here, the museum's official offers us free admission. We pay anyway. The archivists here have provided so much information already.

According to the literature we read, special functionaries, such as prisoners who helped put bodies in the crematoriums, had better chances of survival. They had a "privileged position." They would receive a piece of bread or more soup. Richárd was deported earlier than most of the other Hungarians in that last push to murder in 1944. He was with prominent Jews and Non-Jews who were anti-Nazi politicians. They were deported in early spring. The rest of the Jewish community in Pécs was deported to Aushwitz in July. In Budapest Gábor Schweitzer said that Richárd, "enjoyed a different treatment." According to literature in the archives of Mauthausen other witnesses noted that, in fact, Nazi soldiers set out to make an example of these prominent prisoners and treated them worse than everyone else.

§

We each listen to a self-guided audio tour. We walk slowly. Moving too quickly would disturb this universe. We start at the gate, which opens into a yard, once called the "Wailing Wall," where Nazi soldiers forced Richárd to strip naked outside with other men and women.

They had to surrender their clothes, eyeglasses and false teeth. Soldiers shaved their heads, then poured disinfectant over them. They were given flannel clothes and wooden shoes. SS officers questioned the newly arrived Hungarians, and, as they answered, the SS slapped them and said, "You are a dirty Jew." Then the prisoners stood in line. Prisoner numbers were not tattooed in Mauthausen. This happened only in Auschwitz. At Mauthausen, prisoners wore their number engraved on a metal bracelet as well as on a cloth patch on the chest of their prisoner jacket.

Richárd was number 64240. Records from Mauthausen show his last name *Engel* written in neat black script, without the *de Jánosi*, the part that marked him as nobility. There is also no accent on the *a* in *Richard*. His birth date is listed 31.7.1882. Under profession: *Masch Ingenieur*, Mechanical Engineer. Never mind that by 1943, Richárd owned and ran the family business. Reason given for deportation: 54 *Ung. Jude*. The number 54 might mean that Richárd was among that particular group of Hungarians arrested and committed that day. Fifty-four happens to be the street number of Richárd's permanent address, 54 Rákóczy út. *Ung* was short for *Ungarischer* or Hungarian. *Jude* of course is Jew.

I have read that some people chose to recreate themselves in the camps in order to survive. When they were sheared naked and given a number, they hardened their hearts, created new personalities, changed themselves mentally to suit this unpredictable new world. But at sixty-two, I imagine Richárd was past the point of recreating himself.

We walk past the "Wailing Wall" to the line of unheated wooden barracks where most prisoners were housed. They used straw to cover themselves when they slept. Everyone shared a bunk. Typhoid was spreading. The sick ones got shot.

The SS put most Hungarians in tents. Two thousand in each. If and when they were fed, they received thin potato soup and watered down coffee. For whatever reasons, Hungarian Jews were given less food. Tents got so crowded some prisoners were forced to sleep out in the cold.

The three of us walk these grounds now separately but in the same slow way. Every now and then, we end up together, touching hands. At one point, I watch James stand before the ash dump, where for years the ashes from the crematoriums were dumped. He is wiping his eyes. It's disturbing to think that if the Holocaust had not occurred, my mother would not have come to the United States, and she would not have met my father, and neither I nor James would exist.

I didn't know it then, but I grew up around sad people. Is that what's happening to James? My heart shared the same space with his for nine months. It's impossible *not* to still feel the physical give and take. Am I dooming him to grow up to feel the same pull of the past?

In the cellar of the laundry barracks, we see the showers. I can't help but taste ash in the air. I think I taste blood too, but I recall the mineral smell of the quarry. I lean against the stone walls, and listen for the hum of voices, the whisper of ghosts. I listen for Richárd.

He wouldn't eat. In 1944 Richárd told Rabbi Schweitzer, he was fasting. Political fasting had worked once before for Richárd. In 1918, during World War I, occupying Serbian soldiers arrested and imprisoned Richárd for protesting the ill treatment of Jews. He fasted and they released him. Then the Serbian soldiers left Pécs. People who knew Richárd say that he was "stubborn and rigid and when he decided to do something, it was so." He was an engineer. He believed in a system of order. Maybe he thought it would work again.

But was fasting at Mauthausen really Richárd's way of protesting or was it suicide? If he wanted to commit suicide, there *were* other ways. Some walked to the electric barbed wire fence, which had a 380 V charge. Cyanide tablets went for about $1000 per tablet, but they were hard to come by and few had any money. Some were willingly shot in the neck. By not eating, Richárd had more control. Maybe it was his *choosing* not to eat that made the difference for him. He was controlling his death as much as was humanly possible. Controlling how he died was all he had left of his life.

At school he had studied what his father wanted him to study. He wanted to marry the woman he loved, Theresia, but when his father told him he could not marry her, a Catholic, any Catholic, Richárd did not marry her. He lived with her instead for over fourteen years without anybody ever knowing. That took some doing. When his country told him to fight in World War I, he fought, risking his life for Hungary, his country, the country that sent him to Mauthausen.

Starving is not the same as hunger. The kind of starving Richárd felt surely has no word. As Primo Levi wrote in *The Reawakening* of his time in Auschwitz, "Just as our hunger is not that feeling of missing a meal, so our way of being cold has need of a new word. We say 'hunger,' we say, 'tiredness,' 'fear,' 'pain,' we say 'winter' and they are different things. They are free words, created and used by free men who lived in comfort and suffering in their homes."

It was a cold spring in 1944 and Richárd suffered in the most beautiful countryside. Did someone take his hand? Did Rabbi Schweitzer pray over him, recite the Kaddish in Hebrew, or did Richárd recite it for himself as his body began to shut down? I imagine he yearned for the particulars of his lovely life—his music, his clothes, his food, his familiar routine, his duties at the factory, his synagogue on Kossuth Square, and his home in Pécs.

Did he call out for his brother? His father? Theresia? God? And how did he say goodbye to the world and in what language? *Auf Wiedersehen! Viszont látásra!* שלום

Years later, I find out in Sándor Krassó's account that Richárd collapsed at roll call. Maybe then, in a split second, he thought, *now I will join them. I will join my family, my ancestors, the Engels.* Perhaps in his mind, the Engels were already there—his angels watching over a loyal son.

He fasted for five days.

There is a line drawn through *Engel, Richard 31-7-82 Pécs* on a Mauthausen document dated April 30, 1944, and in the margin, Richárd's number 64240 does not have a line drawn through it, as though the number lives on. The reason for Richárd's death: *collaps; ak Herzschwäche.* Collapse; acute myocardial insufficiency. Heart attack.

Richárd's two brothers-in-law died at Mauthausen a few months later.

On October 7, 1944, the Hungarian Royal Office of Statistics filed a report stating that the "'Engel Adolf and Sons' company, directed by the owner, Richárd who—according to a notice by the German police—has deceased since then."

As it became clearer that Germany was losing, Berlin sent explicit orders for Nazi soldiers at Mauthausen: *do not leave any witnesses behind.* Some Nazis simply ignored these orders, abandoned the sick and dying, and left the camp in a hurry. On April 25, 1945, Hitler committed suicide with his mistress in his bunker in Berlin.

The remaining SS at Mauthausen began burning the paperwork. But two inmates, one Czech, the other Austrian, both political prisoners, both non-Jewish, hid most of the death certificates, including Richárd's. Mauthausen camp was liberated on May 25, 1945. Ernst Martin and Josef Ulbrecht, gave the death certificates to the liberating US army, and because of them, I know more about Richárd's incarceration.

Mourning is different when there is no body. We imagine him before us both alive and dead. Richárd's bones or ashes lay somewhere here on the grounds of Mauthausen. We wander further around the camp, searching for sacred ground until we realize this place is already sacred. I stand with Pat and James between two pine trees.

I can't help but wonder how many others like Richárd have been forgotten or will be forgotten. I recall how in the beginning, Richárd seemed like nobody at all. People wondered why, of all the spectacular people in the family, why focus on *him*, on Richárd, a minor character in a big family of big characters. *He is not an important one.* Why mourn someone who died before you were born? Why mourn anybody for that matter? Because it is in our nature as civilized human beings to mourn and to remember.

A falcon flies overhead. We went all over searching for clues of Richárd's life in order to properly remember him. How could the word remember *not* have something to do with that Eygptian myth about Isis? Her husband Osiris was murdered by his brother, Set, who dismembered him and buried his body parts all over the country. Then, his wife went out, collecting his body parts, putting her husband's body back together, making him whole again in order to re-member him.

There is an ordinary kind of forgetting and a special kind. Many people willed themselves not to know about the murdering or simply to forget about it. *Move on,* they told themselves. We still tell ourselves this everyday when we hear or watch the news. My grandfather forced himself to forget as well, perhaps thinking it was the right thing to do. He wanted his daughter to assimilate. He wanted to further remove her from his Jewish roots so that she might be safe. But when my grandfather, the historian, buried his heritage, he buried Richárd's memory as well.

If my grandfather had been successful, I would never have known about Richárd. But now I know and James knows. We know about other Engel de Jánosis who were murdered too. Not all of them, but most of them. To forget Richárd, is to forget all of them—my family and all the other Jews of Hungary. Each and every one ought to be mourned, missed, and remembered. As Aung San Suu Kyi said in her Nobel Prize acceptance speech, "To be forgotten is to die a little." Forgetting our dead would be murdering them twice.

I have no idea what good this memorializing has done or will do. But I know that it's important to remember. Holocaust-like events could happen again. They *are*, in fact, happening again—hundreds of thousands of people all around the world are fleeing their homes to avoid death and persecution. Swastikas are popping up everywhere.

James finds three stones. Each of us takes one. I have brought candles in my backpack, and put them on a flat piece of ground. Pat lights them. We place our stones next to the candle, our makeshift tombstone for Richárd.

I take out the prayer on the sheet of paper I've been carrying since I learned about Richárd three years ago at Yad Vashem. Is it necessary for us to have a connection in order to feel compassion? We are all of us tied to one another, and according to Jewish tradition, the descendants of the dead have especially strong ties. We have come here together, taken this journey together, searched for him together, and together we read a prayer meant to help the soul of the deceased on his journey.

> May His great name be exalted and sanctified
> In the world which He created according to His will.
> May He establish His kingdom
> And may His salvation blossom and His anointed be near
> During your lifetime and during your days
> And during the lifetimes of all the House of Israel
> Speedily and very soon. And say, Amen.
> May His great name be blessed
> For ever, and to all eternity.
> Blessed and praised, glorified and exalted,
> Extolled and honoured, adored and lauded
> By the name of the Holy One, blessed be He
> Above and beyond all the blessings,
> Hymns, praises and consolations
> May there be abundant peace from heaven,
> And good life
> Satisfaction, help, comfort, refuge
> Healing, redemption, forgiveness, atonement,
> Relief and salvation
> For us and for all His people Israel; and say, Amen
> May He who makes peace in His high places
> Grant in his mercy peace for us
> And for all his nation Israel; and say, Amen.

A slow red sun begins to set. It's getting darker outside and the evening turns burnt orange. We came here out of love for a relative we never knew. I think of the dark graves all around. Have the dead been remembered and grieved for properly? Where are their stones?

Six years of war and six million Jews murdered, my mother's family, and him, Richárd. *Ashes to ashes, dust to dust.* He is here at

Mauthausen. Somewhere his ashes are now dust, languishing in the dark Austrian soil. He is a part of this earth. And he is a part of us now, too.

December
Family

It snows on "Southern Night." One hundred and fifty guests arrive at TRAFIK, the restaurant in Pécs, where James and I serve bowls of Pat's "Hungarian Jambalaya," which is like no other jambalaya we have ever eaten. The Hungarian celery and sausage make it spicier. The chef wants to add the dish to his already voluminous menu.

We have learned that an iron skillet and a wooden spoon is as important to Hungarian cooking as they are in Southern cooking; both require the same curing and scraping to build flavor. In both places, there is love, even adoration for the open fire and freshly killed meat.

Before the screening of "To Kill a Mockingbird," I keep my remarks short and light, but then, at the end of the movie, when we turn up the lights, we see how many people are crying. We have shown a film about our nation's ugly past. Our friends are crying for us, and perhaps, for themselves as well. We are all of us thinking about humanity, hate, and love, and we stay late that night with our friends and students talking about race, religion, and occupying forces.

And then it is December, the end of the semester, and we prepare to leave Hungary. At the ANK school, Pat's students and colleagues throw him a surprise going-away party. They give him gifts of Hungarian linen doilies, photo albums and Christmas chocolates. His colleague, the woman who wanted to know why Americans had not come to rescue Hungarian revolutionaries in 1956, makes him a mixed fruit tart.

Pat fills out another application, obtains four signatures, two seals, and pays an application "fee." In exchange, he receives an envelope fat with forints. This is his entire teaching salary, which amounts to about $400.

James' friends "friend" him on Facebook to stay in touch. On his last day, he stays late to give his music teacher one last bribe of 150 forints to play the drums. After James plays The White Stripes' "Seven Nation Army," his teacher claps. He tells James he's been listening all along.

At the university, Bea hand delivers a package in my office on my last day. The package contains information about Richárd and Erna from concentration camp archivists at Mauthausen and Auschwitz. The envelope has already been opened. Bea looks at me and says in a whisper, "My grandmother weared yellow star." There are tears in her eyes. "She hid at the relatives in Budapest. My relatives had a chances." We hug.

Using Bea's boom box, I play the audio recording of William Faulkner giving his 1950 Nobel speech for my Modern American Literature students. They don't understand a word he says, so I give them copies of the speech, and we discuss what he means when he says "the problems of the human heart in conflict with itself," the old verities and truths of the heart, love and honor and pity and pride and compassion and sacrifice. We go over the part about man prevailing "because he has a soul, a spirit capable of compassion and sacrifice and endurance."

Conspiracy boy with the black lipstick isn't there. He stopped coming to class.

In my last Hungarian creative writing class, we talk about the importance of setting, place, and Eudora Welty. In her essay, "Places in Fiction," Welty wrote about setting as one of the "lesser angels" of stories, and we discuss the importance of place and its permanence in the heart of characters, both real and unreal. I can't help but think of Pécs when I read from Welty. "There may come to be new places in our lives that are second spiritual homes closer to us in some ways, perhaps, than our original homes. But the home tie is the blood tie. And had it meant nothing to us, any other place thereafter would have meant less, and we would carry no compass inside ourselves to find home ever, anywhere at all. We would not even guess what we had missed."

I urge my students to take risks in their stories, their poems, their plays, and in their lives, even if it embarrasses them. "Be courageous," I say. One student, a handsome boy, who has not handed in any work all semester, says, "Why are you preaching to us about courage? Why not sensitivity? Of all the characteristics of an artist, why courage?"

We have a good discussion about being an artist. I go on too long about hard work and determination. They go on about sensitivity and "feelings." I ask them to consider the fourteen Hungarian Nobel Laureates—twelve are scientists and one is Elie Wiesel. At the end of class, I take a picture of the students gathered together, smiling. Then, after they leave, I take a picture of the empty classroom.

Pat and I have one last meeting with one of the gazillion deans at the university. He serves a wonderful *Mákos töltelék*, a Strudel with poppyseed filling, which his secretary made, and his homemade *Pálinka*. It's 10:00 in the morning. Pat and I, and the four other academics in the room drink the *Pálinka* shots because it would be rude not to. We sit and listen to the dean tell a joke about serving a Jewish man pork. The dean laughs at the end of the pork joke. I still don't know enough Hungarian to object. I recall what a former Fulbrighter once told me: *You will never have a meaningful conversation with a Hungarian.* We are the only ones in the room who don't laugh.

Already I have made a list of what I will miss when we leave Pécs. Renáta and Zoli are at the top. "Let's look on the bright side," Renáta says, when we say goodbye. She drops tiny bottles of *pálinka* into our coat pockets. "If you had not come, we wouldn't have this opportunity to be so sad. Life without tears is like goulash without paprika."

At night over dinner, the three of us talk about our travels. James makes a list of Traveling Do's and Don'ts:

Know where you're going.

Be fed when you get to an airport.

Always have money in your pocket.

Always have a plan, even if the plans change.

Always know where your luggage is, and, when you're on the move, stay close to it.

Know that you don't have to stay positive ALL the time. Just stay alive.

In the days left, we go to art galleries we meant to visit. I write down the titles of paintings just because they remind me of Hungary: *Woman in Black Gloves; My Father Leaning on His Arms; Uncle Piacescele in Ladies' Company; Ödón is in a 40°C Fever; Lazarine by the Mirror; Sour Cherry in Bloom; Gloaming in an Intimate Room.*

I visit the synagogue one last time, and attend Sabbath, keeping my coat on because there's no heat. I can't stop shivering. I put rocks on Róbert's grave on the Catholic side of the Mosque. Pat and James go to the market one last time to buy lavender honey and a few more apples. They say goodbye to The Cabbage Ladies.

When I think of Pécs, I consider the light, the wide-open squares, and the yellow buildings. We walk through the town one last time and I can't help but feel I've walked these same streets in some previous life. A friend once told me a ghost is really an imprint. The living leave their imprints on buildings, in chairs, on pillows, in life, and we feel their presence when they are gone. I still feel the Engels everywhere in Pécs. I feel them at my side as I walk. All this time, they were never very far away.

This is where they all lived. The Engels. The Angels. My family.

We stuff our suitcases with Hungarian gifts, *pálinka*, books, recipes, tablecloths, and a dozen delicate, hand-painted eggshells tucked into starched crocheted netting—a foolish souvenir to attempt to bring home. I also have all of my notes on Richárd. I have more now to say for *Circumstances of death;* more to say for *Places and activities during the war.* I have pages to add. It will be part collage, part elegy.

When we finally leave Hungary, we adjust our watches seven hours back to a younger, earlier time. We return that much older.

In Chicago, I present my mother with embroidered Hungarian pillowcases, tablecloths, linens and small Zsolnay saucers. I give my father Zsolnay cufflinks. My parents are both worn out from the radiation treatments and we stay for Christmas break, cooking and re-stocking their freezer.

Every single hollow eggshell I unpack remains intact and perfect. The blown-out eggshells feel as delicate as the material I have collected about Richárd. Richárd will forever be both real and fictional to me. At best, he is half-known. Perhaps he lived as so many of us do—half-known. People only had a sense of him, an idea of him. There are enough details to begin to see the essence of a character. And in this way, maybe I can see Richárd more accurately than I can see any other human being. Too many details can be confusing.

There are so many things I will never know, but I see his face. I see all their faces now, as though they are shadows in the back of my mind, and, periodically, in the middle of a given day or week or year, they reveal themselves.

When I finally mail the Page of Testimony to Yad Vashem in Israel, the archivists research all my research, then reinsert the correct accent marks in Richárd's name. They correct his date of birth. They add the names of his mother and father. They say that he was an engineer and that he was single. There are no blanks left to fill out. They display the pictures Anna gave me of Richárd in their database of Shoah victims and on the Wall of Names. Wherever I am, I find myself calling him up again and again.

Richárd is a character in a story I don't want to finish writing. I don't want him to disappear from my life just because I've finished my so-called assignment. *Stay. Stay,* I think to him, over and over. Richárd is a part of my history. I filled out the last remaining line on Richárd's Page of Testimony with a fact I've known all along. *My relationship to the victim*: Family.

Checkpoint

About a year after our return to the States, my cousin Peter finishes his memoir, which he calls *Reminiscences*. He uses his old, whole name: Peter Engel de Jánosi. I email him another list of questions about Richárd, joking, saying that, now, when I refer to the Engel de Jánosi family, I no longer say "they." I say "we." I don't hear from him. Shortly after, Monica calls to say that Peter has died of a massive stroke.

At his memorial service at The New School in New York, I meet Anna Stein's brother, Gábor, a tall, thin man with big, expressive hands. He is a retired nuclear engineer and he looks like Richárd. I also meet a cousin my own age, Jeffrey, the great-grandson of Alexandor, one of Adolf's sons who had once lived at the *Hofzeile* with my great-grandfather, Moritz. Jeffrey lives in Toronto. For most of his life, Jeffrey knew nothing about his Hungarian family.

Even in death, Peter brings the Engel de Jánosi family together.

Throughout the following year, I keep up with the political news about Hungary and the shift to the right across much of Europe. In one of the Hungarian papers, I read about Gábor Schweitzer's ninety-year-old father, Chief Rabbi Joseph Schweitzer, who was verbally tormented walking home alone on a street in Budapest. "I hate all Jews," one of his attackers shouted. More news appears about increasing anti-Semitic rhetoric and extremist political parties gaining control in the Hungarian parliament and elsewhere. Renáta and Zoli tell us the political and economic situation gets worse every day.

When the credit-rating agency Moody's cuts Hungary's debt rating to "junk," status, we worry about our friends and colleagues. The University of Pécs makes more faculty cuts. Zoli worries about his job. Renáta continues to teach and picks up extra work translating. The publisher doesn't pay her on time. Then he simply doesn't pay.

We make arrangements with the Math department at my university, and host Renáta and Zoli's son Kristóf for a week in southern Indiana. He comes with a bottle of *pálinka* and Hungarian cookbooks, and he helps James with math homework. James' blond head and Kristóf's dark moppy head bend over sheets of equations spread out across the dining room table. We marvel at Kristóf's ability with numbers, formulas, and equations, and we listen spellbound to his dining room table lessons, and later, to his math lectures at the university about the phenomenon of fractals.

"Everything is related to everything," Kristóf tells a group of students in his lecture. He clicks through his Power Point slides, showing the math in clouds, trees, a grain of sand, and a poem by William Blake. "To investigate the beauty of these specific objects is to investigate the universe. These specifics affect all segments of your life. Everything is connected."

I consider the bigger picture and make the connections. Perhaps Hungary's lousy economy is karmic payback. Doesn't Hungary deserve to suffer what it is currently suffering, which is economic disaster? They marched out and murdered their supply of political, cultural, economic and artistic leaders—and future generations of writers, artists, scientists, scholars, and thinkers. Everything is connected.

But what about our friends?

I continue to have trouble explaining the trip to anyone who asks. *It was Great*, I say. *Just terrific!* They make jokes about paprika and goulash and we find ourselves defending Hungary as I spent the better part of my life apologizing for being from Mississippi. I feel myself becoming Quentin again, talking to Shreve in *Absalom, Absalom! I don't hate the South. I don't hate Hungary I don't I don't.*

I have something else left to do. I was not able to bring together Peter with my mother, but Peter's death makes me determined to introduce my mother to her other cousin, Anna Stein.

My father's health declines. For two years, Pat and I take turns caring for him and my mother. Each time, I travel to Chicago, I *will* myself to be strong. I think of what Zita said in the classrrom about Addie Bundren in *As I Lay Dying*. "The mother is decomposing. The whole family is decomposing because their world has fallen apart." I feel my family's world falling apart. What else will? So much of what I know or knew continues to unravel. *Things fall apart; the centre cannot hold; Mere anarchy is loosed upon the world.*

The tumors in my father's brain bloom and broaden, taking up, what his doctor calls, "costly real estate." I stay with my father during chemotherapy treatments while I grade papers beside him.

"Go easy on them," he says, smiling.

Hospice sends religious men who stand at the foot of my father's bed, opening their Bibles. My father sends them away. Then a Rabbi visits. He sits in the chair nearest my father's bed. He reads something from David. My father listens, his eyes as blue and clear as they have ever been. The Rabbi visits again and again.

I feed my father when he can no longer feed himself. I bathe him, nurse him, read to him from the Psalms, singing that song we both love about the wings of a snow white dove. He calls my mother and me his angels. On a beautiful day in April, when the lilacs begin to bloom, my father's color turns. He is darker. Bluer. A line from Matthew comes to me. "Forgive us as we forgive." My mother and I sit with him on his bed, listening. We can feel him leave us. When he's gone, my mother cries on his chest. "Oh Jimmy don't leave me please don't leave me here all alone."

I open the window and watch the lilacs shake as he goes.

I tell James how much his grandfather loved him and will always be watching over him. I admit to him that I believe in guardian angels, and I recall my own guardian angel, my great-grandmother, Marie, and her ever-watchful blue eyes. I remind James of Richárd and all his other angels.

At the funeral service, James wears a pair of his grandfather's shoes and reads from the Hebrew Scriptures.

For a year my mother grieves. I stay with her when she undergoes hip replacement surgery. In the hospital, seemingly out of nowhere, she says now she thinks she is finally ready to visit Hungary. Thoughts of travelling and the urge to walk safely over cobblestone streets get her through physical therapy.

Pat and I make the arrangements, first to visit Paris so that my mother can meet Anna Stein, and, then on to Pécs.

Travel for my mother is an act of defiance and courage. She has been a widow for one year and she has a new right hip. Crowds were difficult before, now even more so. In the airport, she clutches her purse and her identification cards. She will always be *The Immigrant*. Someone will forever be searching her, questioning her, asking to see her papers. It is never just "procedure." For her, her life will always be in danger.

She still calls airpoint security a "checkpoint."

We move slowly through the TSA lines.

"Grandmother?" James says. "Did I tell you about my internship in Paris?" He's seventeen now. He keeps talking. I hear *Utilized Excel spreadsheets, data on competitors in the area, translating,* and *customer experience.* My mother hardly notices when the security guard asks her to let go of her bag.

(left to right) Me, Anna Stein, and my mother, Madeleine

Part V

Paris and Pécs 2013

Paris
French Kisses

A nna invites us all over to her studio and apartment, near
the opera house in Paris. James meets us there after his day,
interning. He knows the Paris Métro and makes his way around the
city alone.

Her rooms smell of linseed oil and mildew. Moving slowly, my
mother and Anna carefully hug each other. They have the same
complexion, the same expressive eyes, the same nose, the same short,
feathery hair, but my mother's hair is all white and Anna's is a pale
grey blond. They are ten years apart in age and they each have a
different kind of beauty. My mother's eyes are wet, but not Anna's.

Was it all leading to this moment, to this time when we could
introduce the two living remnants of a once great family?

We drink wine from Switzerland and sit on shaky aluminum
chairs, which Anna has designed. My mother admires the gold
jewelry Anna makes, especially the big rings.

"Who is she?" my mother says, looking at a gold sculpture in
front of her, a familiar-looking woman with windblown hair.

"She is nobody," Anna says.

Anna takes us downstairs to show us more paintings. She pulls
out a small portrait of an older woman, painted in pale autumn
shades with thick brush strokes. The woman in the painting looks like
my mother, my mother's mother, Anna, Anna's mother—she looks
the way I know I will look someday.

"I would love to buy this, Anna," I say. This painting feels
personal, more personal than the others.

"It's not done," Anna says. "I have to fix her mouth and I have
to sign it." She hesitates. "I can deliver it to you later." I write her a
check then and there. My mother writes Anna a check for the gold
woman.

In her small, cozy apartment upstairs, we all sit down to an elaborate Hungarian feast Anna has prepared: rabbit paté, deer stew, confiture, and poppyseed cake.

"Tonight I sold my mother and my granddaughter," Anna says to her husband, Nourredine, an Algerian academic who spends his days writing in the corner of the room. James, Pat and I lift our glasses in a toast, clinking with Anna and my mother.

The following evening, at the Café de Flore, I sit back, and again, watch my mother talk with her cousin, Anna. It's just us women. They are both dressed up in good summer dresses with colorful scarves, wearing different French perfumes, and, together, they smell wonderful.

They look like sisters. My mother jokes; Anna not so much. They gesture with their hands and fingers in the same way except that my mother's nails are manicured and Anna's nails are imbedded with paint. They are getting used to each other in this second meeting. My mother and Anna really only have each other as family and I can see that neither is sure what to do.

A waiter pours water. He looks like Liam Neeson and Anna charms him, joking, in French, *when will we ever get your attention?* After he takes our orders, Anna reaches into her bag and brings out a paper sack. "It's fixed and dry now," she says, bringing out the painting. My mother and I admire the newly fixed mouth and Anna's signature.

Anna gives my mother a smaller bag, and inside there is a ring. "I saw you admiring this and I thought you might like it."

The ring is hammered gold, misshapen and made with an uneven blue semi-precious stone, the same color and approximate size of of the Engel de Jánosi family ring my mother lost months ago while caring for my father. The ring's imperfections give it character. My mother tears up.

"Oh Anna, thank you," she says, sliding the ring on her right finger. "You can't know what this means."

We thank Anna over and over. Later, I send Anna a copy of József's visiting card, which I receive from the Wagner archives in

Bayreuth, Germany. On it Richard Wagner wrote to József, inviting him to the dress rehearsal of Tannhäuser.

Anna puts her hands together on her lap and watches young women drinking their coffees at a nearby table. My mother loves to watch other women, too. She is often awed and a little stunned when she sees self-assurance in other women. I can see the admiration in her eyes. But I can also see her covetousness. She wants hers back. That's what they really took from her—confidence in being who she was.

Anna wants to catch my mother up on family—who is awful, who is boring, and who are the pretenders—the ones who aren't even *really* related. There aren't many left from which to choose.

Anna asks my mother about her father, Friedrich again—what was he like? Did he love you? Did he love you enough? Was he interested in your life? She's weighing her life against my mother's. It's what one does. In some families, there are always the same questions: who is the most successful? Who is the most loved? Who is the most special? The most brilliant? The prettiest? But here are two women who are related to each other, but never knew. My mother got out of Austria while she was young, and then she was very much freed of extended family because she did not know she had one. Anna stayed behind in Hungary, only to get out much later. Her mother constantly reminded her that what she was doing was not quite right, not quite up to family standards.

"Why didn't he tell you about me?" Anna wants to know why Friedrich never mentioned her to his only daughter. "We could have been friends."

My mother moves her fingers as she listens to Anna. I consider József walking the streets of Pécs, his fingers running up and down his gold-tipped cane, which he gripped behind his back as he walked.

For a moment I worry about what I have done introducing these two. Maybe I should have just taken my mother out with Pat and James to dance to the street music during *Fête de la Musique*. Maybe introducing my mother to Anna will only re-open family wounds. Maybe this meeting will only serve to make them angrier or more impassioned about what has been done to them and to their family.

Why did my grandfather Friedrich say that he was the last Engel de Jánosi when he was not, and he knew that he was not? We will never know why.

"My father didn't want to burden me with the past. It's that simple, I think. He didn't want me saddled with family and all that regret."

Anna takes in my mother's blunt words.

My mother and Anna know how to survive because they know how to adapt. They know how to blend in and not talk about their lives, tempering their aggrieved moods, and anger. Keeping secrets kept them alive but that's also how they lost contact with their families. Perhaps, they also lost the ability to connect intimately with others as well. They both have competitive spirits. They both have to stay busy all the time, often living frantically. They both know about working hard and they know about loss. They know how to suffer and they know how to worry. It's the living they sometimes have trouble with.

"I remember jumping on the boards at the factory in Pécs, before they got loaded on the train headed to Vienna," Anna says out of nowhere. Her eyes crinkle like tissue paper when she smiles. My mother never saw *Jánosipuszta* and Anna never saw the *Hofzeile*.

"And I jumped on those boards too," my mother says. "At the factory in Vienna, before they brought them in. That smell of warm wood when they were unloading." They are smiling and staring at each other now. Are they thinking of those boards, the ones they both played on? Maybe it's finally sinking in, two cousins after all these years, meeting for the first time, like two missing floor pieces sliding into place, reluctantly at first, and then, just like that, they fit together.

Anna puts her hand to her cheek. "My teeth hurt," she says. She has to go home early because the following morning she will work before she goes to the dentist to have the tooth pulled.

We walk Anna to her bus stop in front of the church at Saint-Germain-des-Prés. She tells us about her place in Normandy, where she likes to walk near the water. She describes the place, a place where mountains fall into the sea.

Anna buttons the collar of her coat and says the weather has never been so awful. She says *awful* the way my mother says it. My mother and Anna complain about how "impossible" it is to bundle up in fall clothes at the end of June. They are happily together now in their complaints. A drunk man at the bus stop begins to sing a French drinking song.

The bus arrives and my mother moves away from the noise and the crowd. The drunk man shouts in French that the bus is here and that everyone should hurry. *Attend! Asseyez-vous! Tout le monde!*

It's so difficult to say goodbye because, really, we've just now said hello. Anna and I kiss two times on the cheek. All her life my mother has emphasized her mother's side of the family, her *French* side, always insisting people spell her name, *Madeleine*, the correct way, the French way. But here, now, finally in Paris, the birthplace of her mother, she embraces her one living relative, Anna Stein, in a full, frontal American hug. No two air kisses here. Anna hugs my mother too, looking at me over my mother's shoulder, amused. Her blue eyes twinkle. Her eyes and her smile remind me of my great-grandmother Marie's smile.

Anna steps up on the bus, and then waves as the bus pulls away. We wave back. The drunk man urges us to hurry and get on too. He comes so close we smell the peppery smell of his sweat. My mother squeezes my hand and calls out for her dead husband, my father.

"Jimmy," she says. I hold her hand and help her walk on the wide, difficult cobblestones.

She's afraid of falling into traffic or having her purse snatched by passing gypsies. She is convinced all taxi drivers are cheating her, even if the meters are turned on and audibly ticking. She distrusts most waiters and shopkeepers. But still, she needs people more than ever now. She needs them all around her, needs their stimulation and even their aggravating rub, maybe more so now because she is a widow and alone. She's forgetting things more and more. She repeats. The irony does not escape me: I've asked her to remember and introduced her to people, places and things she never knew at a time in her life when she's forgetting.

When the bus leaves, she begins to cry. Her weeping becomes guttural, the same sound she made the day my father died. Her slight shoulders shake and she puts her head into the crook of my arm. She has gotten so small and frail and I hold her tight. She is crying for everything and everyone—her dead husband, her father, her mother, her lost family and country. She is crying for herself and for all those in her family she knew and never knew.

Pécs
Untying the Knot

Finally, we take my mother to where she has never been, to the cradle of her ancestors.

Renáta and Zoli meet us at the hotel in town. My mother slides into German conversations with Zoli, even though she has not spoken German in over fifty years. Another part of her leaps forth, the rolling *r*'s, her voice a little deeper and more confidant as though she has rediscovered a cornerstone.

"Fantastic!" Zoli says of my mother.

Renáta and Zoli have gotten permission from the mayor and special passes to get inside the Engel de Jánosi home at 54 Rákóczi út. At the door, a city official with Brezhnev eyebrows requests that we give him our passports for the time we spend touring the house, as if we are entering another country. When I give him my passport, I have the booklet open to the page stamped with the word *Hivatalos.* I want Brezhnev Brows to see that one word. *Official.*

Inside, as Pat and James take pictures, my mother admires the high ceilings, the thick walls, the original arches and cut glass windows. She holds onto the railing as we look up the winding wooden staircase, imagining them all coming and going. Outside the building, we stand with my mother before the plaque dedicated to Adolf, reliving the ceremony for her. Making trumpet noises, James hums the coal miner's song.

"It should be bigger," my mother says, staring up at the plaque. She sounds exhausted.

My mother does not want to see what is left of *Jánosipuszta.* Her mother once told her never to go back to either the *Hofzeile* or to Vienna because returning would only make her sad, and my mother is fearful of such returns. Pat and James break away to visit with their friends and former ANK classmates.

We walk to the synagogue. I point out Adolf's name on the marble plaque of founders inside. My mother has never been inside a synagogue. We greet the same elderly gentleman who gave Pat and James skullcaps made of black construction paper, stapled together. He and my mother speak German and hold hands as though they were friends who have not seen each other for some time.

She and I sit in one of the oak pews. She looks up at the blue ceiling. I wonder how long these old buildings can stand as they are, without being maintained or used. Years later, I get an email from a former student saying that the new mayor of Pécs has an "unwritten policy to let all buildings with a Jewish past fall into such disrepair that they will not be in a condition to be saved."

My mother and I stay seated for a while in the synagogue. I know she's ready to leave when I hear her ring, Anna's ring meant to replace her family crest ring, tapping on the wood as she steadies herself to rise. The sound echoes.

For the rest of the afternoon, we take things slowly, stopping frequently at cafés for water. I show my mother where we lived on the corner of Jókai utca and Zrínyi utca. The windows of the apartment are open and we can hear punk rock music playing. We smell the new tenants' cigarette smoke from the street. For a moment, I actually pity The Maestro. The antique shop below on the ground floor is now a travel agency, too, its doors wide open. The man behind the desk is not a man I recognize, and I try not to delight in the antique shop's failure.

A friend once asked me where I wanted to be buried, and when I said Mississippi, he said, "Then that's your home." But a person can have a second home too, a place where you feel the pull of a home, and I feel this way about Pécs. I love it and I hate it the very same way I love and hate the south—for its problematic history and for the fact that it's a part of who I am and where I come from.

We sit at a table where I once sat with Peter.

"Someone should write a book," my mother says, sipping iced coffee. "Not about the *drama* of that time, during the war, but about what it does to the person who's left with all of it, the person who feels it but doesn't quite know it all." She looks around the square.

"Someone should write about what it's like to go ice skating in Vienna and see everyone skating away from you because they *know*." She doesn't say *because they know you're Jewish*.

I see in her eyes that she is back there again, in Vienna at the iceskating rink of her youth. The nice-looking blond boy she likes is there too. She has told me about him before, and she stumbles around in her skates on the ice, trying to slide closer to him, but he is forever skating away. She is a little girl with long black braids, trying not to notice, trying not to care.

"That stays with you." Her eyes tear up. "It becomes a part of you."

In many ways, when she was a little girl, my mother bought into the propaganda. How could she not when it was all around her? She began to believe that Jews *were* lesser people, and when those other children skated away from her, she believed that she was lesser, too.

Retracing my mother's past taught me that she and I are both survivors, not victims of hatred, of World War II, of a difficult family, of anger or regret.

A crucial function of art is to tell the truth, to find the truth, but there are different angles. Can you get at the truth? You can get close. Is the story of my mother's and of Richárd's mine to tell? Only partly.

"I love this ring," she says, holding her hand out for me to see. Already the gold is no longer shiny. "I don't know why, but when I put it on, I feel powerful."

After the *Gulyás* and *Bejgli*, after the *Bécsi szelet, Kolbász* and *Pálinka*, we rejoin Pat and James at the café in Széchenyi Square with Renáta and Zoli, while their son Kristóf explains polynomials. In the fall, Kristóf will begin five years of research and graduate work towards a PhD in mathematics at the Institute of Science and Technology in Austria. The Institute is a former site of Nazi medical experiments conducted during World War II. A few Austrians got together and decided to make something good and meaningful out of what was once nothing but evil.

"It's a tool," Kristóf says. He's talking about a mathematical formula called the *Alexander Polynomial of Knots*. He draws a three-dimensional knot on a napkin as he asks us to imagine it has been tied with a rope with the ends glued together. "The Alexander formula helps you figure out if you can untie the knot without cutting the rope."

I'm confused, but James gets what Kristóf's explaining. James is closing in on adulthood at a dizzying pace. In a few years he'll be in Washington, D.C., majoring in economics and business with a minor in music. He'll wear my father's shoes because they have the exact same feet. He'll attend concerts in a hall called the Lizner Auditorium, down the street from the Lizner Home, where my great-grandmother Marie lived. On his bookcase in his dorm room, he'll keep a slate-colored rock labeled: *rock from where King David encouraged his men to be mighty men.*

Across the table, my mother looks out over Széchenyi Square towards the building her grandfather, Moritz, built, where Richárd had once been held prisoner by the Serbians. Had my great-grandmother Marie ever seen the building her husband, Moritz, built? I recall the knotted bed sheets my mother and I loosened so long ago so that Marie could die the way she wanted: uncovered.

"I feel completely at home here," my mother says. "For the first time in my life." She says it's funny, but she thinks all her life she has been homesick for Hungary. Nostalgia is a kind of homesickness, or, as the Germans say, *Heimweh*. The word *nostaligia* has Greek roots in *nostos* or 'return home' and *algos* for 'pain.'

After my father died, my mother decided she wanted to be buried next to him, in Mississippi. After that there is no more room, no plot left for me or Pat or James. I want to be with her always, but I also know I will have to find my own home, my own resting place.

Sitting there at the café in Pécs, as dusk settles on Széchenyi Square, my mother and I look at each other from across the table. There are tears in our eyes. For a long time, I wanted to blend in, just as my mother had. But with this kind of mother, who could be an ordinary person? She is still one of the most mysterious, difficult and interesting women I know. My father thought so too. It is easy to love people in memory. It's much more difficult to love when the person is in front of you. "Love is so short, forgetting is so long," Pablo Neruda wrote. My mother has lost rings, keys, letters, homes, friends, her mother, her father, and now her husband. She worries about losing her memory. Maybe she's wondering if this will be the last time she sees Pécs and walks the streets of her ancestors, the Engels. *It starts with the father.* But for me, it started with my mother. My mother and all her secrets.

She continues to talk with Zoli in German. She has not lost her languages. She is absolutely comfortable here, with the mix of languages, cultures, and our friends who feel not just close, but part of us now. She grew up not knowing any of this, only to find out that her heart knew all along. Some of us may be able to leave a country, but we can't escape our history.

Kristóf goes on describing the Alexander polynomial with an enthusiasm that makes us smile. He really wants me to understand the computations, and he believes I can. I look closely at the napkin, the knot covered with K's, X's, and H's. I have so many questions. *What if the rope has already been cut? What do you do then? Is there another equation to make fast a bind that has been severed? Or is it ruined forever?* I remind myself of what I now believe to be true - *everything is related. Everything is connected.* I stare at that napkin with the knot. I listen carefully, hoping to understand.

Acknowledgments

I would like to thank Yad Vashem, Mauthausen Memorial Archives, Auschwitz Memorial Archives, the Fulbright organization, the National Endowment for the Arts, Várostörténeti Múzeum of Pécs, and Anikó Kövecsi at the OSA Archivum in Budapest.

My endless thanks go to Dr. Christian Dürr Curator, Mauthausen Memorial for his early assistance and his careful reading of this manuscript; to Lital Beer, Director of the Libraries at Yad Vashem; and to my remarkable editors at Calypso Editions, Robin Davidson, Martin Woodside and book designer Tony Bonds. More thanks to our friends Renáta, Zoltán, and Kristóf Huszár; Adrian Wanner at Pennsylvania State University, and John Meredig at the University of Evansville for their help with Hungarian and German translations.

Thank you to Gary and Cindy Bayer who started me on this journey; Muriel Joffe for her faith in this project; Peter Engel de Jánosi, who told me "they weren't *all* bad;" Anna Stein, who took the time to explain to me just what being an Engel means; Christof Bairsdorf for trusting me with so many of his documents; Ryan James and Ron Schmitz for their friendship and hospitality at BudaBaB in Budapest; Gábor Schweitzer for his time and honesty; Jeff Engel for sending me Moritz's play; Josip Novakovich for his friendship, help, and advice; Annamária Sas of the Fulbright organization in Budapest for paving the way; all my students and colleagues at the University of Pécs, especially László B. Sári, Mária, Bea, Monika and Gabi, for everything; Tena Heck for her reliability; Melvin Peterson; Mark St. Germain, "The Playwright" for giving me courage; Dr. Seewann; Dr. Leonhard Kühschelm for his thesis "*Die Engels-Die Anfänge Einer Jüdischen Familie in Ungarn*"; Ambassador Ed Loos; former Ambassador to Hungary Eleni Tsakopoulos Kounalakis; and Mayor Zsolt Páva of Pécs for their kindnesses and hospitality; all my students and colleagues at the University of Evansville, especially those in the Department of Creative Writing—Bill Baer, Rob Griffith, and Paul

Bone; Melanie Bishop for her patience, careful reading, and heartfelt enthusiasm; and Erik Larson for his interest in this project.

My biggest thanks go to my finest traveling companions, Pat and James O'Connor who are always up for an adventure, no matter how challenging.

Family members, scholars, students, and friends, please forgive any factual errors. I did my best with the sources I had.

Portions of this manuscript have appeared in *The Los Angeles Times, The Washington Post, The Huffington Post, The Sun, Boulevard, Palo Alto Review, Anchor* magazine, *Literary Bohemian*, and *The Montréal Review.*

About the Author

Margaret McMullan is the author of nine award-winning books including the novel, *In My Mother's House*, the story collection *Aftermath Lounge*, and the anthology, *Every Father's Daughter*. Margaret's young adult novels *How I Found the Strong*, *When I Crossed No-Bob*, and *Sources of Light* have received best book awards from Parents' Choice, School Library Journal, the American Library Association, and Booklist among many other educational organizations.

Margaret's essays have appeared in *USA Today*, *The Washington Post*, *The Huffington Post*, *The Los Angeles Times*, *The Chicago Tribune*, *The Boston Herald*, *Glamour*, *The Millions*, *The Morning Consult*, *Teachers & Writers Magazine*, *The Montréal Review*, *National Geographic for Kids*, *Southern Accents*, *Mississippi Magazine*, and other periodicals. Her short stories have appeared in *Ploughshares*, *Deep South Magazine*, *StorySouth*, *TriQuarterly*, *Michigan Quarterly Review*, *The Greensboro Review*, *Other Voices*, *Boulevard*, *The Arkansas Review*, *Southern California Anthology*, and *The Sun* among other journals and anthologies. The recipient of an NEA Creative Writing Fellowship and a Fulbright professorship in Hungary, Margaret has served as a faculty mentor at the Stony Brook Southampton Low-res MFA Program in New York where she also taught on the summer faculty. She was the Melvin Peterson Endowed Chair in Literature and Creative Writing at the University of Evansville, where she taught for 25 years. She writes full time now in Pass Christian, Mississippi.

Connect online: *www.margaretmcmullan.com*

Bibliography

Arendt, Hannah. *Eichmann in Jerusalem: A Report on the Banality of Evil.* London: Faber & Faber, 1963.

Bánffy, Miklós. Translated by Patrick Thusfield and Katalin Bánffy-Jelen. *They Were Found Wanting.* London: Arcadia Books, 2000.

Barnás, Ferenc. Translated by Paul Olchváry. *The Ninth.* Evanston, IL: Northwestern University Press, 2009.

Biro, Adam. Translated by Catharine Tihanyi. *One Must Also Be Hungarian.* Chicago: University of Chicago Press, 2006.

Bowring, Sir John. *Poetry of the Magyars.* Hungarian edition, Budapest: Allprint, 2006.

Denes, Magda. *Castles Burning; A Child's Life in War.* New York: Simon & Schuster, 1997.

Duras, Marguerite. Translated from the French by Barbara Bray. *The War: A Memoir.* New York: The New Press, 1986.

Engel de Jánosi, Adolf. Translated by Peter de Jánosi. Életemből. Pécs, Hungary: Pannónia Könyvek, 2008.

Engel-Jánosi, Friedrich. Translated by Adrian Wanner. *...aber ein stolzer Bettler.* Vienna, Austria: Verlag Styria, 1974.

Engel-Jánosi, Friedrich. *The Growth of German Historicism.* Baltimore: The Johns Hopkins Press, 1944.

Engel-Jánosi, Friedrich. *Remarks on the Austrian Resistance, 1938-1945.* Washington, D.C.: Journal of Central European Affairs, Volume XIII, Number II, July, 1953.

Engel-Jánosi, Friedrich. *Austria and the Conclave of 1878.* Washington, D.C.: The Catholic Historical Review, Vol. XXXIX, No. 2, July, 1953.

Engel-Jánosi, Friedrich. *The Return of Pius IX in 1850.* Washington, D.C.: The Catholic Historical Review, Vol. XXXVI, No. 2, July, 1950.

Engel de Jánosi, Carlette. *The Forest of Fontainebleau in Painting and Writing.* Washington, D.C.: The Journal of Aesthetics and Art Criticism, Vol. XI, No. 4, June, 1953.

Engel, von Moritz. Translated by John Meredig. *Transactionen.* Leipzig, Germany: Verlag von Eduard Uvenarius, 1902.

Engel de Jánosi, Peter. *Reminiscences.* Self-published.

Esterházy, Péter. Translated by Judith Sollosy. *Celestial Harmonies.* New York: HarperCollins, 2005.

Fruend, Florian. Translated by Max R. Garcia. *Concentration Camp Ebensee, Subcamp of Mauthausen.* Vienna: Austrian Resistance Archives, 1998.

Gáll, István. Translated by Thomas DeKornfeld. *The Sun Worshiper.* Budapest: Corvina, 1999.

Gruber, Ruth Ellen. *Letters from Europe (and Elsewhere).* Budapest, Austeria, 2008.

Gundel, Ferenc and Imre. Tranlated by Ágnes Kádár. *Károly Gundel Hungarian Cookbook.* Budapest: Corvina, 2010.

Haunschmied, Rudolf A. *St. Georgen Gusen Mauthausen.* Austria: St. Georgen an der Gusen, 2007.

Heltai, Jenő. Translated by Bernard Adams. *Jaguar.* Budapest: Corvina, 2009.

Hilberg, Raul. *The Destruction of the European Jews.* New York: Holmes & Meier, 1985.

Hoff, Agatha. *Burning Horses: A Hungarian Life Turned Upside Down.* El Paso, Texas: Sweet Earth Flying Press, 2010.

Horwitz, Gordon J. *In the Shadow of Death: Living Outside the Gates of Mauthausen.* New York: The Free Press, 1990.

Huszár, Zoltán and Rill, Martin. *Ungarns Erbe in Flugbildern von Georg Gerster.* Budapest: Verlag, Wort, Welt, Bilt, 2010.

Ibsen, Henrik. Translated by R. Farquharson Sharp. *Four Great Plays.* New York: Bantam Books, 1984.

Kenez, Peter. *Hungary From the Nazis to the Soviets.* Cambridge: Cambridge University Press. 2006.

Kertész, Imre. *Fateless.* Translated by Christopher C. Wilson and Katharina M. Wilson. Evanston, IL: Northwestern University Press, 1992.

Kertész, Imre. Translated by Christopher C. Wilson and Katharina M. Wilson. *Kaddish For a Child Not Born.* Evanston, IL: Northwestern University Press, 1997.

Koestler, Arthur. *Scum of the Earth.* London: England, 2006.

Konrád, George. Translated by Jim Tucker. *A Guest in My Own Country; A Hungarian Life.* New York: Other Press, 2002.

Kosztolányi, Dezső. Translated by Richard Aczel. *Skylark.* New York: New York Review of Books, 1993.

Lascault, Gilbert. *Les Figures, Les Matériiaux, Les Mythes D'Anna Stein.* Paris: L'Harmattan, 2001.

Lendvai, Paul. Translated by Ann Major. *The Hungarians: A Thousand Years of Victory in Defeat.* Princeton, New Jersey: Princeton University Press, 2003.

Levi, Primo. *The Reawakening.* New York: Touchstone, 1995.
Márai, Sándor. Translated by Carol Brown Janeway. *Embers.* New York: Vintage International, 2002.

Márai, Sándor. Translated by Albert Tezla. *Memoir of Hungary 1944-1948.* Budapest: Corvina in association with Central European University Press, 2000.

Maršálek, Hans and Hacker, Kurt. *Concentration Camp Mauthausen.* Vienna: Österreichische Lagergemeinschaft Mauthausen, 2001.

Maugham, W. Somerset. *The Summing Up.* New York: Penquin Books, 1938.

McCagg, William O. Jr. *Jewish Nobles and Geniuses in Modern Hungary.* New York: Columbia University Press, 1972.

Meyer, Michael. *Ibsen.* New York: Doubleday & Company, 1971.

Molnár, Ferenc. Translated by Louis Rittenberg. *The Paul Street Boys.* Budapest: Corvina, 2005.

Molnár, Miklós. Translated by Anna Magyar. *A Concise History of Hungary*. Cambridge: Cambridge University Press, 2005.

Nádas, Péter. Translated by Ivan Sanders with Imre Goldstein. *A Book of Memories*. New York: Picador, 1994.

The New Yorker Magazine Editors. *The New Yorker Book of War Pieces*. New York: Schocken Books, 1947.

Örkény, István. Translated by Judith Sollosy. *One Minute Stories*. Budapest: Corvina, 1995.

Pressburger, Giorgio and Nicola. Translated by Gerald Moore. *Homage to the Eight District: Tales from Budapest*. London: Readers International Inc. 1990.

Radnóti, Miklós. Translated by Francis Jones. *Camp Notebook*. Budapest: Arc Publications, 2000.
Ranki, Vera. *The Politics of Inclusion and Exclusion: Jews and Nationalism in Hungary*. New York: Holms & Meier, 1999.

Richler, Mordecai, editor. *Writers on World War II*: *An Anthology*. New York: Vintage Books, 1993.

Snyder, Timothy. *Bloodlands: Europe Between Hitler and Stalin*. New York: Basic Books, 2010.

Snyder, Timothy. *The Red Prince*: *The Secret Lives of a Habsburg Archduke*. New York: Basic Books, 2008.

Stein, Rózsa, Transcript Interview, interviewed by Marx Károly, translated by Renáta Huszár, University of Economic Sciences, Budapest: Corvinus University, 1987.

Summary report on the activities of the War Refugee Board with respect to Jews in Hungary. Franklin D. Roosevelt Library, records of the war refugee board, box 34, Folder: report on Hungary, October 9, 1944.

Suleiman, Susan Rubin and Rorgács, Éva. *Contemporary Jewish Writing in Hungary.* Lincoln, NE: University of Nebraska Press, 2003.

Szép, Ernő. *The Smell of Humans: A Memoir of the Holocaust in Hungary*, translated by John Bátki. Budapest: Central European University Press, 1994.

Tihany, Leslie Charles. *The Baranya Dispute 1918-1921: Diplomacy in the Vortex of Ideologies.* New York: East European Quarterly, Boulder, Distributed by Columbia University Press. 1978.

Trahan, Elizabeth Welt. *Walking with Ghosts.* New York: Peter Lang, 1998.

Turgenev, Ivan. Translated by Richard Freeborn. *Fathers and Sons.* Oxford, England: Oxford University Press, 2008.

Vali, Fekete. Translated by Orzóy Ágnes. *The Works of Anna Stein.* Paris: L'Harmattan, 2012.
Von Rezzori, Gregor. *Memoirs of an Anti-Semite.* New York: New York Review of Books, 2008.

Weissberg, Alex. Translated by Constantine Fitzgibbon and Andrew Foster-Melliar. *Advocate for the Dead: The Story of Joel Brand.* London: Andre Deutsch, 1958.

Wheatcroft, Andrew. *The Habsburgs.* London: Penquin Books, 1996.

Wiesel, Elie. *Night.* New York: Bantam Books, 1986.

Wiesel, Elie. "Introduction." *The Holocaust in Hungary: Forty Years Later.* Eds. R. Braham and B. Vago. New York: Columbia University Press, 1985.

Winter, Miriam. *Trains.* Jackson, Michigan: Kelton Press, 1997.

Zweig, Stefan. Translated by Joel Rotenberg. *The Post-Office Girl.* New York: New York Review of Books, 1982.

Zweig, Stefan. Translated by Phyllis and Trevor Blewitt. *Beware of Pity.* New York, New York Review of Books, 2006.

About the Publisher

Since 2010, Calypso Editions has operated as a cooperative, artist-run, press. As a 501(c)(3) non-profit organization, our mission is publishing quality literary books of poetry, fiction, and creative non-fiction with a global perspective.

By unearthing literary gems from previous generations, translating foreign writers into English with integrity, and providing a space for talented new voices, Calypso Editions is committed to publishing books that will endure in both content and form.

In a world of digital saturation, we believe that the global literary community is strengthened by books that represent diverse voices and serve as physical artifacts of empathy, beauty, and wonder.

Calypso Editions

info@CalypsoEditions.org | www.CalypsoEditions.org

CPSIA information can be obtained
at www.ICGtesting.com
Printed in the USA
BVHW041253181119
564171BV00008B/65/P